Fitzgerald Library

St. Mary's College
Winona, Minnesota

✜ ✜ ✜

Gift of
Bro. James Farrell

Data Communications for Distributed Information Systems

DATA COMMUNICATIONS

for

Distributed Information Systems

DIMITRIS N. CHORAFAS

a petrocelli
book

new york / princeton

Copyright © 1980 Petrocelli Books, Inc.

All rights reserved.
Printed in the United States.

1 2 3 4 5 6 7 8 9 10

Designed by Joan Greenfield

Library of Congress Cataloging in Publication Data
Chorafas, Dimitris N.
  Data communications for distributed information systems.
  Includes index.
  1. Computer networks   2. Data transmission systems.
I. Title.
TK5105.5.C485   621.38   79-28113
ISBN 0-89433-108-6

To E.B., for some creative thoughts

CONTENTS

Introduction   xi

1. What Is Telecommunications?

The Investment 3   Communications Costs 5
Estimating Communications Requirements 7   Calculating Unit Charges 10
Expected Benefits 12   New Perspectives 13

2. Space, Frequency, and Time   15

Space Divisions 16   Frequency Division and Time Division 17
Code Conversion 20   Time Slots and Alohanet 21
Time-Assignment Speech Interpolation 23
Intelligent Time-Division Multiplexing 25   The Problem of Vocabulary 27

3. Concepts and Devices   29

Switching 29   Quality of Service 31   Modems 32
Technical Issues with Modems 34   Types of Modem 35   The User Site 36

4. Terminals   41

The Use of Terminals 42   Building Blocks 45
Transmission Speed and Interfacing 48   The Line Controller 50
Computers, Minicomputers, Microprocessors, and Terminals 52

5. Communications Gear   57

Multiplexers and Concentrators 58   Front Ending 61
Breaking Down the Front-End Tasks 67   The Data Communications Machine 70

6. From Data Processing to Data Communications   73

User Levels in Data Communications 74   System Perspectives 76
The Three Main Classes of Communications 81
Electronic Message Systems 81   Future Developments 83
A Message Service: Ontyme 84

7. Transaction-Based Systems   87

The Transaction Network Service 87   The Choice of Facilities 89
Types of Communications Link 91   Change of Structure 93
System Requirements 95

8. Message Theory   97

Message Technology 97   Principles of Message Systems 98
Conventions 100   Performance Criteria 102   The User's Requirements 103

9. What Is a Protocol?   105

Protocol Reliability 106   The Access Method 108
Procedural Requirements 110   Synchronous and Asynchronous 110
Synchronous Protocols 112
Terminals for Synchronous and Asynchronous Protocols 115

10. Circuit-Switching and Polling and Selecting   121

Circuit-Switching Principles 122
Control Procedures: Fixed, Switched, and Multipoint 123
The Coming Possibilities 129

11. Bit-Oriented Protocols   131

The Data Link 131   The Fields of XDLC 136
Frame Sequence and Acknowledgment 141
Using a Bit-Oriented Protocol in a Loop 143   Objectives of XDLC 145

12. The Nesting of Protocols   149

Standards for the Physical Circuit 150   Second-Level Protocols 151
Framing and Link Management 152   The Higher Levels 153
Applications Protocols 156

12. Networking Functions   159

Routing 160   Virtual Circuits and Datagrams 164
Choosing Virtual Circuit or Datagram 166
Connection and Transmission 167
Node-to-Node Protocols for Communications 168
IMP-to-IMP Protocols 169   IMP-to-Host Protocols 169
Host-to-Host Protocols and Higher 170

14. The X.25 Recommendation   171

What Is X.25? 172   The Communications Session 175
Comparing Protocols 176   Flow Control 179   Goals in Flow Control 181
Congestion Control 181   Internetworking 182

15. Session and Presentation Control   185

The Purpose of Session Control 187   ANSI and Session Control 189
Presentation Control 190   A Process-Level Protocol 192

16. Communications Software   195

Developing the Software 197   Software Functions 198
Downline Loading, Upline Dumping, and Loopback 202
Data Base Support 203   System Design Requirements 204
The Implementation Schedule 206

17. A Network Operating System   209

Designing a Basic Operating System 210   The Software "Constant" 212
Some Historical Background 214   Executive Functions 217
System Management 218   Data Maintenance 218
Terminal Handling 218   The Server System 220
Distributed Operating System 223

Index   225

INTRODUCTION

The rapid increase in the demand for data communications services has brought forward the need for more efficient structures than those now available. The great steps technology has been making during the last ten years substantiated many of the users' demands. In turn this increased the requests for terminal-to-terminal, terminal-to-computer, and computer-to-computer communications, and for remote access to data bases.

The aspect that distinguishes a computer from a communications network is the shared data base capability. This is precisely the subject which involves the highest grade of skill, and the one in which experience, worldwide, is the thinnest.

Though we still lean on data bases, we do know beyond doubt that data communications and data processing are converging. Before long there will be no distinction between them at all. The common ground is distributed information systems, or networking. Its impact will transform our lives, our professional and personal interests.

The emphasis in communications is shifting toward digital networks, which include not only voice traffic and digital transmission facilities but also intelligent devices for providing services previously impossible. The problem is that the most basic of the available resources, the telephone network, represents in the United States alone an investment of $130 billion, and such investments cannot be changed overnight.

Data traffic differs from voice traffic. It may be queued for delivery; it calls for bit error rates three orders of magnitude lower; it is subject both to preprocessing and postprocessing; it can be transmitted discontinuously in blocks or packets; it has different holding times; and for efficient services it requires simultaneous transmission and reception—something beyond people's abilities but not machines'.

What is more, the new networks should be designed to support a wide variety of services from teleconferencing to document-handling (electronic mail) and data and voice requirements. Imaginative developments are called for, because the solutions currently existing and those projected for the near future are not as radical as they need to be. Arthur A. Collins and Robert D. Pedersen aptly remark:*

> The question today is not simply how do we improve upon the telephone set of Bell and Edison. *Telecommunications systems have outgrown not only the classical telephone set, but also Bell's vision of a "grand system."* Communications today is not only "by word of mouth with another in a distant place." Not only men, but also machines require systematic communication—and not only by means of "branch wires with private dwellings, country houses, shops, manufacturers, etc." but also with jet aircraft, ships at sea, land vehicles, and spacecraft.

Satellites and optical fibers are the coming transmission media. And time-space-time (TST) switching technologies will one day become commonplace. But networks cannot be simply turned on, complete, from the word "go."

Conceptually, we have left behind the old world of hard metal contacts and moving mechanisms. We have entered the era of exceedingly small structures. Yet in telephony the mechanical devices are still around, and probably they will continue to be until the year 2000—creating the problem of symbiosis between the new technologies and the old.

One of the keys to the developing capabilities lies in the use of electronic switching and transmission technologies under software control. Another great issue is the integration of traffic. Voice, data, and image must be carried in a general-purpose network whose speeds, quality of service, and mode of operation should reflect future, not past, requirements.

The next five years will be crucial, not because of the number of networks to be developed and implemented, but because companies, both large and small, must make some major decisions about capital investments. And these will have to take into account the most probable shape of communications and data processing facilities during the next ten, fifteen, and twenty years.

Let me close by expressing my thanks to everyone who contributed to making this book successful. From my colleagues, for their advice; to the organization I visited in my research, for their insight; and Eva-Maria Binder for the drawings and the typing of the manuscript.

---

*Arthur A. Collins and Robert D. Pedersen, *Telecommunications: A Time for Innovation*. Merle Collins Foundation, Dallas, Texas, 1973.

1
What Is Telecommunications?

Telecommunications encompasses all transfer of information, both internal and external to an organization, by electromagnetic means. This includes voice telephone, data transmission, telegram and facsimile, and picture transmission.

The term *network* is often used in a broad sense to designate not only the circuits (and lines) for voice and data transmission but also terminal equipment, such as telephones, teletypewriters, switching equipment (PBXs, computers, etc.), and operating personnel.

Telecommunications and data processing both continue to penetrate the mainstream of the business and scientific environments. We see the combination of both in office products and services. And where previously the responsibilities for telecommunications, data processing, and office facilities were divided, we now see large, integrated departments that encompass all three. It is clear that very soon the telecommunications function will be everywhere one of management's most powerful tools.

The emergence of telecommunications as a key management discipline has several causes: (1) the growing demonstration of benefits to management functions, such as marketing, production, and finance; (2) the explosion of telecommunications technology, enriched by inventions in electronics and in production technology; (3) the increasing role of telecommunications at the corporate level, where it is easier to move information electronically than by the traveling of people and paper; (4) the advent of alternative suppliers in both equipment and services; (5) the increasing sophistication required for optimal choice; and (6) the alternatives in ways of spending the telecommunications dollars (Figure 1.1).

Today *telecommunications is one of business's biggest and fastest-rising expenses.* In the United States the cost is between $15 billion and $20 billion annually, or about 1 percent of the nation's gross national product. Some companies spend as much as 12 percent of their annual operating expenses on telecommunications.

2   *Data Communications for Distributed Information Systems*

Figure 1.1
Business telecommunications costs by class

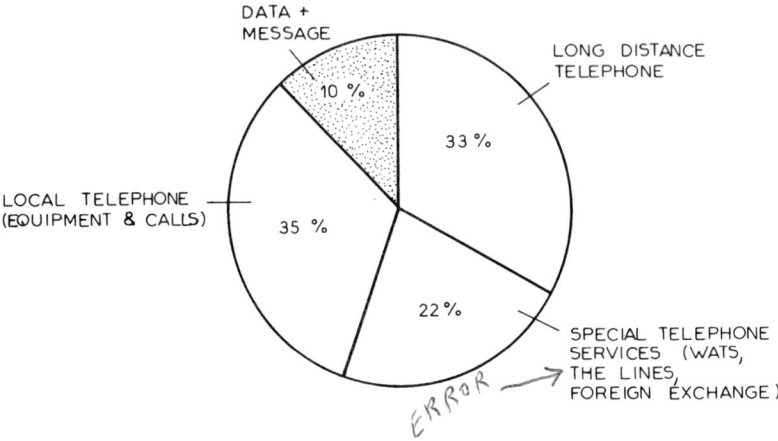

The national average is somewhat below 4 percent (Table 1.1). In the past these costs rose somewhat in line with sales; nowadays they rise much faster (Table 1.2). There are three reasons for this. First, new uses, such as data and facsimile, have only recently emerged in a service that otherwise remained basically unchanged for thirty or forty years. Second, corporate management is beginning to regard telecommunications less as a necessary evil and more as a vital management tool. Third, the effects of inflation are especially bad in some areas of telecommunications, particularly those that are noncompetitive, such as local services. This means that increasing professionalism is required to cope with costs.

Table 1.1
Telecommunications Cost Ratio by Industry

Industry	Communications Costs Range (%)	Average (%)	Of Total
Manufacturing	0.3–1.0	0.5	Turnover
Retailing	0.2–0.7	0.4	Turnover
Insurance	1–3	2	Premium income
Banking, Finance	0.6–4.2	1.5	Operating expenses
Airlines	3–7	4	Operating expenses
Securities	8–12	10	Operating Expenses

What Is Telecommunications? 3

Table 1.2
Telecommunications Markets/Carrier Only

	Billions of Dollars			*Annual Growth*
	1978	*1980*	*1984*	*Rate (%)*
Voice	45.00	54.00	80.00	10.9
Message	0.95	1.10	1.30	5.6
Data	3.80	5.60	8.50	20.0
	49.75	60.70	89.80	

The Investment

There are 160 million telephones in the United States and American Telephone and Telegraph, AT&T, serves 82 percent of them. Telephone equipment costs represent only 20 percent of the total telephone bills; 80 percent is for use. This is the area that has the greatest potential for cost control.

Capital investments are made in telephones, data sets (modems), private branch exchanges, switching centers, short lines (loops), long lines, the installation system, and the maintenance network.

The total investment in plant and facilities at AT&T was estimated in December 1977 at a colossal $98 billion. To this should be added the investment in plant and facilities of the GTE Corporation and the independent companies, about $24 billion. AT&T's planned expenditures for 1978 stood at $12.5 billion (their employees exceed 930,000), with another $3.8 billion per year for the independent companies. The cumulative total stands at $136 billion. For an estimated 160 million telephones in operation in 1978 this makes the capital investment $890 per telephone. The station (telephone) cost is 2 percent. The rest is the network, the switching centers, and the overall services. All this capital investment and operating expense is financed by the household market and by business and industry.

In early 1978 it was projected that in that year alone in the United States the telephones would carry more than 300 billion calls. Let us see what the share of a single function would be: cheque clearance, performed by the banking sector. The cheques processed by the banking system in 1978 were projected to be more than 40 billion. The ratio of calls to cleared cheques is 7.5 to 1. Approximately 75 percent of the cheques require bank clearance. Each clearance message is about 1,000 bits long; this means that 30 *trillion bits* are transmitted over lines for cheque clearance alone. If a telephone is used in every American home for direct access to computer memory at the local bank and for subsequent processing of payment orders and money transfers, then 50 percent of the current volume of cheques may be eliminated. This is one of the new frontiers for computers and data communications.

Statistics from the Department of Commerce show that telephone and teletypewriter traffic alone will constitute a $100-billion industry by 1986. By that year—or sooner, according to AT&T—it will cost less to transmit a facsimile letter than to send a conventional letter through the mail. By 1980 or '81 from 80 to 85 percent of all computers in the world should have at least one remote terminal on-line. In the same period more than 30 percent of the hardware budget will go to communications-related products and by 1986, more than 50 percent.

A variety of services can be provided by data communications, from sub-voice-grade lines (Telex being an example) to specific data communications-oriented networks (Figure 1.2). Packet switching is a special subject, which will be treated later in detail.

Is industry ready for this changeover? Statistics—and a good number of executives—say it is not. A couple of years ago a study made among seven medium-sized United States firms showed the following:

	Cumulatively spend	*While employing*
For computer gear	$56 million	1,089 persons
For communications	$20 million	15 persons

Figure 1.2

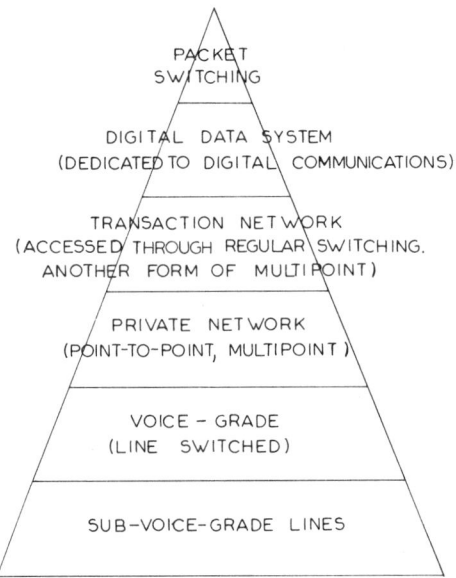

What Is Telecommunications? 5

In terms of know-how in systems applications and cost effectiveness, in 1979 we stood in the field of data communications exactly where we were in 1953 with computers. Yet in terms of money it is projected that the budget for equipment in the early 1980s might be as follows: 40 to 45 percent for data communications, 30 percent for data processing, and 25 to 30 percent for terminals.

By 1980 data communications would amount to a 30 percent share of expenditures for electronics data processing (Figure 1.3). As time passes, communications costs will represent 40 percent or more of the total budget. Already with Arpanet, a network developed by the Department of Defense, the cost of data communications is greater than the cost of data processing, and this is the best teleprocessing example we have today. With private lines the costs can even be higher. One telephone company (SIP, in Italy) stated that on the average the telephone lines cost $1,750 per year per terminal, for more than 200 terminals, as over against $2,100 per year for the terminal itself—and the terminal cost decreases sharply.

International Business Machines (IBM) predicts, however, that with satellites, optical fibers, and microelectronics the communications costs will drop dramatically, by 1982 to 1984, to a fortieth or a fiftieth of those prevailing today.

Communications Costs

Most companies look upon communications expenditures as a bothersome but necessary cost of doing business. Despite the magnitude of the costs, decision-making in this area is often fragmented among local offices or purchasing managers who have little or no technical experience in communications.

The essentials of the current situation are these: First, manageable telecommunications costs are rising because of inadequate controls. Secondly, the technology is proceeding at an extremely rapid pace, opening up innovative ways of deploying communications to competitive advantage. Thirdly, advanced products and services are being introduced, offering every firm an opportunity to upgrade its service and reduce its "fixed" costs.

Figure 1.3
Estimated telecommunications costs versus electronic data processing costs

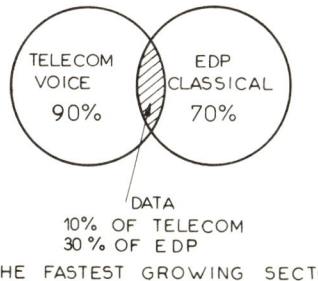

DATA
10% OF TELECOM
30% OF EDP
THE FASTEST GROWING SECTOR
IF DIMENSIONED AT DATA COMMUNICATIONS LEVEL

Contrast, for example, the typical decision-making process concerning communications hardware with that of acquiring a medium-scale computer. In the case of the computer the lessons of the 1960s taught everyone that a great deal of analysis, planning, and weighing of alternatives is needed before any decisions are made, yet a 500-line private branch exchange system (PBX) is equivalent in leased cost and service charges to a fully equipped medium-scale computer. Further, the new PBX system will incur a firm a contractual liability of three to five years, making this decision a $1-million commitment.

Telephone communications expenses involve both direct and indirect costs. The *direct-cost* elements are the easier to pinpoint and analyze; examples are the telephone company's charges for service and equipment, salaries associated with switchboard attendants, and the value of the floor space used by the telephone plant. The *indirect costs* are involved in establishing general criteria of cost-benefits that suit the organization as a whole and its operating departments.

It is equally important to determine the degree or quality of telecommunications service to be purchased. This requires a comprehensive analysis of the entire telephone network, the communications loads imposed by different functional organizations within the corporation, and the effectiveness of the present service.

Some employees have so-called telephone-intensive job requirements. Purchasing agents, reservations clerks, and sales persons, for example, often require a higher degree of service than many middle-management and junior executives. These people deliver messages to a client, to a supplier, to the company's own factories or sales offices, often by voice.

Voice, however, is not an efficient medium. A message delivered by voice must be transcribed; then it must be transported as hard copy, transcribed again onto a computer support medium, and then checked, validated, and processed. Transcriptions mean opportunities for errors and errors always cost.

It is not necessary to talk of computer networks to dramatize the issues of choice and the costs that lie behind them. We can stick, for that purpose, to the simpler example of a PBX, which is able to answer the voice requirements. The number of trunks needed to serve a specific PBX system is determined by an Erlang analysis and a queueing study. Erlang's formula may be used to postulate the probability that a randomly arriving call will encounter a busy condition. Because the caller must hang up if the line is busy, the call is lost in the network. A queueing analysis determines the number of attendants needed to ensure a high probability that all calls will be answered within a predetermined time. Response-time requirements are not the same for every class of PBX user nor for the normal or peak-hour use by the same subscriber. In determining the type of PBX needed it is wise to use a checklist; an example is given in Table 1.3.

Concerning the technical specifications we should examine both the minicomputer that will reside on the premises and the postprocessing software that will transform the computer's output into meaningful management reports. The flexibility of both the hardware and the software is important; a company's communications use is constantly changing. The equipment should be modular, expandable in both size and features, and easily upgraded from a passive to an active and dynamic system.

We should also be convinced of a supplier's dedication to a continual improvement of his wares, and this includes software.

Estimating Communications Requirements

In this and the following sections we shall concentrate on the voice-grade service. Estimating the requirements of a communications service is not always easy, particularly when a company is large.

First of all we must find out how the existing system is being used, what needs are not being met, and what the future needs will be. Three types of study may be very helpful in this: the executive interview, the employee questionnaire, and an operations-load study.

In the first study the manager of each department is interviewed to determine what his department does, what its future plans are, and how it uses the telephone system.

Several important questions need answers: What is the function of the department? How will the function change in the next five years? Who or what other departments are contacted most often? What are the best and worst features of the existing telephone system? How could the telephone system help the department in the future?

Operations-load studies are vital because they afford an insight into what is happening on a day-to-day basis.

We can determine several factors that are important in assessing the desirability of a PBX service: number of incoming calls in a month, number of outgoing calls in a month, number of operator transfers in a month, percentage of incoming callers who know the name, department, or extension number of the person they wish to speak to, and dates when additional operators, positions of switchboard, or station lines were added. Information available from operators, such as the number of incoming and outgoing calls handled, should be collected periodically and graphed for an analysis and a projection of trends.

When all these studies have been completed, we shall have a pretty good picture of the company's communications requirements now and for the future. The following four items should be given attention.

Number of lines: We should know the company's plans for the next five years and how they will affect the telephone system. Then we can determine the system's growth by projecting the past and present ratios of telephone lines to number of employees into the future.

Number of operators: We can determine the current number of attendant call operations each day and forecast this for at least five years. By relating the forecast

Table 1.3
A User's Checklist for a Telephone Monitoring System

A. *Equipment*

1. Modular, expandable units: to more lines and trunks, to active or dynamic features, to allow for company expansion and for more sophistication.
2. Connection to line or trunk: has flexibility; can be tailored to user needs; an initially low-cost system can be upgraded later.
3. Wide breadth of line and trunk toll restricting abilities; tailoring of telephone usage to management responsibilities.
4. Proven technology.
5. Enhanced reliability.
6. A minimum of one month of magnetic-tape storage saves necessity to change tapes frequently.
7. On-line diagnostics and on-line reports through teletypewriter: immediate monitoring of points of developing bottlenecks.
8. Rotary or touchtone or both, as input: saves system conversion, enhances flexibility.

B. *Software*

9. Ability to capture only the calls required (not local or intracompany calls): saves postprocessing expenses.
10. Ability to capture call records in real time: saves postprocessing, increases capacity of magnetic-tape storage.
11. Complete and wide array of software capability available now: increases breadth of management reports available, enables customizing of reports.

Table 1.3 (cont.)
A User's Checklist for a Telephone Monitoring System

---

12. Supplier service center facilities available: relieves user of electronic data processing.
13. Service-center programming and data base updated as tariffs change: ensures timeliness and accuracy of management reports.
14. Automatic recommendations on optimized network configurations: enables responsive, rapid configuration.
15. Hourly distribution of call minutes per trunk: pinpoints congestion, enables smoothing of peaks and valleys.
16. Line or trunk correlation: trunk identification for accurate engineering, performance analysis, charge back.
17. Alternative methods of cost distribution such as between Wide Area Telephone Service (WATS) and WATS overflow lines: enables fair allocation of telephone expenses.
18. User data base easily changed: maintains accurate and up-to-date- cost allocation and management reports.

C. *Crucial Factors*

---

19. Variety of short- or long-term rental or lease programs available, also purchase or lease and purchase: customizes acquisition to meet financial policies.
20. Breadth of maintenance ability: to ensure uptime, to enhance credibility of references available.

---

to an operator's call-handling capacity we can establish the number of operators that will be required in the future.

Problems with existing system: We should know what the current problems are and what the employees' opinions are on how to improve the system.

Minimal in-dial percentage: We should know the percentage of persons calling in who know whom they wish to speak with and who would dial the extension if they could.

Having now determined the current and future communications requirements, we must decide whether the existing system will meet them and, if not, whether PBX service should be obtained. Some of the factors to consider are the following:

Capacity: Can the system meet the future station line requirements? Is there room for future growth?

Equipment: Can the important existing communications problems be solved? Is the system maintenance-free or old and out of date?

Size: What is the initial number of lines? What is the needed growth capability?

Features: Which are mandatory features? Which are the desirable features?

Maintenance: What is the expected reliability? What are the type and frequency of maintenance required?

Site: Which are the site limitations (floor space, ceiling height, floor loading, power requirements, and environmental conditions)?

Schedule: What is the schedule for starting installation? For cutting over the system?

Cost: What is the cost of equipment? Of the service, installation, maintenance (if extra)? Of the moves and rearrangements?

Objectives: Does the system enhance our corporate objectives? Can it be expanded to meet objectives as requirements develop?

Future costs: How much will it cost to expand or modify the system to meet the company's future needs? How much will additional operators cost? How much is the necessary floor space worth?

It should be understood that this impressive list of questions relates to a PBX, not to a computer and data communications network; the requirements for the latter are much broader.

Calculating Unit Charges

In calculating message unit charges, the following issues are of importance.

Message unit: A measure of telephone service used on station-to-station calls within an area, based on time and distance.

Message-rate service: Every call is message unit or long distance; calls within certain areas are only one message unit, regardless of length of time of call.

Local-area service: A flat rate for a small area, message unit or long distance for others.

Metropolitan service: A flat rate for a large area; message unit or long distance for others.

Flat-rate service: A more expensive flat rate for unlimited calling within a limited area.

Metropolitan-area service: Calls timed within the area, such as WATS.

Foreign-exchange (FX) service: One of the above from another location.

In controlling abuses and misuses in order to lower costs, management must:

Determine the overall problems; find out where calls go and why.

Train the employee in telephone usage.

Study the equipment and line configuration, considering alternative services and removing unused equipment to reduce exposure.

Evaluate the wisdom of restricting individual telephones to cut down on unauthorized calling.

Lock telephones after hours, to prevent unauthorized calls by after-hour personnel.

Employ equipment that can check for proper use and block improperly selected calls; hardware devices monitor and control calls.

Establish exception-reporting and analyze results on a continuing basis.

The common background of the aforementioned points is the need to analyze the costs of communicating on a regular and systematic basis to ensure full value received for each dollar spent.

For a documented cost control (and billing), call records must be consistently kept. They include the authorization number, the number called, the duration of call in minutes and tenths of minutes, the time of initiation of call, the type of long-distance line desired, and the actual type of long-distance line used. This information is the basis for billing the individual users in their departments for their use of the telephone network. It also provides the data for systems usage analysis and reconfiguration.

A cost-control scheme is of fundamental importance if we wish to evaluate the means of communications used so as to ensure that the best available method is being utilized, commensurate with the job at hand. The more limited, and more immediate, object of calculating unit charges is to establish a cost allocation procedure, which would permit the company to take advantage of shared services and produce cost breakdowns that are acceptable and equitable in the various divisions. The findings may be instrumental in defining a number of other issues. For example:

Developing employee education programs designed to encourage good communications habits.

Promoting an awareness and appreciation of communication costs.

Developing a working knowledge of equipment capabilities and limitations.

Optimizing, within the existing tariffs and regulatory changes, the use of the telephone facilities.

Studying the applications of new equipment, systems, and offerings, as they may be profitable and effectively used by the company.

Companies that have studied the cost effectiveness of their current systems have found that they should use the following: data terminals to reduce transaction-recording (clerical) costs, data concentrators to cut the line costs, special common carriers, interfacility private-line costs, an advanced PBX for combinations of voice and data and to reduce operator needs, and the "interconnect" PBX to gain the advantages of industry-specialized design and of lower costs.

Expected Benefits

The control of costs, though absolutely necessary, is not enough. If costs were the only problem, we should not use cars, the telephone computers, or electricity at large. Money is spent to produce a useful product, and the most appreciated benefit of any product is that which materially improves the user's productivity and ultimate profit. The most direct route to the top in any corporate organization is via the management discipline most crucial to success: the enhancement of profits. Industry has seen the marketing "whizz kids" climb to the top in the 1960s and the computer specialists climb to the top in the 1970s; the telecommunications experts may be there in the 1980s.

The reasons behind this new field of interest are structural. They include the growth and concentration of service facilities, the fragmentation of nonstandardized production runs, the growth of marketing organizations, a plethora of government regulations, and an acceleration both in the volume of recording and in time scales.

Corporate personnel are less and less concerned with the actual management techniques and more and more with the recording and monitoring of production, marketing, and finance functions. The information flow becomes the lifeblood of an enterprise. Without adequate supplies of relevant information, management is increasingly unable to reach rational decisions.

Another reason for this field of interest is that information theory has lagged behind the demands placed on it. The layer upon layer of management reporting structures is distorting the information flow.

The combination of computing and telecommunications technology has made itself felt. Banks are an obvious example. No major financial institution today would contemplate running its business without on-line systems that not only serve their clientele more efficiently but also are an invaluable marketing tool. The banks are consolidating credit and credit-card information, offering services to a far wider range of customers than formerly allowed.

Electronic mail is another example, though it is still in the experimental stage.

The airlines, too, have long computerized their reservation systems and their arrival and departure information, so that the traveling public may be better informed on actual flight arrivals and departures.

Through point-of-sale terminals the retail trade is moving toward credit authorization, and almost instant information on the sales of particular products, using that information for rapid reordering, so as to avoid heavy inventory positions.

The potential is hardly scratched. As the price of long-haul communications facilities drops, the size of communications channels widens to suit the information flows, and computing power is focused on the manipulation of the flow of data, voice and image. It is in this way that the full potential of telecommunications begins to emerge.

New Perspectives

To manage communications effectively a firm must look to the future and, in some cases, the far future. Communications today are more manageable than they have ever been, and communications managers have more useful tools available to them to do a better job. Future systems promise a total upset of the present values. Which are the systems that will have far-reaching impact? They are the communications satellites and waveguide transmission, the large-scale terminal-oriented computer systems, the lines that will carry 250,000 telephone calls simultaneously, and the computer-switched telephone exchanges (already here). As they grow, these systems will enable information to be transferred a full order of magnitude more quickly, accurately, and broadly.

Interactive television, allowing one to see as well as hear the other party, and two-way broadband cable (CATV) communications systems are in limited use today. When perfected and accepted widely (probably in the early 1980s) the developments will spark major shifts in marketing techniques, in the deployment of physical facilities, in travel patterns, and in work habits.

The developments are timely, because the current systems and the procedural solutions are both overburdened. There are more than 120 million telephones in the United States and 130 million more in other countries. The telephone exploits a basic electroacoustic technology that is difficult to improve on, given very tight economic bounds; yet, simple as it is, it acquires enormous power by virtue of the network to which it offers access. One of the reasons for exploiting to the fullest degree the potential of a telephone system is its general use. Since it is in almost every home, the telephone reaches many strata of a working population. The network embraces more than 200 countries and territories, making it possible for virtually any pair of telephones among the more than 250 million to be interconnected on command. The new needs (data solutions) extend this perspective.

Facsimile terminals in the home or business office will supplement and, later on, replace the mail carrier. New approaches to Telex communication will aid in this direction. At present most Telex terminals are of the type using 50 bits per second or the 5-bit Baudot code, with 75 bits per second being used in recent years. Since the data transmission capacity of a telephone line, however, can be 9,600 bits per second, the Telex authorities, or users with large numbers of terminals themselves, combine the low-speed data streams and transmit them over a single high-speed facility (time-division multiplexing).

Many areas in the use of telephony are still unexploited. For example, a simple attachment to the telephone handset makes it possible to transmit a patient's heart signals to the office of a physician, where the signals are reproduced on a cardiograph. Other developments, still in the experimental stage, are transmission via optical media, electronic mail, and voice-input recognition. All these will offer strong economic incentives for executives to change some of their basic ways of conducting business. That is why we cannot foretell tomorrow's solutions on the basis of what is available today. New systems are being developed that will revolutionize the current communications services.

2

Space, Frequency, and Time

The four basic design parameters characterizing a data communications network are transmission, switching, storage, and control. In this chapter we shall be concerned with the technology of transmission: space, frequency, and time.

Transmission is the function of the links, or channels. The links may be twisted wire, coaxial cable, waveguides, radio bridges, satellite channels, or other media. They may be arranged in a star or in a loop shape, to interconnect a switching center with other switching centers and with subscribers. As regards the technical aspects of transmission, we must account for electrical characteristics, such as conditioning, synchronization, regeneration, and the frequency spectrum. Across the electromagnetic spectrum even the nomenclature changes. *Discrete frequencies* are used mostly for audio and speech. *Conventional wavelengths* are radio waves through microwaves. *Rays* are heat, light, and molecular-electron emissions (which are also frequency-related phenomena). *Wideband* usually refers to media that allow the handling of any type of signal whatever, including transmission and switching. (In this sense, if one had to transmit only voice and Telex, a 1,200-band line is a wide band. A wideband solution means, essentially, transmission and switching that do not have limits due to band.)

Voice traffic has classically been accomplished with half-duplex links (requiring one pair of wires). In half-duplex it is necessary to invert the line in order to change the direction of transmission. This fits voice requirements, since in person-to-person communications the two stations do not need to transmit at the same time, but it is inadequate for data communications, with the so-called intelligent terminals and computers, which can transmit and receive simultaneously. Simultaneous two-way transmission requires full duplex (two pair of wires).

Another major difference between the lines for voice grade and those for data communications is in the bit error rate (BER), which is the number of bit errors transmitted per, say, one million bits. Bit error rates of 10^{-4} to 10^{-5} are acceptable for voice-grade lines, but they must be upgraded by nearly three orders of magnitude, to 10^{-7}, for data communications.

Two other factors differentiate voice-grade lines from data communications, one being the call-holding time and the other the store-and-forward capability.

The call-holding time in voice-grade communications averages three minutes. The average for data traffic depends on the type of transmission being treated: very large messages may take one or two hours, whereas queries and real-time update will take only a few seconds. But data transmission can be spaced in convenient ways: very large messages are usually sent during the night hours, when traffic is least, so that by helping to fill the slow times an optimal use of the network is made.

Store-and-forward was implemented with message-switching. The receiving node stores a message, if traffic is too great, until it can forward it down the line. Today this process is largely reserved for data traffic, but we may expect changes in the general character of voice traffic due to the evolving requirements, the increasing speed of the lines, and the limited sensitivity of the human communicator to minute interruptions.

Space Division

Information is transmitted over channels so that an end-to-end communication may be established. The search for channel capacity has led to significant developments in switching technology. The process of switching necessitates the activation of some sort of physical connection or path to allow a conversation between two stations, whether they are telephone sets or terminals. The connection may occur by electromechanical means (a relay contact closure) or by electronic means (activation of a diode) without any difference in the basic switching principle. An actual metallic switch point (cross-point) must be there and be available to make the switched connection. Space-division switching is one of the most commonly used in telephone systems (Figure 2.1). The "space" is to the physical metallic path, which always exists for a given switch connection. This kind of switching is done with a multiplicity of individual wires, the talking paths over which the voice or data are carried. All conversational electromechanical telephone switching systems are of this type. Most electronic systems today also use space-division techniques.

Space-division switching is not the only means of connecting two points; time and frequency division are two other approaches, fundamentally different from that of switching, so that there is a total of three different methods. Frequency division and time division differ from space division in that separate physical paths or circuits are not required for each voice or data transmission. One advantage of using frequency and time separation for switching is that the number of elements (cross-points) is reduced and, hence, the cost in the interconnection network.

Figure 2.1
(a) Space-division switching (space = actual metallic physical path);
(b) frequency-division switching

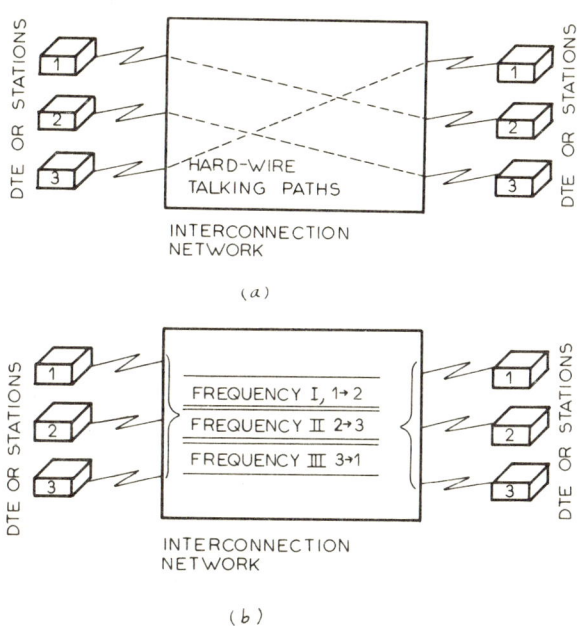

Furthermore, time switching provides an elegant basis for the transmission of voice, data, and image on a single channel.

Frequency Division and Time Division

If simultaneous conversations that are to be switched are established in different frequency bands with a means at both ends of discriminating and recognizing the assigned frequencies, then we have a switching technique based upon frequency separation. Since voice occupies a bandwidth of only about 4,000 cycles per second, a transmission scheme that has a bandwidth of some multiples of this allows many conversations to be sent over a single piece of wire.

The use of frequency for channel separation is common enough; it is known as frequency-division multiplexing (FDM). It is applied in two major areas: carrier transmission systems and data multiplexers. Transmission systems employing it are used widely by common carriers on computer communications systems. Concentrating low-speed terminals onto a single high-speed line makes use of frequency-division multiplexing.

At present frequency-division multiplexing is not used to any great extent in telephone switching, being limited to applications with relatively few subscribers because of the physical size and cost, but it has specific technical advantages in certain applications.

The use of time for channel separation, like frequency, is becoming common for carrier transmission systems and data multiplexing (Figure 2.2); it is commonly referred to as time-division multiplexing (TDM). It is used chiefly when large numbers of subscribers' lines need to be accommodated.

Time-division multiplexing has the advantage of becoming more economical as the number of lines increases; this makes it eminently suitable as a replacement for space-division switching in telephone applications (data, voice). All subscribers, lines, or channels, share the same portion of the frequency spectrum, as does space-division switching, but they do it in a time-dependent manner. The channels are separated on a selective, sequential basis. Thus both time-division and

Figure 2.2

(a) Time division switching and (b) time-division multiplexing

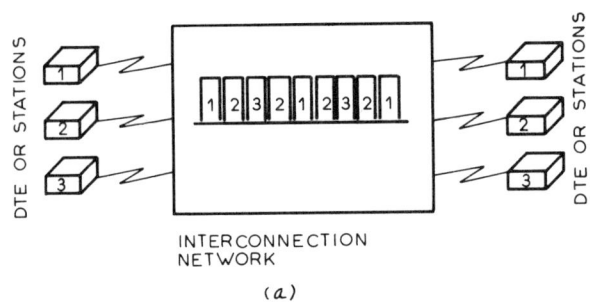

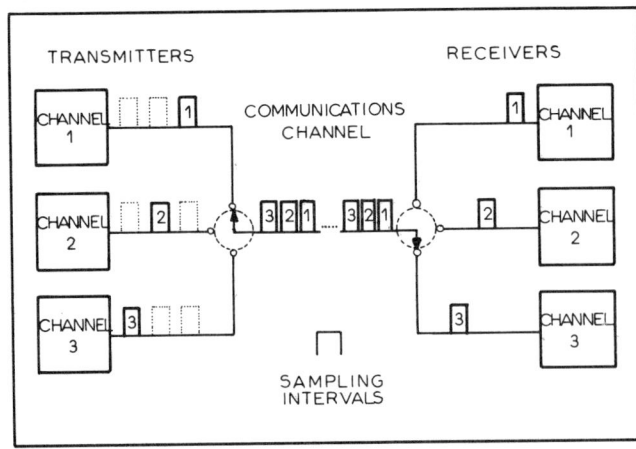

Space, Frequency, and Time 19

frequency-division have the ability to multiplex many channels onto a single wire or cable while remaining, as in space-division switching, independent of frequency considerations within a particular system; see Figure 2.3.

In time-division multiplexing all information is represented in a digital format in order to achieve the required time separation between channels and drive the synchronization at both ends of the link. This presents no problem for the transmission of data, but for voice it requires that analog information be converted into digital form. The process by which this is accomplished is called sampling (see the next section).

Long-haul digital transmission is rapidly emerging as the next logical step in the conversion to time-division multiplexing of trunk data communications systems. To accomplish this conversion and to take maximal advantage of existing communications facilities, we need both frequency-division multiplexing and digital processing and modulation techniques; they should make efficient utilization of the existing allocated bandwidths.

Figure 2.3

FREQUENCY–DIVISION MULTIPLEXING (FDM)

AND TIME DIVISION MULTIPLEXING (TDM)

A1, B1, C1, A2, B2, D1, ...

THE CHANNEL DIVISION CAN BE CARRIED OUT AT BOTH ENDS WITH FDM

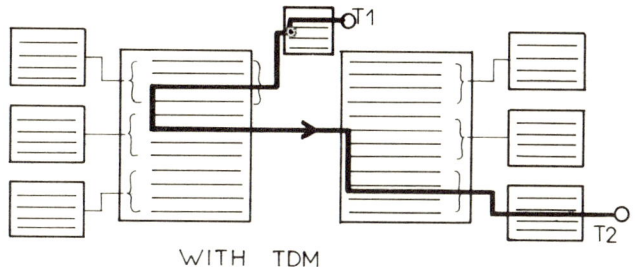

WITH TDM
THERE IS A CASCADING OF ARRANGEMENTS WHEREBY TERMINALS COMMUNICATE THROUGH TIME SLOTS.

Let us recapitulate. To connect one point with another for the transmission of information we need a link, that is, a communications channel. The link may be created by pulling from point 1 to point 2 a twisted wire (which we really would not do), or by putting a coaxial cable or a private radio bridge between them or by getting the telephone company to provide the line. The information will travel over the line by means of multiplexing with space, frequency, or time division.

Code Conversion

In the preceding section we spoke of the process of sampling, the conversion of analog information to digital. There are both economic and technical advantages in converting voice and image signals into digital forms (Figure 2.4). This calls for a code-conversion procedure, of which there are three types: pulse code modulation (PCM), differential pulse code modulation (DPCM), and delta modulation (DM). Pulse code modulation has been traditionally used for the digitization of voice and it still constitutes the standard form, but delta modulation is the simplest and most economic of the three.

As Figure 2.3 shows, voice-encoding involves sequential steps. First an analog input signal is band-limited by a low-pass filter to the cycles per second (Hertz) corresponding to the frequency band of speech, 3,000 to 4,000 Hertz. Then the signal is sampled at a frequency rate greater than the frequency band. Thus, for voice a sampling base of 8,000 times per second is used. The sampled signal is held in a sample-and-hold device during the period between two sampling intervals. Then it is quantized into one of 2^n levels (if the coder is designed to produce n-bit words per sample). The larger the n, the more accurate the representation. To code, for instance, the signals in Figure 2.3 we need at least $n = 5$. American telephone-quality standards require $n = 13$ to encode low-level signals. Next is needed a linear coder with uniform quantizing step sizes; this produces linear pulse code modulation (LPCM). This then reduces excessive bandwidth requirements by compressing words in linear pulse code modulation according to standard algorithmic methods; this is called compressed pulse code modulation (CPCM). The functions of equalization and compression are often combined. In decoding, the 8-bit compressed pulse is converted into amplitude level, and the pulse samples are low-pass filtered at the original bandwidths.

The delta modulation principle is quite different in several ways. The band-limited input signal is compared with a "prediction" of the input derived from the encoder's digital output. All intervals are controlled by clock. The output of the error signal is quantized into 1-bit words. Finally, if the error signal is positive, the quantizer's output is 1; if negative, it is 0.

The code structure of delta modulation is inherently simpler than that of pulse code modulation. Its clock rate is much higher. This suggests the use of much simpler band-limiting filters. Furthermore, the feedback network is designed so as to allow the output to be a close approximation (estimate) of the input signal at the

Space, Frequency, and Time 21

Figure 2.4
(PAM, pulse amplitude modulation)

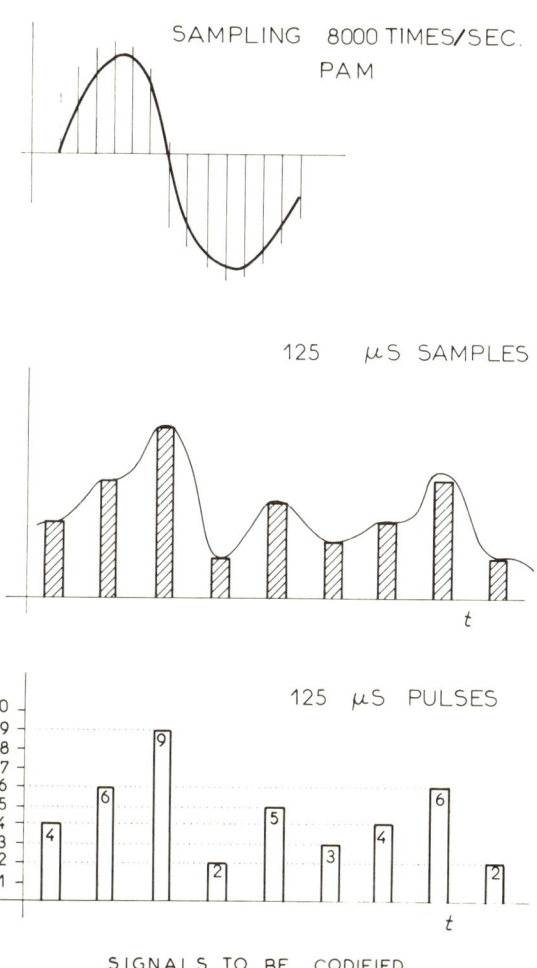

next clock pulse. And improvements can be applied, such as adaptive delta modulation (ADM).

Time Slots and Alohanet

Though frequency and time division may be used equally well with voice and with data communications, the fast-growing demand for data and image transmission underlines the need for new techniques or else the generalization of old ones that are so far quite specialized. A different way of saying this is to say that the growing use of distributed information systems and the increasing intelligence of terminals make imperative better solutions to the problems of communications from computer to computer, from computer to terminal, and from terminal to terminal. One may say that the real need is for a communications system with the following characteristics.

A large number of terminals transmitting data in a very "bursty" or "low-duty-cycle" fashion.

A small number of nodes (hosts) transmitting data at a "high-duty-cycle."

A medium number of devices exchanging synchronous data, e.g., facsimiles.

A medium number of devices with asynchronous data concentrated in clusters. (*Asynchronous* means start-stop, or character by character; each character is preceded by a start bit, the zero condition, and followed by one or more stop bits.)

A high priority on full connectivity for a large number of subscribers. Full connectivity means that ability of any subscriber to communicate with any other subscriber or group of subscribers simultaneously.

One solution is time-division multiple-access (TDMA) bus, or satellite broadcast; in this system time is divided into intervals called slots, which are combined into larger intervals called frames.

The pioneering effort in this field was made in Hawaii, where the Alohanet was developed. The system uses small radio transceivers connected to interactive terminals, to provide communication between these terminals, which are scattered throughout the Hawaiian islands, and a central computer. Each terminal buffers several characters and then forms a message with an address and a checksum; it then attempts to transmit this message to the central computer. If it accepts the message correctly, the central computer sends back an acknowledgment. If the transmission is in error (for instance, when there is competition between that message and another terminal's message), no acknowledgment is returned, in which case the terminal waits for a given amount of time and retransmits the message. Transmissions from the central computer to the terminals, on the other hand, do not suffer from "contention" since there is only one source of traffic in that direction.

A project that, like Arpanet, is sponsored by the Department of Defense, is Satnet. Among its features are the following.

A number of satellite nodes, called interface message processors (IMP), are connected to satellite earth stations and share a broadcast satellite channel.

The same principles as in the Alohanet hold here, with a few exceptions.

All the interface message processors act as sources of traffic as well as receivers, so there is contention in both directions.

The traffic over the channel consists of long file transfers as well as interactive traffic.

The speed of the channel is very high, for instance, speeds of 50 kilobits per second have been tested, and speeds of 1.5 megabits per second are intended for the future.

Such are the factors that have influenced the designers of satellite contention systems to provide for more efficient mechanisms than so-called random Aloha.

The simple expedient of synchronizing all interface message processors so that packets fit into time slots leads to only half as many "collisions." Further refinements, including advance reservations of time slots, are also possible.

Another system using contention is Ethernet, developed by the Xerox Corporation for local network connection. A number of subsequent developments in this field have also begun, such as the Network System Corporation's Hyperbus and various projects around the country at, for instance, the Massachusetts Institute of Technology.

These systems have in common a coaxial cable as transmission medium, with cable adaptors connecting the various computers and terminals in a local area to this cable. The typical transmission speeds are in the range of 1 to 10 megabits per second. Contention for transmission over the cable happens in exactly the same manner as over a radio or satellite system. Messages are addressed and carry checksums. Collisions between messages can be noted by the senders.

The cable-based systems are often implemented in such a way that it is possible for a potential sender to sense the carrier on the cable before initiating its own transmission; if the system is already busy, it can wait until the cable is free before transmitting. This is impossible in satellite systems because of the long propagation times, but it is not impossible in radio systems such as Alohanet. Thus, the collisions in a cable-based system can be much fewer than those in transmission systems with long delays, such as satellite channels. The basic principle underlying transmission with and without slots is shown in Figure 2.5.

Time-Assignment Speech Interpolation

Costly communication links can justify extraordinary signal-processing at the terminal if their traffic capacity can be materially increased. One such signal-processing adjunct is the time-assignment speech interpolation (TASI). It was developed for the very expensive transatlantic cable (for voice transmission). The method is a concentration by what is called stuffing. It differs from multiplexing, in which different voice paths require their own discrete time slot on a frequency-division channel. It takes advantage of the brief silences in normal conversation to achieve channel savings of more than 2 to 1. The silences are simply not transmitted. When the speaker pauses, the channel is taken away from him and assigned to an active speaker. With this strategem 96 overseas telephone channels can carry 235 simultaneous conversations spread over different trunk lines.

Figure 2.5

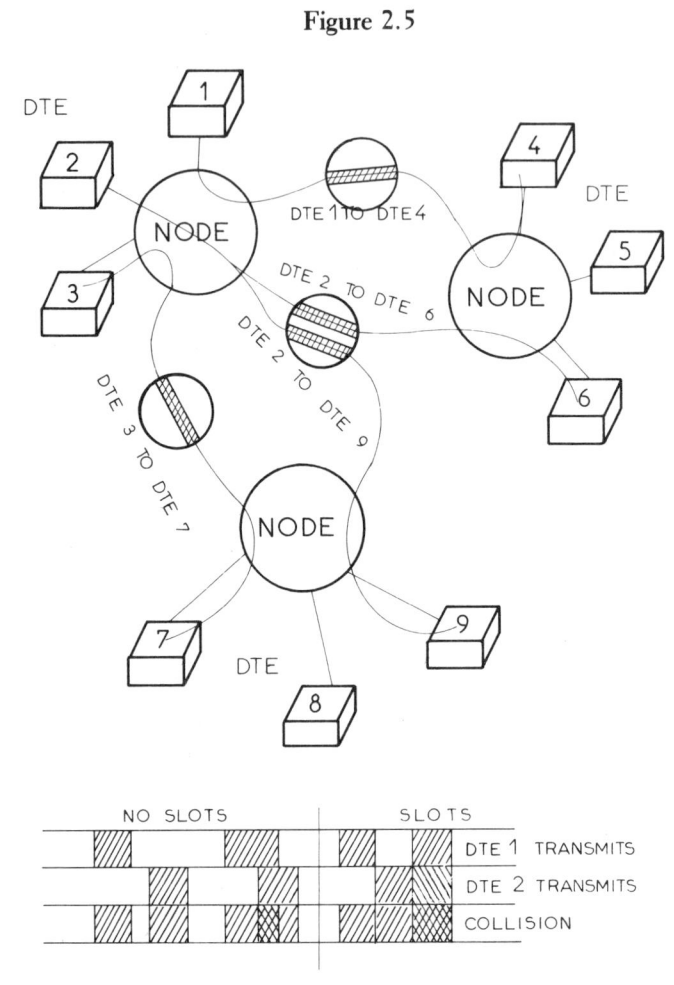

The procedure is based on a characteristic of normal conversation, which is that there are many short pauses between words and phrases and very lengthy pauses when one person is listening or searching around the telephone for a pencil or some such. In a two-way conversation the average speaker is actually talking somewhat less than 40 percent of the time. The TASI monitors each speaker's time and compares its signal 25,000 times per second against five distinct reference levels. The speaker is assigned a channel only when he is judged to be active. In general, a speaker will retain a channel for the second or so taken up by a word or group of syllables. Only after a pause of a fourth of a second is the channel taken away from him. When he resumes speaking, he is likely to be assigned a different channel.

This is an excellent example of a technology that fits perfectly into a data communications environment. Let us see why.

Space, Frequency, and Time

Data terminal equipment—a computer, minicomputer, or terminal—may be linked to a network via single physical circuits and employ packet-interleaved asynchronous time-division multiplexing (ATDM), which is a hybrid of multiplexing and concentration. This type of multiplexing differs from other time-division multiplexing in that a dedicated time slot is not provided for each circuit being multiplexed. It exploits the fact that a typical circuit to remote data terminal equipment may actually be carrying data only a small percentage of the time. It dynamically allocates the bandwidth to an active circuit, thereby increasing the overall utilization of the line and decreasing the bandwidth needed by the circuit connecting the terminal equipment to the network node. The bandwidth of the physical circuit must be based on queueing delays for handling the average busy-period loads for the virtual circuits being multiplexed.

This can be said in summary: the transmission of data, by means of logical solutions, on the same physical facility, have developed in the way in which voice transmission disciplines have developed with the telephone lines since the 1950s. Without such fundamental evolutionary steps it would not have been possible to talk today of the multiplexing of voice, data, and image nor of the exciting new perspectives in data communications.

Intelligent Time-Division Multiplexing

More demands for services and better capabilities produce better tools. Such is true of the recently developed "intelligent" time-division multiplexers. The immediate attraction of the new TDMs is the significant improvements in network utilization that they offer. They provide the network with the efficiencies of a concentrator and the network transparency of a hard-wired TDM, at a cost only slightly higher. They accomplish greater network efficiencies by taking advantage of network statistics. If we regard a circuit as the path between a terminal and the port of a central processing unit (CPU) we can view its use from three statistical aspects.

The statistics of circuit use: The dimensions of the periods of complete connection between a terminal and its port vary from the occasionally used terminal, such as in time-sharing applications, to the full-period dedicated terminal.

The statistics of data activity: The periodicities of data transmission on a connected circuit vary. Keyboard entry is at the low end of the activity range, and devices that transmit data without interruption, such as the high-speed aggregate of the TDM itself, are at the high end.

The statistics of language use: Individual characters within a set vary in the frequency with which they are used. Morse code, for instance, has a set twenty-six letters, ten numbers, fourteen punctuation marks, and some operational characters. The length of each coded character is inversely proportional to its frequency of use in the language. In English, for example, the code symbols for the letters E and T have one signaling element each, whereas the code symbols for punctuation marks have six.

Different multiplexing techniques are used, each with its own characteristic advantages and disadvantages, but all are statistical in nature, and the term *statistical multiplexing* has come to mean those techniques that are based on the statistics of data activity.

On a typical active circuit there are periods when no data are being transmitted, such as between keystrokes in a manual-entry circuit or between ACK and NAK transmissions on the return path of a bisynchronous circuit. In statistical multiplexing only active data are transmitted. They are formed into packets, together with channel-address information and error-protection coding. The packet length varies from system to system and depends very much on the applications. For instance, when propagation delay is important, the packets are kept relatively short, perhaps 32 characters or bytes. There may be also the requirement to transmit "short packets," such as the last few characters of a typed line. The intelligent TDM must therefore monitor all the transmissions in search of packet-terminating characters.

Statistical multiplexers are transparent to the standard code sets, but their use is limited in random-pattern transmissions because packet-terminating characters are generally unidentifiable. Since the packets consist of channel-addressing information and error-protection coding besides data, the proportion of the high-speed aggregate data stream occupied is somewhat greater than the circuit data rate, the actual proportion being determined by packet length.

The network traffic statistics must be monitored very closely when statistical multiplexing is used. If traffic forces a channel to wait for "space" on the high-speed aggregate data stream for a period longer than the buffer length assigned to the channel, then subsequent data are lost. This potential blocking may be reduced by extending the channel buffer lengths, by increasing the high-speed aggregate data rate, or by reducing the number of circuits that have access to the statistical multiplexer.

Data-compaction multiplexers gain their efficiency through the statistics of language use. This technique can be very efficient for a very specific language application, since the more frequent characters are assigned few signaling elements, and the less frequent characters are assigned to code words, the number of signaling elements being roughly in inverse proportion to their frequency of use.

The same characteristic that makes a code set very efficient for a specific language application can make it very inefficient for some other application. For instance, a code set intended for the transmission of an English-language text can be very inefficient for the transmission of numerical data (as in the case of Morse code). For maintaining a high level of efficiency the terminal code set, such as ASCII, is abbreviated when converted to the data-compaction code set for transmission. The efficiency is therefore obtained at the sacrifice of data transparency.

Space, Frequency, and Time

The data-compaction characters define, in their bit sequence, their own termination. This is necessary for determining whether a sequence of, say, 10 bits represents one 10-bit character from one channel, two 5-bit characters from two different channels, or perhaps two 3-bit characters and one 4-bit character from three different channels. This being the case, a bit error in a data-compaction character destroys the identity of its termination. This loss of character synchronization permeates the succeeding characters of other channels, although eventually a true character ending is recognized, and character synchronization is restored. This error-multiplying characteristic means that data-compaction multiplexers must operate with a sophisticated error-protection scheme.

The data-compaction channels will, when the code is properly matched to the language, utilize a proportion of the high-speed aggregate data stream that is, on the average, less than the overall circuit data rate. The instantaneous proportion will vary above and below this average, depending on the specific character transmitted. The minimal bandwidth is utilized when there are no data on the channel and only the terminator for that channel is transmitted. By the same token, data compaction will, like statistical multiplexing, exhibit variable propagation delays during periods of high network activity. It is also susceptible to blockage if the data activity of its channels exceeds the capability of its buffers to bridge the transmission delays encountered.

With the intelligent time-division multiplexers we have techniques that all offer significantly higher levels of network utilization than are possible with the hard-wired kind.

The Problem of Vocabulary

Before closing this discussion of the fundamentals of our subject, we must speak of definitions. One of the psychological barriers in data communications is the technical jargon. The following is a discussion of the most basic terms.

The first subject is *signals*. There are three basic functions of signals: control, clocking, and data transfer. *Control* constitutes the *conversion* that takes place between terminal and modem; equipment are "on" or "off." *Clocking* regulates the speed of the data transfers. *Data* are transferred in a *serial* manner; they may be converted (by the modem) into an analog form or carried through the network in a digital form.

The difference between a *baud* and a bit per second is important.

A *baud* (the word is a derivative of *Baudot*, a telegraphy code) is (1) a unit of signaling speed in data transmission, (2) a function of bandwidth, (3) a figure indicating the number of times per second that a signal changes, and (4), in an equal-length code, a rate of one signal element per second; (for example, with a duration of a signal element of 20 milliseconds the modulation rate is 50 baud).

Modulation is counted in Hertz (one Hertz being one cycle per second). A sine-wave signal repeating itself once every second travels at 1 Hertz; if it repeats itself once every millisecond (1/1,000 sec) at 1,000 Hertz, each repetition of a signal is called a cycle.

A *bit per second* is not exactly the same as a baud. Bits per second are (1) a function of transmission (quality of equipment, lines, modems) and of noise, and (2) the measure of the true bit data transfer rate. Further, the *levels* at which a modem operates may be measured in *dibits* or *tribits*; for example, a 2,400-baud modem operating on dibits works at 4,800 bits per second (two bits in one baud), and a 3,400-baud modem operating on tribits works at 9,600 bits per second (three bits in one baud). To operate in this way we must *pack* and *unpack*.

The maximum capacity of channel is C (in bit/sec) = bandwidth (in Hz) × $\log_2$ (1 + (signal/random noise)). Hence, bits per second are a function of the means with which the communication is done. Bandwidth is bits per second; it is the difference expressed in cycles per second (Hertz) between the highest and the lowest frequencies of a band.

A *wideband* is a bandwidth greater than that required for a voice channel; in a wideband the capacity to modulate is critical.

A *carrier* is an electrical signal chosen because of its ability to travel through the transmission medium utilized; hence, "to carry the data." In data communications the medium is the telephone line. The presence or absence of a carrier refers to the presence or absence of transmitted energy.

Broadcast is the dissemination of information to a number of stations simultaneously.

Information that is transmitted over lines is, at its origin, in the form either of analog signals or of digital signals. *Analog signals* represent voice, music, television, images (charts, drawings, frame freeze, picturephones). *Digital signals* are telegraphy, Telex, data, and facsimile.

The following are the transmission alternatives available today for data communications purposes. The first three are for the low-speed transmission of binary signals; the networks are direct current with voltages of 40 to 120. *Telegraphy* was the earliest transmission medium (transmission of binary signals or pulses). *Telex* is a dial-up message-switching network for the transmission of binary signals at not more than 50 baud (originally). *Datex* is a dial-up network for the transmission of binary signals at 200 baud and more. *Telephones* are line-switching voice-grade lines operating at 300 to 400 Hertz and 48 volts. *Broadband* is lines with an extended frequency range (better than 4,000 Hertz). *Dial-up circuit* is a switched public network, generally of low quality with noise interference. *Leased circuit* is a dedicated line; it allows specification of the quality required (*conditioning*); it operates at higher speeds for a given transmission error rate than in a dial-up connection; it is very costly.

3
Concepts and Devices

In the opening statement of chapter 2 we said that the four basic design parameters characterizing a switched network are transmission, switching, storage, and control. These are the basic issues around which revolve the concepts and devices of a communications mechanism. Many of the outstanding problems in the field of telecommunications relate to, and derive from, the voice-grade network. Others are proper to the origin and evolution of the data communications discipline. But, as is true of all professions, the origin and evolution relate highly to each other.

The evolution of data communications has long been founded on the people, the technology, and the capital connected with the voice-grade lines. One of the issues facing the specialists is this: How are we going to integrate computer-based requirements with the existing telephone company's voice-grade networks? Extend? Overlay? Separate?

There are advantages and disadvantages with each alternative. The telephone companies themselves have not made up their minds. And there are other questions: Is it rational to put horizontal (user) solutions on basically star telephone-company networks? How radically will the current network concepts be altered by the coming "user" requirements of 10,000, 12,000, or even more terminals? How can we protect our investments while keeping the door open to the steady stream of technological advances? Financial, operational, and technical criteria will influence the answers.

Switching

The technical problems with telecommunications start with transmission: the choice of medium, of speed, and of quality, as we have said in chapter 2. Our first parameter was transmission; our second is switching, which is the key to distribution: signals have destinations and must be channeled from sender to receiver.

The mission of a telephone exchange is distribution. The distribution may be either two-way (bidirectional) or one-way. The needs of a two-way distribution brought about the development of switching mechanisms (step-by-step, crossbar, electronic switches). Two-way solutions are necessary for interactivity (conversational). Some processes do not require bidirectional switching; for instance, television, music, telegraphy, and, to some extent, facsimile (given current slow speed). Telegraphy was the earliest to be used.

In general, present-day networks are *not* able to transmit or distribute in a homogeneous manner the different types of information with which we deal. Furthermore, present-day technology has limitations. For instance, the switching centers (the telephone companies) are not made for the transmission of television signals; they are made for voice, at about 4 kilohertz, and television needs 5; if signal-switching for the handling of images is wanted, then wideband should be taken at the 5-kilohertz level for the different types of signal to travel—regardless of their nature. In any case, switching is the cornerstone to the modular construction of networks, to their interconnecting, and their growth. Switches are a simple method of increasing the size of the network, its expansion ratio, and its flexibility, but they also are points of congestion and delay. A little noticed fact about switches is that they remained unchanged for almost a hundred years, thereby restricting the capability and also increasing the cost of communications systems. All this is now ready for a radical change.

A switch can work in successive stages (the Strowger principle, 1889) or be of the crossbar type (1919) or work according to the latest techniques. During the last twenty years the tendency has been to convert from the basic design principles used for electromechanical media to modern devices, such as semiconductors. Keeping the design principles the same, though, itself has slowed the advance of technology. Only recently a determined effort has been made to modernize the circuit-switching principles; the time-space-time (TST) solution is an example.

Two basic switching disciplines have been used since the beginning of technology, the step-by-step, which is the older, and common control. Both are characterized by twelve objectives that are quite similar in their fundamentals, as follows. Note that the data terminal equipment is hereinafter called the DTE.

1. Recognize a communications request.
2. Determine the identity of a DTE.
3. Connect the requesting terminal to the switching facility.
4. Decode the address and signal the destination terminal.
5. Terminate the status of the destination terminal.
6. Arbitrate among DTEs contending for the use of facilities.
7. Select and allocate a communications path.
8. Establish the connection.
9. Monitor the session.

10. Assure recovery procedures in the event of errors.
11. Disconnect when the session is completed.
12. Guarantee quality of service, providing the needed data for error detection and correction.

In the step-by-step solution a single mechanism combines contact switching action and address coding. An incoming line is connected to several line finders, one of which will be used on a given call. This is also called *progressive control*, because successive digits of the address are directly employed in the operation, correspondingly defining successive switch stages.

Switching allows the communication to be established between terminals or, in voice networks, stations, temporarily connected as point-to-point. Since the late nineteenth century, although the goals of switching have not changed, modern design has aimed to drive out the switching machines, with their bulky electromechanical devices located in large and costly buildings. The new switching techniques aim for economy and efficiency. Some of the solutions brought forward challenges; for instance, the problem with time-division multiplexing is that of interconnecting channels occurring at different times on different links.

Common control evolved through a number of phases. The oldest is crossbar switching, with a hard-wired mesh, in which the switching is done by means of relay contact. The newest is computer-based, in which the switching is effected through software support.

Common control is unlike the step-by-step solutions. It has different levels of sophistication, but all involve logical operations for generating control signals. Decoders, senders, and markers are necessary, and they may be effected through hard-wire logic, as in crossbar switching, or stored programs, which is the modern computer-based alternative.

Quality of Service

The quality of service is improved through computer-based control. If nothing else, the growth rate in communications and the dropping prices in computer gear imposed certain demands: statistics on use and failure rates must be kept, the allocation of expensive equipment must be optimized, setup time must be minimized, and delays must be controlled. Such problems must be solved automatically, not manually, for reasons both of efficiency and of cost. Furthermore, to sustain substantial voice and data loads, the switching units must be designed for unattended operation. They must allow remote monitoring, locating of faults, and on-line maintenance. Switching centers should, through software, provide for efficient resource allocation and routing algorithms—which leads from the notion of the simple switch to that of the intelligent switch, or node.

When we speak of intelligence in relation to a node or terminal we mean memory, that is, the storage of both data and programs. The connection of storage devices to a switching center has produced new methods; message-switching and packet-switching have developed out of this. Storage elements are changing the whole outlook on switching. They have influenced the flow of traffic, the speed, the error rates, the delays, and the cost and the quality of service. Most importantly, in the interrelationships of storage, transmission, and switching, storage is the connecting link.

Switches need to be redesigned with data, voice, and image in mind. The available switches were originally designed for voice only, and they hold traffic for three or four minutes. What we really need is call processors that are fast, modular, and able to work with short intervals of time, and that are projected for a transmission of, say, 60 kilobits to 200 megabits per second.

Finally, storage capability enlarges the concept of control. In communications, control means monitoring, logical functions, traffic analysis, testing, reconfiguration, deferred traffic, and reporting for management purposes. We shall return to these subjects when we talk of communications software.

Modems

If we look conceptually at a terminal-to-computer connection, end to end, we shall see at the extremities the terminal equipment, the DTE, linked by channels and switching points. The purpose of the links is transmission, and transmission takes place through physical media, such as twisted wire, coaxial cable, and optical fibers, or through microwaves, used in radio links and by satellites.

Transmission may be effected at different speeds and different capacities. A low capacity is, say, from 2 or 3 to 24 voice-grade channels, a medium capacity is up to 300 voice telephone lines (which, incidentally, corresponds to an image, or picturephone, channel), a high capacity is from 300 to 10,000 or more. The range in speed is enormous: sub-voice-grade lines operate at 50, 70, 100, 300, 600 bits per second, voice-grade lines at 1.2 and 2.4 kilobits per second, and wide-bandwidth lines at 56 and 64 kilobits and up to 100 and 200 megabits per second.

Finally, the lines may operate on analog or digital transmission. The former is the older, the voice-grade type, and the one that has made evident our need of modems. We may say that computers and terminals are user-level devices. Space, frequency, and time division are techniques that concern the efficiency of the line; between the line and the terminal is the modem, the modulator-demodulator, also called a data set or data communications equipment (DCE).

Digital data, as it is manipulated by a computer, or by a terminal, is represented by pulses, or square waves. Such waveforms cannot be applied directly to the telephone network, because their frequency spectrum would not be faithfully preserved. The pulse signal must first be converted to a modulated-wave format which has no direct-current component and fits well into the voice-transmission band. The new format must also be rugged enough to survive impairments of transmission, perhaps in the frequency. At the same time it must permit an

Concepts and Devices   33

accurate recovery of the original signal. This signal conversion and reconversion is the job of the modem.

To repeat, modems have been designed to operate on voice-grade lines. A voice-frequency signal transmitted between modems is modulated into intervals that vary in amplitude or phase or a combination of the two. Digital data have been represented on telephone lines by waves that are amplitude-modulated, frequency-modulated, and phase-modulated (Figure 3.1). Many of the modern modems use phase modulation because it is relatively insensitive to transmission impairments. Amplitude modulation was favored for the early data channels; at the present time it is chiefly of interest in transmitting multilevel symbols.

The type of modulation chosen should be a function of the application. Binary frequency modulation by means of the frequency-shift key (FSK) is preferred, for reasons of simplicity and economy, but it does not support bandwidth efficiency. The differential phase-shift key (DPSK) is a good choice for medium bandwidths. (In differential phase-shift key the phase of the cycles in a particular time period is compared with the phase of the cycles in the previous time period.) Figure 3.2 compares these methods. Most modems are designed to accept and deliver a serial stream of binary data at the terminal interface, but some handle a character at a time by accepting and delivering binary signals on several parallel interfaces, and others use acoustic coupling to telephone handsets.

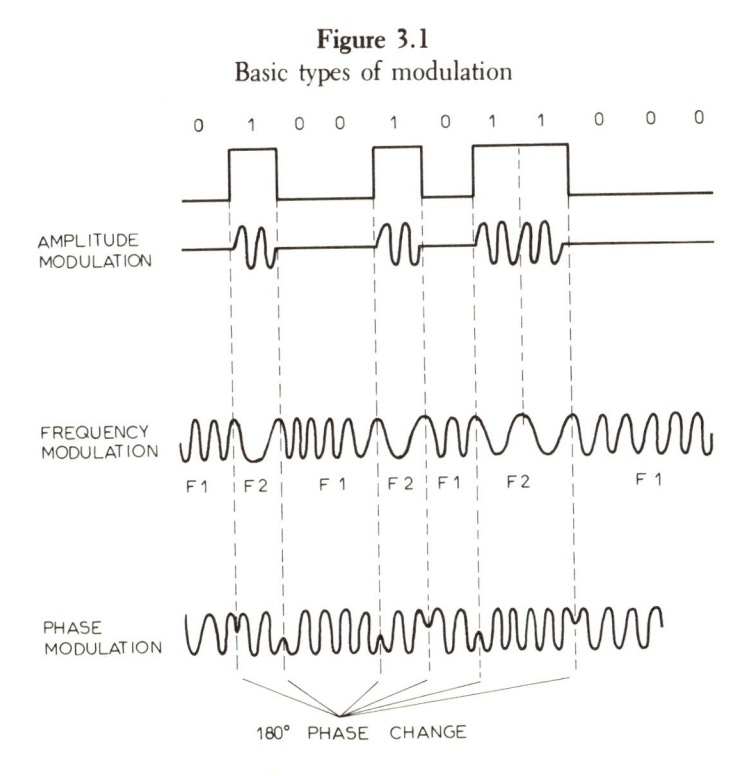

Figure 3.1
Basic types of modulation

Figure 3.2

FSK: FREQUENCY SHIFT KEYING

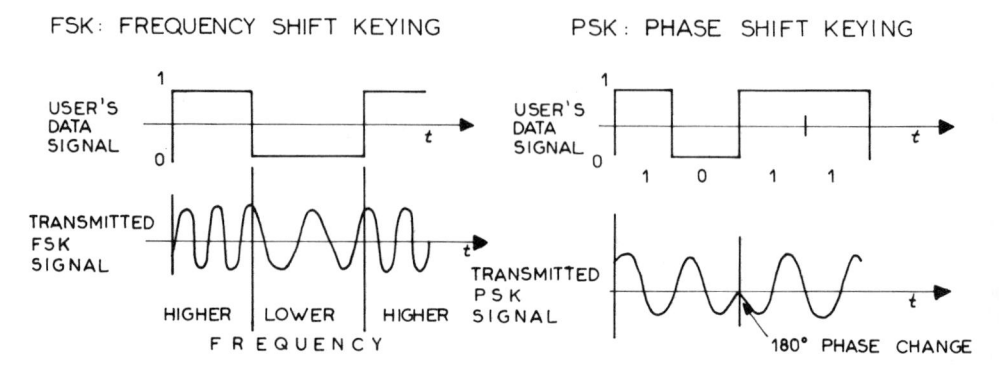

PSK: PHASE SHIFT KEYING

Technical Issues with Modems

A number of technical distinctions must be made in considering or choosing a modem. One of the most basic is that of synchronous and asynchronous communications. For asynchronous transmission two signal states are used, and the lengths of the intervals are prescribed by the transitions of the binary data wave. In synchronous transmission the intervals are uniform in duration; the choice of signal states is usually made an integer power of 2, to simplify the relationship to the binary data being handled.

Another technical question concerns the half-duplex and full-duplex capabilities. Many modems are so designed that they may be operated over two-wire or four-wire circuits. When half-duplex operation is acceptable, then the two-wire circuit may be used, saving the cost of one line, but the operation is logically more complicated, because equipment must switch between the "transmit" and "receive" modes.

Parenthetically, a complication with synchronous data sets is that a pattern must be transmitted after each line turnaround so that the receiver clock may be locked to the transmitter clock. Because the resulting lost time may be important in certain circumstances, some data sets need four-wire circuits, as do most line drivers and receivers, for either type of bidirectional transmission.

A further distinction should be made between units designed for short-haul and long-haul transmission. Short haul, referred to as a modem, usually means a device operating at distances of three to five miles. Many data communications requirements call for long-haul design characteristics.

Finally, it is part of the technical function of a modem to provide good service. Three topics are specifically related to this reference: conditioning, equalization, and scrambling.

Conditioning has to do with tolerances. A voice-quality line presents electrical characteristics conditioned by tolerances, which indicate how far you can go within the specification. Hence, the "purchase of conditioning" is essentially the price paid for high quality.

Equalization is telling the modem how to compensate for the characteristics of a particular telephone line, for a tremendous variety of transmission characteristics can exist on any given telephone line. Equalization is enhanced through a microprocessor and through algorithms, which allow reacting automatically to changing conditions. This minimizes errors due to line distortions.

The digital-loop mode of operation is a way of testing the modem. Test equipment is connected to the near-end set, and both the transmitter and receiver are tested by having the receiver's output connected directly to the input of the transmitter at the far end of the connection.

Scrambling is an interesting process. The scrambler changes the data so that it appears to be in a random pattern. The purpose may be something like avoiding long strings of 1's that might cause problems in the clocking circuitry.

A new family of modems with diagnostic features is keeping pace with many of the changing market needs: small size, efficient handling of short messages, fast startup, and compact touchtone receivers. Laboratories also are actively working to devise an efficient signal that will watch the channel characteristics, provide automatic compensation for signal distortion caused by the channel, and a means of automatically correcting errors caused by unavoidable bursts of noise.

Types of Modem

Modems were developed in the late 1950s and early 1960s. The first modem was introduced about 1960. Since then many technological developments have taken place. We are now a long way from the modem that had to be installed, tested, and maintained by specialists. One of the earliest and still extensively used modems is the Bell System's 103 Series. It can now be purchased from many manufacturers as a standalone unit. It is an asynchronous modem that operates at any speed up to 300 bits per second. This speed is adequate for a large number of applications, such as the operation of computer terminals at 300 characters per second.

To review briefly the types of data sets available today, we must return to the fundamentals. The traditional voice-grade channels provide an operational bandwidth of 600 to 4,000 Hertz. The restriction to this bandwidth has profoundly influenced the design of modems, since they must fit the limitations. Furthermore, higher data-transmission rates have required modems of greater and greater complexity and with very low error probabilities. To compensate for line errors, modern modems also include forward error-correction procedures.

The Bell System's 201 modems have given, in the past decade, synchronous-mode service at 2,400 bits per second. The first member of a new family, the 208A, was introduced in 1972; it uses a bandwidth of 4,800 bits per second and is primarily for private-line use. This modem, designed with attention to cost, grew out of the 201 modem. They use a four-phase signal format in which successive pairs of bits, dibits, are encoded as one of four possible phase shifts of the carrier signal. In 1974 AT&T introduced the 209A, for 9,600 bits per second. Yet a large percentage of all modems is still on 600 bits per second.

Among technical advancements for switched lines we distinguish automatic answering and automatic dialing. To make feasible automatic computer-to-computer communication and hence reduce in a significant manner human handling costs, automatic call and receive units have been developed. The 212A modem is an example. A typical application for the automatic call–receive modem is in a manufacturer's headquarters. Every day a computer calls each of the sales offices across the country using the automatic calling unit (ACU) and the wide-area telephone service (WATS). After making the connection, the ACU puts the modem on the line, and the ordering information is automatically transmitted to the headquarters. The information is loaded onto disc memory, the computer processes it, and then, with another modem link, the offices or plants are given instructions.

The 212A is called bilingual, because data are transmitted in two different formats at two speeds, high and low.

At the low speed the network operates with a frequency-shift-keyed carrier signal. The frequency of the carrier signal transmitted over the telephone channel is controlled by the data signal from the customer equipment. The carrier frequency assignments are such that the modem can operate with other frequency-shift-keyed low-speed sets.

At the high speed the modem can furnish timing signals to the terminal, and the data bits must be phase-locked to those signals; this is what is called a synchronous operation. Also in the high-speed mode, but without the timing signals, the operation of the set is called character asynchronous. In the character asynchronous operation the data bits are fed to the modem as "characters," which are groups of nine or ten bits, depending on the type of data terminal.

These are the Bell System's equipment. Since the Carterphone decision of the Federal Communications Commission many independent (interconnect) companies, about a hundred, offer their modems to the market. Table 3.1 presents the CCITT (International Telegraph and Telephone Consultative Committee) and Bell standards for modems.

Table 3.2 reflects into the future in terms of existing, transitional, and the next generation of data sets. Two broad classes are identified: analog and digital transmission.

The User Site

At user sites modems can be much needed but a continually nagging problem. Modem manufacturers install the unit but do not recommend to the user what options should be included. This is entirely up to the hardware and software

Table 3.1
CCITT and the Bell Standards for Data Sets

Bell Type	CCITT recommendation*	Speed (bit/sec)	Line, no. of wires	Line usage	Modulation**	Mode†
103/113	V.21	0–300	2	Dial or leased	FSK	Asyn.
202	V.23	0–1,200	2, 4	Dial or leased	FSK	Asyn.
201B	V.26	2,400	4	Leased	PSK	Syn.
201C	V.26bis	2,400	2, 4	Dial or leased	PSK	Syn.
208A	V.27, V.27bis	4,800	4	Leased	DPSK	Syn.
208B	V.27ter	4,800	2	Dial	DPSK	Syn.
209	V.29	9,600	4	Leased	QAM	Syn.

*CCITT is the International Telegraph and Telephone Consultative Committee. These standards are generally implemented in Europe.
**FSK, frequency-shift key; PSK, phase-shift key; DPSK, differential phase-shift key; QAM, queued access method.
†Synchronous or asynchronous.

Table 3.2
Generations of Data Sets

	Interfaces*	
	Analog	Digital
Existing	DTE, DCE 20 kbit/sec	—
Transitional	DTE, DCE 60 kbit/sec	DTE (No modem) Public data networks 60 kbit/sec
New Generation	—	DTE, 10 Mbit/sec; "Digital modems" (DCE) to handle > 5 km distance

requirements in the computer system. Computer manufacturers, therefore, will be well advised to make those recommendations in a technical note in their manual.

Since the use follows the choice, it is also well to emphasize that choices should be made on the basis of both technical and economic factors. The following examples describe the technicalities of some types of modem, each type being more or less expensive than another.

Modem A is synchronous, at 4,800 bits per second over voice-grade four-wire lines or the public switched network. Its fast turnaround time of 50 milliseconds is standard and ensures maximal data throughput rates. A comprehensive package of light-emitting diodes (LED) monitors the overall operation. Options include an asynchronous-to-synchronous converter and a remote diagnostic test system that permits checking the entire data communications system from a single master site.

Modem B is low-power solid-state for transmission and reception of synchronous 2,400 bits per second as serial binary data. Front-panel test switches permit fast selection of test modes. Front-panel indicator lamps display control and data functions to simplify fault diagnosis.

Modem C provides automatic answering of incoming calls and will automatically switch to the original mode of operation when calls are dialed.

Modem D will transmit data at 1,200 bits per second over private lines with conditioning at rates as high as 1,800 bits per second. The operation is half-duplex on two-wire private lines or full-duplex on four-wire private lines.

Modem E is designed for low-speed data transmission in the acoustic mode. The unit is portable and can be utilized with any one of a number of data terminals. A carrier indicator light is provided to monitor the operation of the unit.

Since the problem of choice is complicated by the purchase price, and the user's requirements can and do change, the best selection by today's criteria might turn out tomorrow to be a poor one. Both present and projected needs must therefore be considered, and due attention paid to technological advances, for technology sometimes moves faster than we think.

4

Terminals

Terminals are typical components of a communications system, which consists of a chain of several terminals and channels. A terminal converts a signal appropriate to one channel to a signal appropriate to the next channel, while preserving the signal's information content. For example, a message may originate in a human brain, be transmitted to the fingers, pass into a teletypewriter, travel over a wire line to a radio transmitter, journey through space to a radio receiver, be typed out onto a sheet of paper, be scanned by a pair of eyes, and, finally, enter another human brain.

The communications engineer often regards a terminal as any apparatus at either end of a discrete electromagnetic channel. More commonly, however, a terminal is viewed as an apparatus for converting a visual, acoustic, or tactile signal into an electrical signal, or vice versa. This is a basic definition, a good one to be kept in mind. Telephone sets and their logical extension into data communications are the most common terminal devices, and they are the least expensive.

Telephone sets, unintelligent or intelligent terminals, computers—that is DTEs in general—are built with certain blocks; the electronic components, such as the microprocessor, the memory, the decode and control, and the peripheral interface adapter, are nowadays made of semiconductors.* The most striking feature of the semiconductor industry is its continuous and rapid change. During the last five years many opportunities have presented themselves as a result of investments made in research and development and in manufacturing engineering.

---

*A substance, as germanium or silicon, whose conductivity is poor at low temperatures but is improved by minute addition of certain substances or by the application of heat, light, or voltage; used in transistors, rectifiers, etc.

Since the beginning of the computer era, the cost per bit of information has decreased a thousandfold.† Since 1951 the cost of 100,000 calculations has fallen from $1.56 to one penny! These reductions are due to the advance of on-line operations. The user of a computer and data communications service can now have his own DTE at very low cost. Right after World War I the radio became a household item. A third of a century after World War II the same has happened to the computer.

Such developments require time to mature. The circuitry had to be simplified and controls had to be redesigned to make their function as obvious as possible and the chances of a mistake in operation as minimal as possible. More importantly the prices had to be brought down to a level appealing to the users' market.

These developments have come to maturity. The products available in the market now and in the years ahead make the microcomputer necessary to the consumer, just as are the telephone, the radio, and the automobile. That is why the early 1980s will be very exciting in the computing field.

The Use of Terminals

Terminals capture, buffer, transmit, and receive data. They fall into two categories: the inexpensive, passive units, and the intelligent units.

The first has limited functions that serve the basic needs of sending and receiving messages. The transaction telephone, for instance, performs those functions from the customer's card and manual entry and then transmits the data from memory when an answering signal is received. This data terminating equipment is new. It has a number repertory for repeated calls to the same number, it can dial out from a private branch exchange or on a foreign-exchange line, it automatically tests proper operation, and it may be equipped with an auxiliary manual-entry card so that the customer at a bank or store can enter a personal identification number (PIN) if necessary.

The second category, intelligent terminals, have expanded capabilities and functions, processing message data before they are transmitted and after they are received. To do this they require self-contained storage and local data-handling facilities. This means they are programmable. The user would have hands-on experience with such terminals and could obtain both hard copy and soft copy (CRT). Figure 4.1 presents the output alternatives.

An intelligent terminal usually will be programmed to check that the data received are accurate and in correct sequence, so that the computer does not find errors at processing time. If errors are found, the terminals will inform the operator accordingly (for example, through a video screen or in printed form), so

---

†During the last few years the cost of computer memory is down by an average 40 percent per year, that of computer logic by 25 percent per year, and that of communications by 11 percent per year; conversely, wages are high, at an annual rate of around 6 percent.

Figure 4.1

OUTPUT / TERMINAL

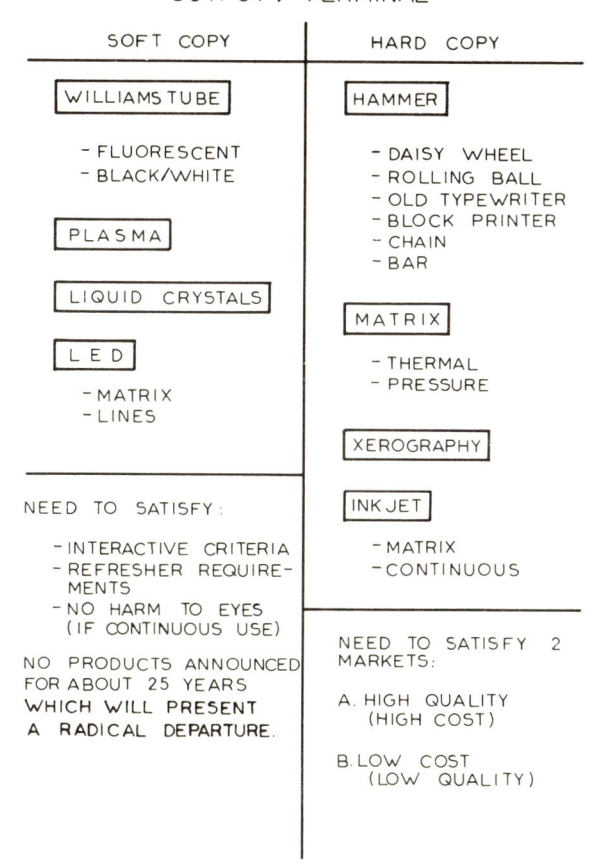

SOFT COPY	HARD COPY
WILLIAMS TUBE	HAMMER
- FLUORESCENT - BLACK/WHITE	- DAISY WHEEL - ROLLING BALL - OLD TYPEWRITER - BLOCK PRINTER - CHAIN - BAR
PLASMA	
LIQUID CRYSTALS	MATRIX
LED - MATRIX - LINES	- THERMAL - PRESSURE
	XEROGRAPHY
NEED TO SATISFY: - INTERACTIVE CRITERIA - REFRESHER REQUIREMENTS - NO HARM TO EYES (IF CONTINUOUS USE) NO PRODUCTS ANNOUNCED FOR ABOUT 25 YEARS WHICH WILL PRESENT A RADICAL DEPARTURE.	INK JET - MATRIX - CONTINUOUS NEED TO SATISFY 2 MARKETS: A. HIGH QUALITY (HIGH COST) B. LOW COST (LOW QUALITY)

that corrective action may be taken (probably canceling the information just entered and repeating the input).

Data clearance at the point of origin is important because it permits the operator to know at once whether the input has been accepted, prior to the next batch of data. This requires a set of instructions. An unintelligent terminal will be instructed what to do by the computer (or minicomputer) with which it operates on-line; an intelligent terminal will have its own programs to perform.

The end-to-end position (in a network) will be maintained by the terminals, irrespective of whether the link is wire, radio, or other. Figures 4.2 and 4.3 make the point. Data terminating equipment are so called because of this simple fact. We shall speak of DTEs, however, generically—not only as terminals but also as any device occupying an end position in a network; a computer may be a DTE.

Since there may be many terminals, from one to hundreds, connected to a computer, they must be simple in design, easily maintained, rational in terms of

44 *Data Communications for Distributed Information Systems*

Figure 4.2
Components of a data communications system

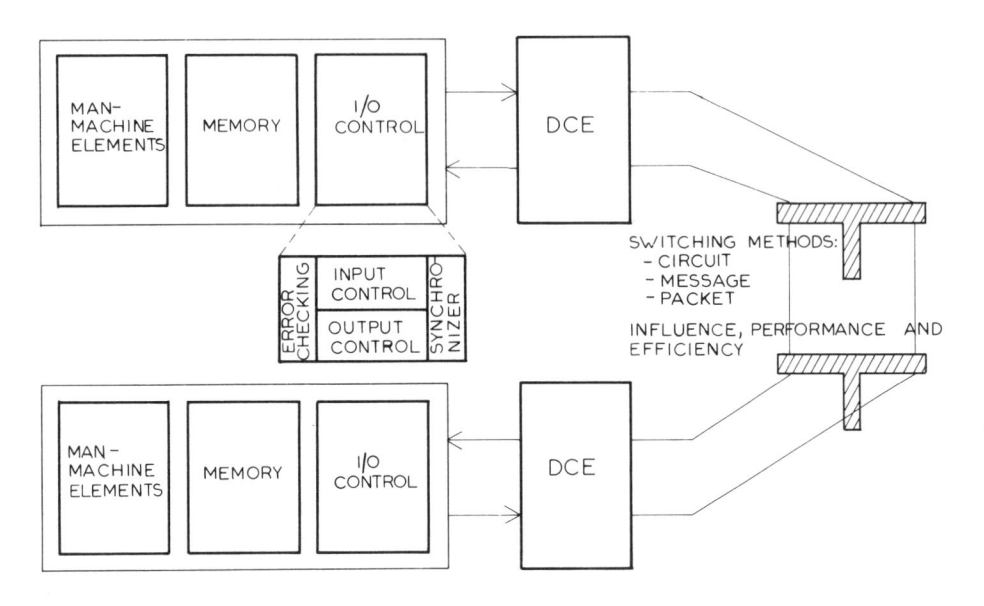

Figure 4.3
DTE to DTE data communications

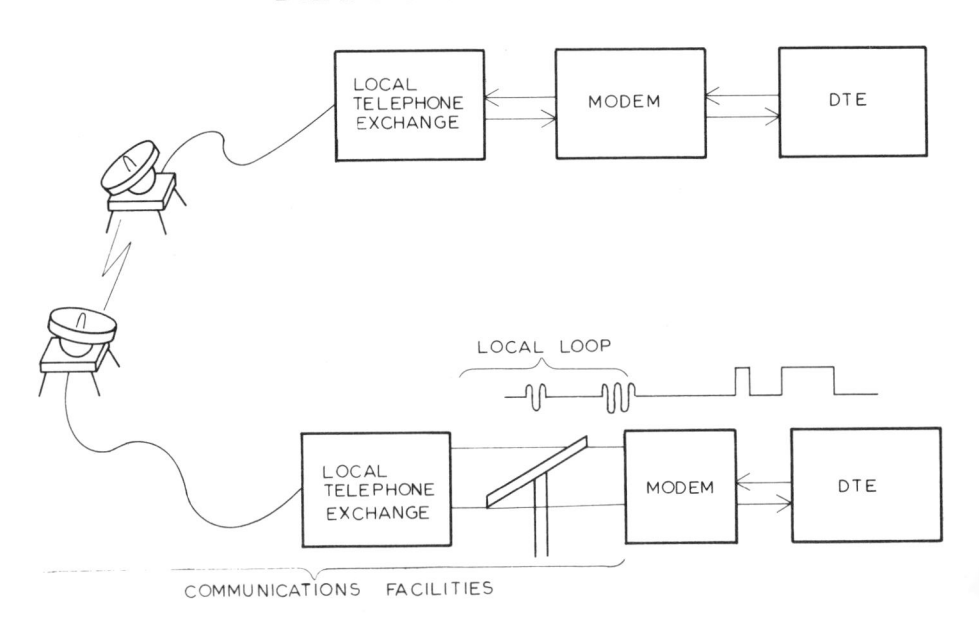

resources, and straightforward to communicate with. The operator should have only to key in data and be able to examine the results. Since the terminals are the interface between persons and computers, they must be characterized by a working simplicity; they must appeal to the nonspecialist. This means that a terminal must reduce the description and presentation of data to an easy-to-follow form. It must communicate the information it receives to the central computer (or minicomputer resource), transmitting it on-line. And it must receive data, store it temporarily, and present it to a human being.

We have spoken of interfaces, and of the terminal as an interface. Actually, as the term is used in computer technology, an interface is a set of rules covering the relationship among dissimilar functions within the same node of an information-processing system.

This bring us to the issue of codes and coding. A code is a set of signals, representing letters or numerals, used in sending messages. A person must give information to a terminal in some form, as by touching keys or using magnetic striped cards, but once the data enter the terminals, they will be coded, so to speak, in a form intelligible to the computer, as, for instance, a string of bits.

This is one of the basic functions a terminal will perform. It is not the only one.

Building Blocks

The typical DTE consists of a microprocessing unit (MPU), which is something like the central processing unit of a bigger computer, a read-only memory (ROM), which is a storage device that a user can only read, not write on, a random access memory (RAM), which is a storage device on which a user can both read and write on, and a peripheral interface adapter (PIA), which handles the devices attached to the mainframe, such as the input-output units. These parts combined with an appropriate power supply, and bus drivers,* make up the DTE; see Figure 4.4. The function of the control bus is to carry control signals to all the electronic components of the system. Such signals originate at the control unit ("decode and control" in the diagram) and more particularly in the timer section. Control means, simply, ensuring that the right thing happens at the right time. The data bus transfers the information between the different components of the DTE or, to be precise, from the peripheral interface adapter to the memory, from the memory to the microprocessor, and then back, etc. The control bus and the data bus are, for all practical purposes, two distinct subsystems, each with its own functions.

An integral part of the DTE, and a very important one, is the real-time clock. It serves as an interval timer. Let us look at its functions.

---

*A conductor or group of conductors in the form of a bar, serving as a common connection for circuits; also called a busbar.

Figure 4.4

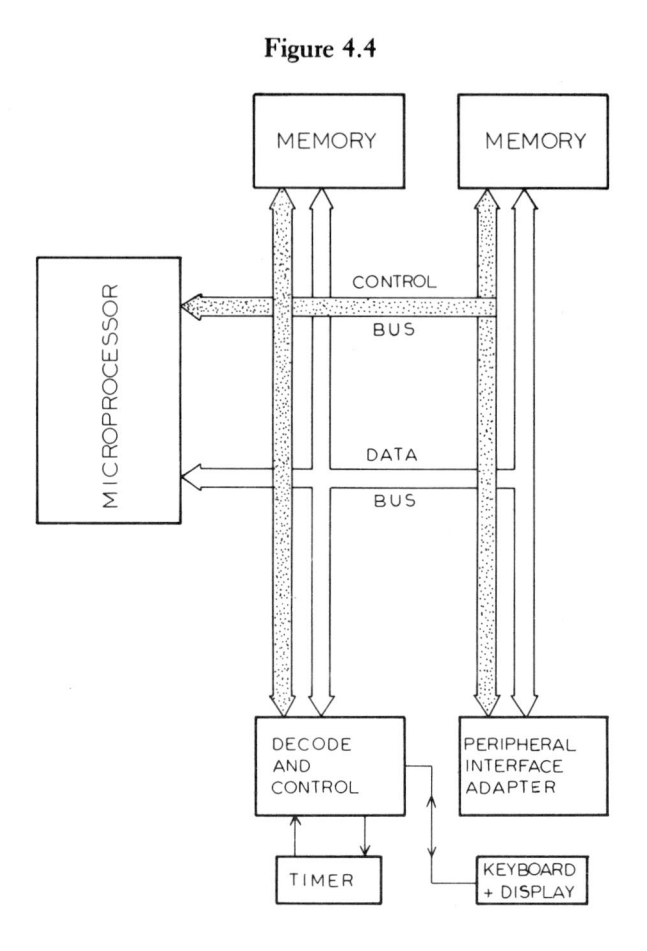

[Figure 4.4: Block diagram showing MICROPROCESSOR connected via CONTROL BUS and DATA BUS to two MEMORY blocks, a DECODE AND CONTROL block (connected to TIMER), and a PERIPHERAL INTERFACE ADAPTER (connected to KEYBOARD + DISPLAY).]

It gives the right timing and control impulses to all units of the machine.
It makes it possible to measure a given time interval.
It ensures that the different units of the computer begin actions at fixed times.
It helps check that the duration of a certain program does not exceed given limits.
It also provides the time of day in operations for which this is necessary.

The peripheral interface adapter (PIA) allows the attachment of such terminals as the keyboard, the printer, the video, and, eventually, the line controller for teleprocessing; see Figure 4.5. The minimum the user will need is a unit for input and output. Through this unit he will enter a control program in memory, which will tell the DTE what it should be doing. The user will enter data for storage and for treatment. He will receive the answers. Input and output units are designed to help the user communicate with the machine, and vice versa.

Figure 4.5

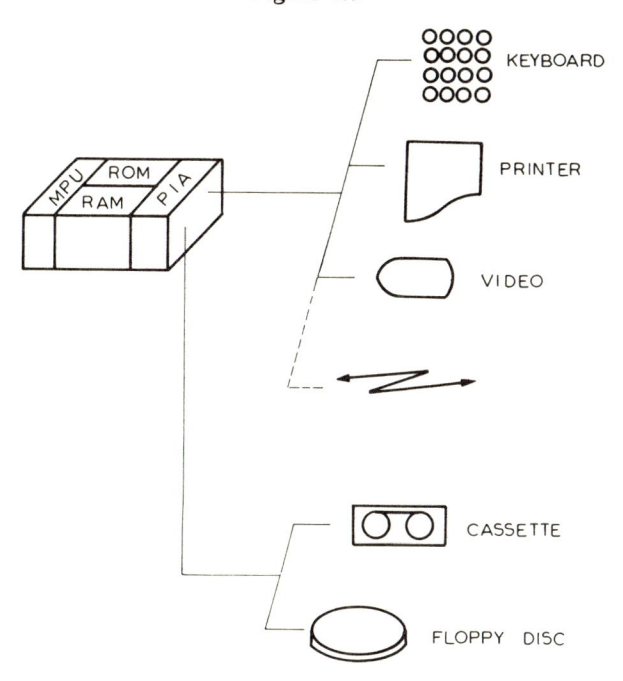

```
                                  ○○○○
                                  ○○○○   KEYBOARD
                                  ○○○○
                                  ○○○○

     ┌──ROM──┐
   MPU│   │PIA        ┌──────┐    PRINTER
     │RAM│                  
     └───────┘        

                      ┌───┐     VIDEO


                      ┌───┐
                      │○○│      CASSETTE
                      └───┘

                       ⬯         FLOPPY DISC
```

Some of the vital peripherals are the storage devices. A storage device contains data and programs, as does a memory device, but it differs from memory in several respects. For one thing, whereas a memory device in a typical terminal holds 16, 32, or 48 kilobytes (thousand bytes), a storage device will hold 256 or 512 kilobytes. For another, the cost per byte will be much lower on a floppy disc than on a central memory device. The access time will be much higher in the floppy disc than in the central memory. The memory devices are directly attached to the microprocessor; the storage devices are coordinated through the peripheral interface adapter, also known as a peripheral control unit.

To recapitulate: *Memory* and *storage* mean different things with DTEs. We usually speak of "memory," "central memory," or "high-speed memory" when referring to random-access memory. We say "storage" when referring to external devices able to hold information, such as floppy discs, cassettes, magnetic tapes, or high-capacity discs.

A floppy disc—so named because of its resemblance to the discs in a jukebox—is a handy extension of the storage capabilities of an intelligent terminal or a minicomputer. The addition of a cassette recorder to a system which had only floppy discs is an example of the increase in the number of component units. Whether a floppy disc or a cassette is used in connection with a terminal, and for transmission purposes, data will be retrieved from storage, sent to the central memory, and forwarded to the device asking for it.

The characteristics of storage are capacity (expressed in characters or in bits), access time (expressed in milliseconds), rotation time (expressed in milliseconds for drums and discs), and transfer time (expressed in bits per second). They should be kept in mind when choosing a device to add to a DTE. If the work is mainly batch, a cassette device may be best; that would be so even in the case of data transmission, provided that the transmitted data may be forwarded serially. If, on the other hand, messages are received with random reference to information in storage, as a file, a floppy disc is better, because, as we shall see, it allows direct access. *Direct access*, also known as *random access*, is a prime matter in information technology.

Transmission Speed and Interfacing

An important characteristic of a DTE is its transmission speed. The most widespread standard speeds of data transmission vary from 50 to 300 to 2,400 bits per second, but 9,600 bits per second and higher are possible; the ratio of 50 to 9,600 is 1:192. Though the moving gear behind the transmission speed is the modem, the terminal also plays a key role, applied to a network.

Given the abilities, and limitations, of the human operator, and other factors, the speed of transmission is in direct relation to the possession of buffer memory, which is a transit memory that helps distinguish the high speeds of the electronic equipment and transmission line from the far lower speeds of the electromechanical devices of a terminal.

Although most of the terminals installed today operate in less than 600 bits per second, the trend is definitely for terminals to work faster and faster, especially in business, industrial, and financial applications. Higher transmission speeds are advisable in case of heavy data loads and also for a better exploitation of the central computer resources and of the available line capabilities.

From a projection of the interfacing work it should be doing, a terminal is designed for a certain speed of transmission. To satisfy the requirements, not one but a whole lot of component units must be properly projected, in particular the input devices, the memory, the physical interface, and the modem; see Figure 4.6.

If all data processing equipment and transmission facilities were designed and built by one vendor, the relationships might have been, by design, sufficiently interrelated to preclude the need of hardware and software interfaces. As matters stand, however, data are handled by equipment from several vendors and are sent over telephone lines that were never intended for their use. The operations executed during the transmission phase include the following:

Storing the messages to be transmitted

Queueing them

Converting them from computer code into various transmission codes

Figure 4.6

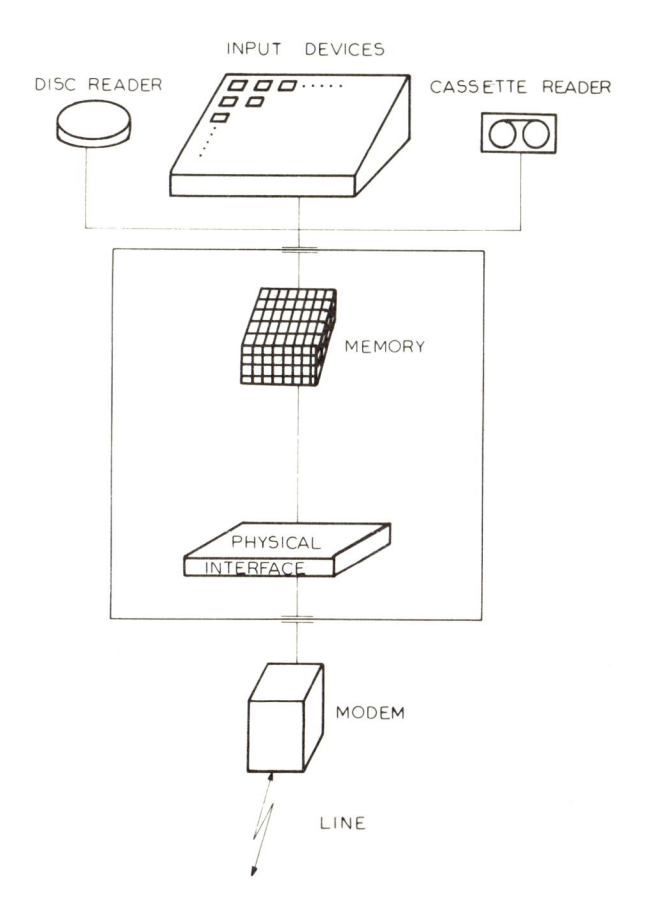

INPUT DEVICES
DISC READER
CASSETTE READER
MEMORY
PHYSICAL INTERFACE
MODEM
LINE

Introducing the needed characters for transmission

Transforming the messages into characters

Breaking up the characters into bits

Initiating the message proper

Forwarding the bits on-line in a timely manner

Supervising the transmission process, with the possibility of repeating messages in case of error

Giving a warning of the end of text, end of transmission, and the like

The Line Controller

The on-line connection of a computer to a terminal, and vice versa, required a line controller. A line controller is an interface between the lines and the terminal. Its structure may range from a very simple one to a sophisticated one that is equipped with a large memory and has several line control programs (Figure 4.7). Sophisticated line controllers are capable of running the transmission network autonomously and also managing the flow of messages.

Some line controllers only effect a physical connection between the line and the computer, providing an interface; others carry out network management functions autonomously by supplying corrected input messages to the central computer and by receiving output messages to be relayed to the computers or terminals. In any case, the line controller is a necessary interface when computer devices talk to one another over short- or long-distance telephone lines. Its basic tasks are to initialize, signal for errors, add and delete, and start and stop, and signal the end of the transmission.

The simple line controllers can transfer data between the central memory and the terminals, transform characters, serializing them by bit, do the opposite, i.e., give a character (parallel) structure to serially transmitted bits, and synchronize with the computer for incoming messages and for those to be transmitted.

We must bear in mind that to take advantage of the central processor's or microprocessor's high speed, it is necessary to have at least a small buffer (for example, one character size) present in the line controller. The exchange of characters between the central unit and the line controller takes place through this buffer. Other tasks include checking the received data for freedom from error, eliminating the start–stop bits during the phase of receiving, transforming the code received into the character structure desired by the computer and, during receiving and transmission, signaling "end of text" or "end of transmission."

In the literature the line control procedures are also known as data link control (DLC). The easiest way to remember about them is to know that they are hardware and software conventions, used for transferring data and controlling information devices. To provide a link between separate and often diverse information-handling units a connection must be established, synchronization of the parties to the exchange obtained, messages passed, and the inevitable errors detected and corrected.

Eight technical characteristics help differentiate one line controller from another:

1. The number of connecting lines: line control units may be designed to handle just one line or a hundred lines; generally, for a given line control, the number of lines is variable, from a minimum to a maximum. This choice, once made, brings the other seven technical criteria into perspective.

2. Speed of transmission: the speed of the various lines can either be the same or not.

Figure 4.7

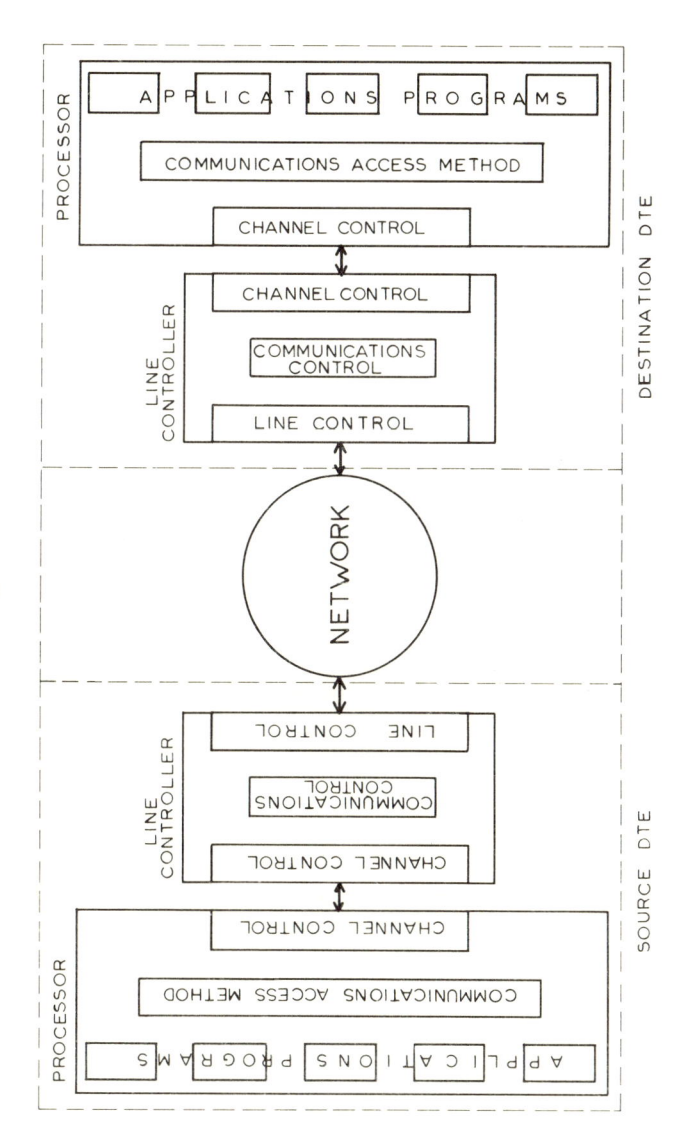

3. Permitted transmission techniques (telegraph, modem).
4. Codes of transmission: the line controllers may be divided into three main groups: those that accept all codes, those that accept only some codes, and those that accept only one code.
5. Connecting line: public (message-switching) or private (point-to-point, multidrop).
6. Number of wires making up the single lines (2 or 4, or 2 and 4 wires).
7. Direction of transmission: simplex, half-duplex, full duplex.
8. Type of transmission: asynchronous, synchronous, or packet.

The type of transmission is defined by the number of connecting lines. This is a fundamental aspect, which helps distinguish the various line controllers.

Computers, Minicomputers, Microprocessors, and Terminals

Terminals are made of semiconductors, as are microcomputers, minicomputers, and computers. All are composed of five basic units: input, output, memory and storage, arithmetic and logic, and control (and so, incidentally, is the finest information machine to date, made by nature: the human nervous system). What then is the difference between them?

To start with, to some people the term *microcomputer* means "microprocessor." To others the two words do not mean the same thing. We shall say that a microcomputer is a full system with input–output, memory, arithmetic logic unit, and so on. A microprocessor is a central processing unit on a chip, and does not have self-standing capabilities; it is a machine within another machine (a computer, an auto, a refrigerator).

Fundamentally both consist of a single, integrated circuit "chip," which contains (according to some reckonings) at least 75 percent of the power of a very small computer. A microprocessor usually cannot do anything without the aid of support chips and memory. By contrast, a microcomputer is a fully operational computer system based upon a microprocessor chip.

A computer is any device, usually electronic, that is able to accept information, compare, add, subtract, multiply, divide, and integrate, and then supply the results in some form of human-to-machine communication. The operations are indeed performed just as well by a minicomputer, a microcomputer, and a person who computes.

But a computer, as we habitually think of one, is a complex piece of equipment; it may have many input–output units, billions of bits of high-speed memory, different storage devices, and, lately, many processor units. Furthermore, over the last fifteen years computers have been supplied with sophisticated software whose development usually costs more than that of the hardware.

Computers are designed to solve a large range of problems both technical and scientific and are adaptable to a variety of operations. Minicomputers are computers at miniprices; indeed, by today's standards Univac I, the world's first commercially available computer, is a minicomputer. (This fact alone dramatizes the sharp drop in production costs due to technological developments.) But while a modern large-scale computer (at a cost of, say, fifty times that of the minicomputer) will be characterized by multi-access, multiprocessing, and multiprogramming, the user of the minicomputer will be well advised to keep his machine on monoprogramming. The more limited software support (offered by the minicomputer manufacturer) of the maintenance service and of assistance in system skill are variables that partially (not wholly) justify the price difference between minicomputers and their larger brethren.

We come to the conclusion, therefore, that the main difference between computers, minicomputers, and, eventually, microcomputers (not microprocessors) is one of end use. End use includes the software libraries, which are available, the system's support, and the "multi" properties mentioned above. Whether one needs all these or simply wishes them, a price must be paid to have them.

Terminals, we said, are installed to collect, maintain, and extract data from memory. In extracting data they operate upon a data pool kept at the central computer resource. The memory at the local terminal may be no more than a buffer, but some terminals possess substantial memory capabilities, the intelligent terminals. Intelligent terminals are programmable. Although the terminal is the peripheral device of a computer, a minicomputer, and even a microcomputer, an intelligent terminal may incorporate in itself a whole microprocessor.

The early terminals were mostly of the teleprinter type: a typewriter with a line controller. Today the mechanical parts—the keyboard and the printer—remain the most expensive and the least reliable of the components. Figures 4.8 and 4.9 illustrate this difference. Figure 4.8 presents the functional blocks of the now famous terminal, the IBM 2780, which has been the most copied in the history of computing. The input–output buffer, the line buffer, and the encode–decode unit are the heart of this equipment. But an intelligent terminal, while preserving this structure, is a much more sophisticated device, as Figure 4.9 shows. Microprocessors are built into the terminal so they can perform and control the various operations of the units. Microverification, for instance, helps check the operational integrity of the arithmetic and logical unit (ALU), channels, buffers, and storage units, which operate automatically when the system's power is on. They validate the integrity of the data flow, write in and read back a specified bit pattern in memory, control the integrity of the DTE by running through a set of instructions, compare an accumulated checksum to a preprogrammed checksum, and validate the overall integrity of the device. Thus, if an error is detected in the processor or channel or a problem in an input–output attachment, a condition of error will be presented to the user.

Intelligent terminals evolved as a function of demand and also of the sharp drop in the prices of storage devices; see Table 4.1. The abilities of the DTE are a

54 Data Communications for Distributed Information Systems

Figure 4.8
Functional block diagram of the IBM 2780

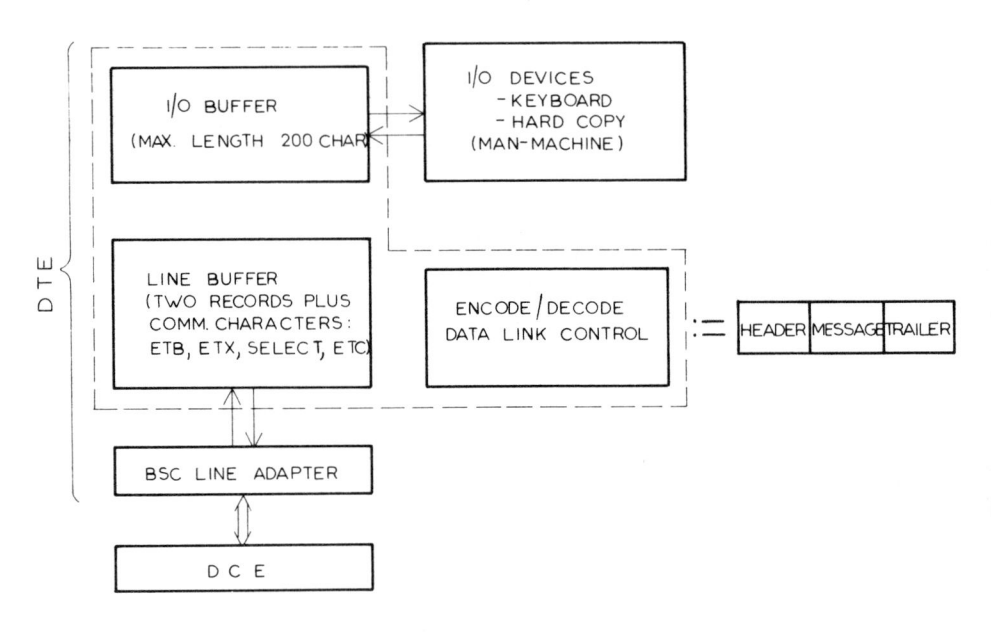

Figure 4.9
Functional block diagram of intelligent terminals

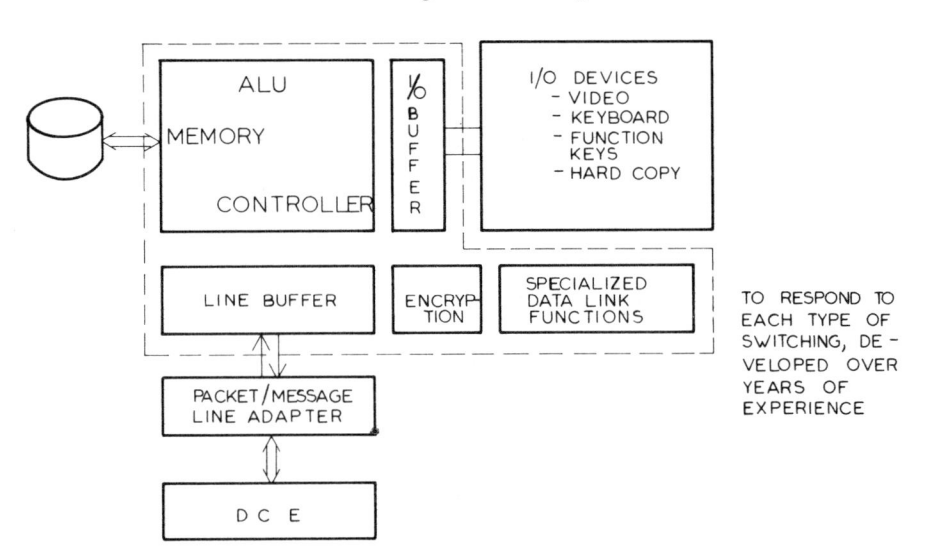

TO RESPOND TO
EACH TYPE OF
SWITCHING, DE-
VELOPED OVER
YEARS OF
EXPERIENCE

Table 4.1
Storage Devices for the 1980s

Type	Possible Capacity (megabytes)	Access Speed (seconds)	Cost Goals ($/megabyte)
VLSI	0.25 to 5	nanosecond	2.000 to 5.000
Bubble memory	1 to 20	k microseconds < 1 millisecond	400 to 1.400
Moving head disc	50 to $k \times 1{,}000$	millisecond	15 to 25
Mass storage	Trillions	second	0.3 to 1.0

For any type of storage, the basic selection criteria are: cost, access speed, capacity limits, reliability, other performance criteria, and availability. VLSI, very large-scale integration.

powerful extension of computers and minicomputers. With the increasing use of telephone lines for processing purposes, new perspectives are opening up. No wonder that terminals and the communications gear are getting the lion's share of the market (Figure 4.10).

Figure 4.10
(*The American average is 10%; however, organizations well-launched in real time have about 20% and this chart concerns this population.) (PTT is Poste, Telegraph and Telephone, in Europe)

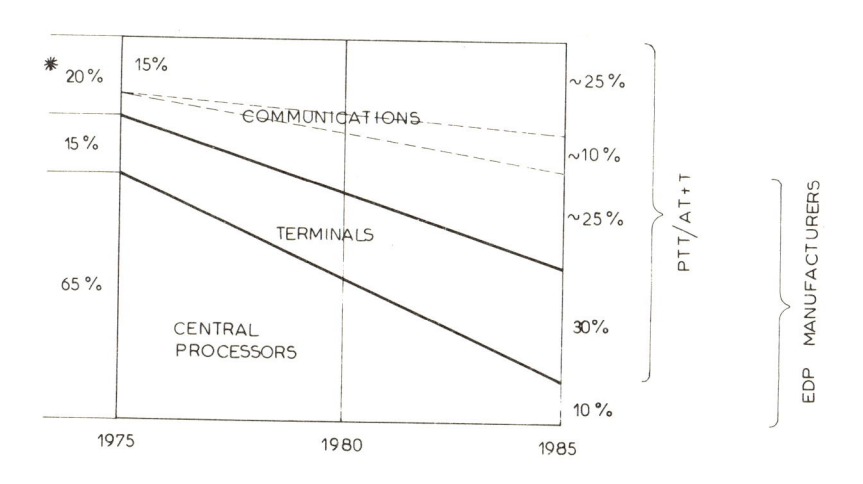

5
Communications Gear

The preceding three chapters described a good deal of the gear necessary for data communications. Lines, switches, control programs, modems, computers, and terminals are part and parcel of this gear. The subject has not been exhausted, however; we must talk of multiplexers, concentrators, and front ending.

Multiplexing is a regrouping of signals into a one-way transmission. This can be done at the line; physical media, such as coaxial cable and optical fibers, permit a high level of regrouping, and so does satellite broadcasting. The practical limit is set by interferences. The best examples of multiplexing technology are those we discussed in chapter 2, frequency-division multiplexing and time-division multiplexing.

Rules and standards for frequency-division multiplexing have been specified by the international committee CCITT:

12 channels: 60 to 108 kilohertz

60 channels: 312 to 552 kilohertz

960 channels: 60 to 4,028 kilohertz

2,700 channels: 3,122 to 12,388 kilohertz

10,800 channels: 4 to 61 megahertz

Computers and communications networks, though they use extensively frequency division and time division, still require a higher level of intelligence.

Multiplexing and concentration interface between the source and the destination of the data, and by so doing they bring forward the need for conventions, or protocols.

Protocols are formal sets of conventions governing the format and the control of data. They constitute logical levels of connection to the physical line (carrier). The simple, early ones were of the Stop–Start variety; the modern ones contain advanced concepts. Primarily, they standardize known, not new, functions, of which there are two. The first is contact which is identification, synchronization, and creation of a virtual channel; these facilities concern source and destination. The second is transfer, which includes error detection and correction (EDC) and delivering of the message. Given the importance of the subject, we will devote several chapters to the basic notions and the variety and use of protocols.

Multiplexers and Concentrators

In a data communications process the line may act as a multiplexer of messages from different DTEs connected to that line. This is especially true of an intelligent line.

An intelligent line, which is a line equipped with a microprocessor and memory, can act in one or more of the following ways:

    Polling, addressing

    Polling, unpacking; compacting

    As high-speed accelerator

    As asynchronous or synchronous gateway

    Buffering

    Error controlling, including ACK, NAK, repeat, time-out

    As a multiplexer

Lines are only now becoming intelligent, and they are controlled by the telephone company; for this reason there is an interest in developing and implementing separate media: the concentrators and multiplexers.

Multiplexers are physical devices and are selected on the basis of supported channels, line interface modules, automatic testing capabilities, and display facilities; see Figure 5.1.

Data concentration is a logical function that combines a series of communication links into one physical line; see Figure 5.2. This may be done with hardware (multiplexers) or with software and hardware (processors).

Concentrators also are physical devices; they are selected according to efficiency, traffic load, reconfiguration capabilities, configurations of line interfaces, and diagnostics (centralized and local loopbacks).

Both multiplexers and concentrators regroup low-speed lines into a high-speed trunk, but there are differences; see Figure 5.3. With the multiplexer n lines, corresponding to an equal number of terminals, are multiplexed into n channels. Normally, all lines coming from the terminals to the multiplexer are of the same speed. At the output side the line uses frequency division or time division. The messages are of fixed format. The n lines feed into the concentrator, but the output is one channel. The lines connecting the n terminals to the concentrator

Communications Gear 59

Figure 5.1
Multiplexer

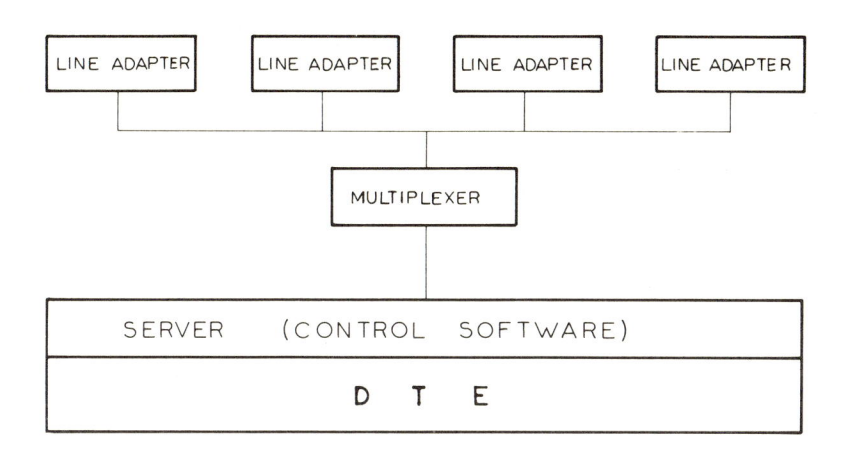

```
[LINE ADAPTER]  [LINE ADAPTER]  [LINE ADAPTER]  [LINE ADAPTER]
                       |
                  [MULTIPLEXER]

| SERVER   (CONTROL   SOFTWARE) |
|         D    T    E           |
```

Figure 5.2
Concentrator

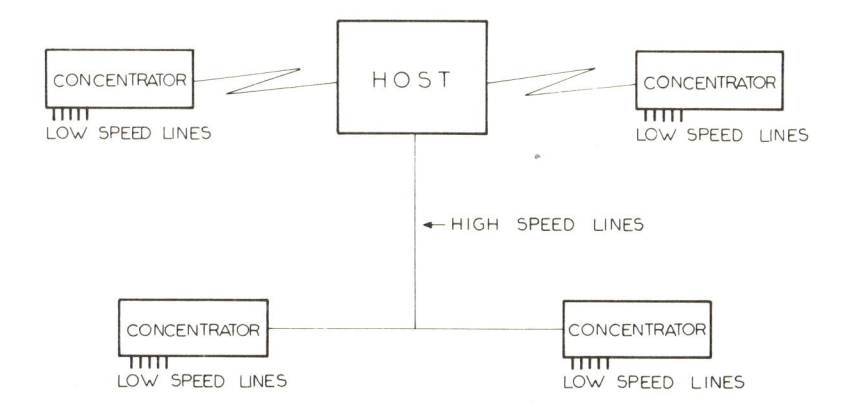

```
[CONCENTRATOR]      [ HOST ]       [CONCENTRATOR]
 LOW SPEED LINES                    LOW SPEED LINES

              ← HIGH SPEED LINES

[CONCENTRATOR]                     [CONCENTRATOR]
 LOW SPEED LINES                    LOW SPEED LINES
```

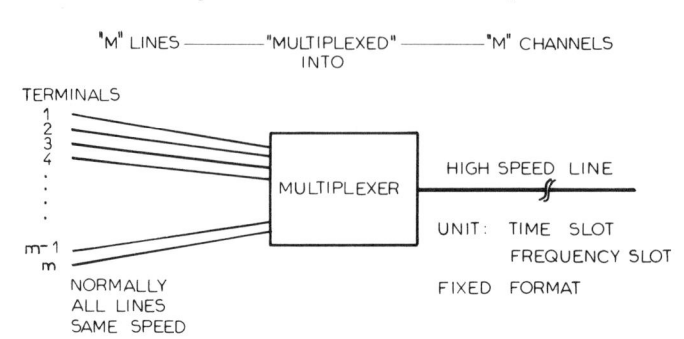

60   *Data Communications for Distributed Information Systems*

Figure 5.3
Multiplexer and concentrator compared

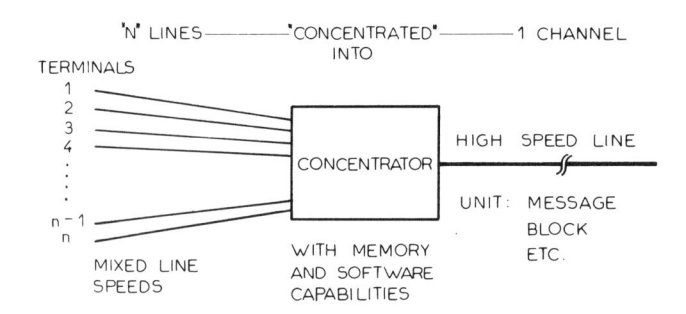

```
'M' LINES ———"MULTIPLEXED"——— 'M' CHANNELS
                  INTO
TERMINALS
  1
  2
  3
  4
  .                            HIGH SPEED LINE
  .          MULTIPLEXER
  .                            UNIT: TIME SLOT
 m-1                                 FREQUENCY SLOT
  m
 NORMALLY                       FIXED FORMAT
 ALL LINES
 SAME SPEED


'N' LINES ———'CONCENTRATED'——— 1 CHANNEL
                  INTO
TERMINALS
  1
  2
  3
  4                            HIGH SPEED LINE
  .          CONCENTRATOR
  .                            UNIT: MESSAGE
 n-1                                 BLOCK
  n          WITH MEMORY        ETC.
 MIXED LINE  AND SOFTWARE
 SPEEDS      CAPABILITIES
```

may have various (mixed) speeds. The high-speed line at the output side will carry formatted messages and blocks of messages.

The concentrator has to be an intelligent machine. It requires software. Multiplexers have long been unintelligent equipment, but this is changing.

Line adapters, if programmable, provide maximum flexibility and throughput. Their capabilities may include character of frame synchronization, special-character detection, filler-character transmission, control-code generation, programmable data set control displays, and diagnostics. In general, the functions of line-management interfaces are to:

Serialize and deserialize the bits

Control transmission

Control procedures (points 2 and 3 via software)

Bring traffic into equilibrium, to manage different lines

Control the code of the transmission with the help of tables in memory

Supervise the speed of transmission

Interface on the channel, as a function of the type of lines used

These functions may be realized through hardware or software. Hence the line-management device has a dual interface: with the operator and with the mainframe.

The input-output possibilities are enhanced through data communications capabilities, and they involve direct memory access with start and end of block detection; the interrupt-per-character systems are less efficient and less costly.

Microcomputers may be used as interfaces to existing network structures, central processing units, and terminal and software modules.

Miniprocessors and microprocessors are fairly inexpensive tools that maximize throughput, provide gateways, build concentrators, extend the life of available hardware and software, and, in general, create the structure for flexible and expandable communications systems. The architecture of the central processing unit must ensure that the instruction set is adequate for the protocol to be utilized, provide byte operation for the bisynchronous mode and bit and byte operation for bit-oriented protocols, and ensure Boolean and shift operations for error-check codes.

Subnetworks, literally parts of a network, are characterized by dynamic bandwidth allocation, alternate routing, partitioning into distinct subnets, each subnet being dedicated to a user, resource selection, "hunt groups" (groups in which to make automatic search for available facilities), and "camp on" (automatic stacking of requests for facilities, until they become available).

Front-Ending

Front-ending is the means of moving data to and from the lines and the data communications software. Front ends must offer aggregate throughput support, subject to numbers and combinations of line adapter, special features (switching, queueing, first-in and first-out (FIFO), and contention), standalone test capability (automatic and manual), reliability, and price comparison of per-port costs. Historically, the development of front ends started with the time-sharing experiments at Dartmouth College (General Electric's solution). Two approaches have been followed ever since; see Figure 5.4.

The first approach is the use of the mainframe to front-end for communications purposes, through software support. This solution was promoted by International Business Machines in the early 1960s until the announcement of its 3705, which performed front-ending functions on a self-standing basis. IBM seems to hold to these later designs, judging from the characteristics of its 8100, even though the latter has much broader capabilities.

The second approach is the use of a dedicated front-end machine to handle the communications part of the process. This solution is now giving way to the data processing and data communications functions that are handled separately on distinct equipment. The data-transport facility (both switching and transmission) no longer exists as part and parcel of the mainframe work. Even so, whether data

Figure 5.4
Front-ending as developed by International Business Machines and General Electric

	IBM	GE
1963/1965	FRONT-ENDING BY THE CENTRAL COMPUTER TERMINAL MANAGEMENT THROUGH MAINFRAME	SEPARATION OF THE FRONT-END MACHINE FROM THE MAINFRAME TERMINAL MANAGEMENT BY THE FRONT-END
	THIS HAD AN IMPACT ON: - TIME SHARING - REAL TIME - VIRTUAL MEMORY SOLUTIONS	
1967/1968	BSC PROTOCOL	VIP PROTOCOL (PROJECT 4001/TRIAD/115) MILANO / PHOENIX

communications are performed through a horizontal, dedicated network or by means of a relatively centralized engine, the ideas brought forward by the front-end experiences have found fruition in the use of the rear end of the mainframe, in the management of the data base.

Figure 5.5 shows the maxicomputer of the coming decade as composed of three major building blocks: the front end, and its derivatives, for handling communications, the mainframe, for handling the applied programs and, hence, the processes, and the rear end, or back end, for managing the data base.

Data base management systems (DBMS), which today are largely software implemented, will be moving into the rear-end machine and be converted to hardware, software, and firmware solutions. The reason that the now classic front-end standalone approaches cannot meet the evolving requirements is the sheer increase in the communications load. Solutions that might have been excellent with ten, twenty, fifty, or at most a hundred terminals do not respond as the need of five hundred terminals grows, and they are totally inadequate after that. Because of the ever-growing load the front-end machine became the system's bottleneck, while it should have been a data highway toward the mainframe (Figure 5.6).

The sought-after advantages are that the mainframe load be reduced: line polling, line management, terminal management, and both the physical and logical terminal mapping should be done by front-ending. To reduce the load of the mainframe we need communications programs, line tables, terminal tables, queue

Communications Gear 63

Figure 5.5
Maxicomputer, projected for the 1980s

TERMINALS

FRONT END → QUEUE

MAINFRAME

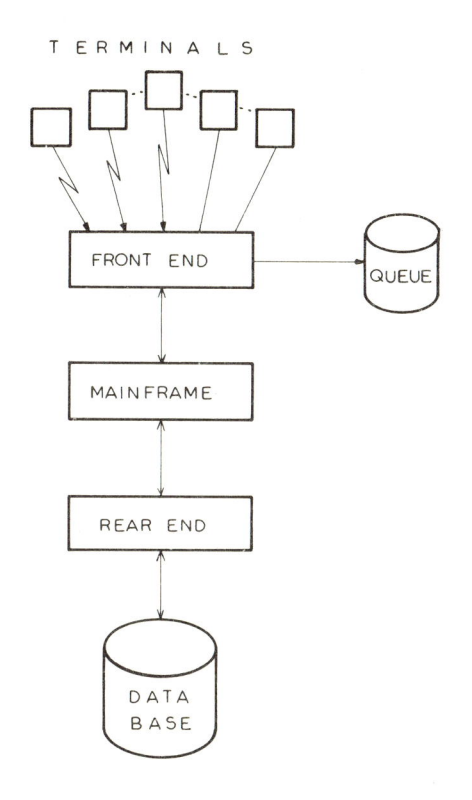

REAR END

DATA BASE

Figure 5.6

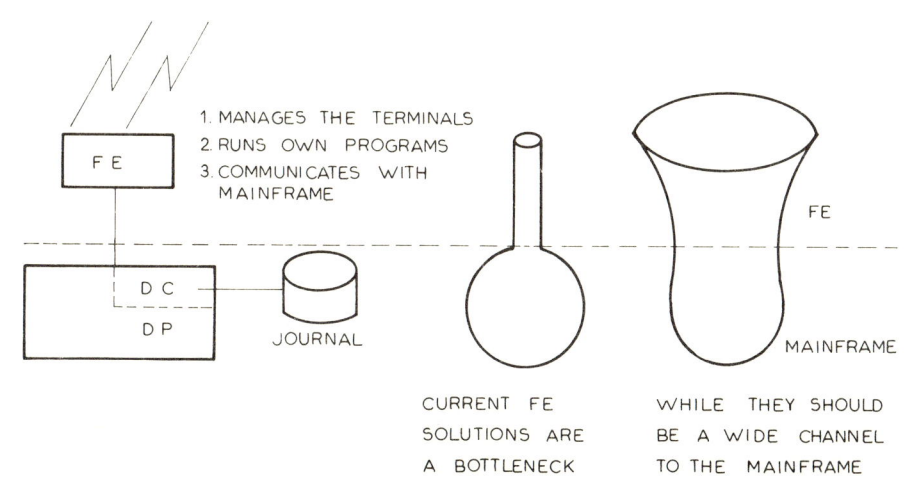

F E
1. MANAGES THE TERMINALS
2. RUNS OWN PROGRAMS
3. COMMUNICATES WITH MAINFRAME

D C
D P
JOURNAL

CURRENT FE SOLUTIONS ARE A BOTTLENECK

FE
MAINFRAME
WHILE THEY SHOULD BE A WIDE CHANNEL TO THE MAINFRAME

management, and journaling done by the front end. A message queue may require 70 to 100 kilobytes, which is a relief for the mainframe. It also creates two problems.

First, the software for the front end tends to be rather complex. To ease the requirements manufacturers often use the transaction-oriented software of the mainframe to do, for instance, the journaling and intermediate data storage; obviously, in this case the memory is not relieved after all.

Second, in complex communications systems the front end tends to develop heavy "housekeeping" requirements: it must at one and the same time communicate with the mainframe, manage its own operations, and handle the lines, the terminals, and the concentrators attached to it. The turnaround time is thus increased, and as the number of terminals grows, a bottleneck develops, as Figure 5.7 indicates.

To summarize, the functions of front ending are message switching, communications, line concentration, and interaction with the central processing unit (sometimes even used to connect two such units, as a hot switch). To these functions may be added data conversion, editing, and networking, depending on the available software support.

Editing and validation by front-ending will help reduce costs and, to some extent, increase the flexibility and portability of the data. For instance, we can store the data in the front end in a format compatible with the subsequent han-

Figure 5.7
Data communications time/KK

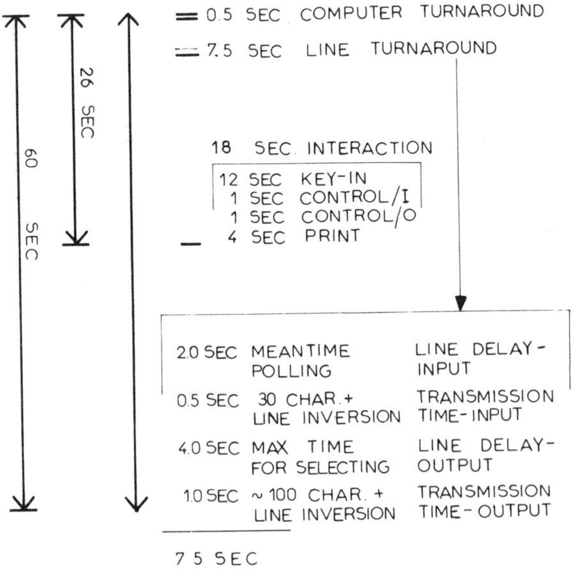

```
                    = 0.5 SEC  COMPUTER TURNAROUND
                    = 7.5 SEC  LINE TURNAROUND

                      18 SEC. INTERACTION
                      ┌─────────────────────┐
                      │ 12 SEC  KEY-IN      │
                      │  1 SEC  CONTROL/I   │
                      │  1 SEC  CONTROL/O   │
                      │  4 SEC  PRINT       │
                      └─────────────────────┘

              ┌──────────────────────────────────────────┐
              │ 2.0 SEC  MEANTIME       LINE DELAY-      │
              │          POLLING        INPUT            │
              │ 0.5 SEC  30 CHAR.+      TRANSMISSION     │
              │          LINE INVERSION TIME-INPUT       │
              │ 4.0 SEC  MAX TIME       LINE DELAY-      │
              │          FOR SELECTING  OUTPUT           │
              │ 1.0 SEC  ~100 CHAR.+    TRANSMISSION     │
              │          LINE INVERSION TIME-OUTPUT      │
              └──────────────────────────────────────────┘

                              7 5 SEC
```

(60 SEC, 26 SEC shown as vertical time bars)

dling by the mainframe, which is not necessarily the same format as that used at the terminal.

Front-ending may enhance the security of data as in the entry and preparation of messages by the SWIFT network. At relatively low cost it carries out authentication, uses multiple terminals, formats, and security checks.

To a certain extent, especially in environments that are not very complex, front-ending helps cope with functional heterogeneity; we refer to off-loading the host processors by moving as much communications processing as possible into the front end.

By the same token, front-end processors affect the availability and reliability of the communications paths from each terminal to the host, the more so if they produce acceptable data throughput and guarantee minimal delay characteristics. But the job may become too complex for one front-end machine and may disturb the response time. We must recall that computer-based equipment and its handling are influenced by human nature, contention, queues, and connects, by the nature of data (interactive or question–answer), and by the control requirements, interfaces, and protocols.

The software organization at the front end is typically as diagrammed in Figure 5.8. The software are most effective when the parametric approaches to it take into consideration environment, topology of hosts and terminals, technical characteristics of the transmission system, such as carrier, trunks, subsystem switches, and concentrators, and, if possible, the adequacy of the procedures (for instance, of fallback configuration).

Diagnostics should be an integral part of the network software. They are routing error detection, testing capability, malfunction isolation, failsoft requirements, reporting, and backup. Software should also provide for a number of architectural prerequisites, including points for expansion, throughput increase, modular design, and the necessary interfaces. In the last analysis, the quality of software has a great effect on response time, network delays, and general interface capacity.

To recapitulate, the differences between computer communications systems with and without front-end capability is as follows.

Without front-ending

Much of the central processor's time is devoted to servicing the teleprocessing network.

The access method has logical control of all lines and processes the data from the station.

The access method communicates directly with each station; each line has a different subchannel address.

Concentrators, if used, will have only physical control of the lines.

The number of lines in the teleprocessing network can be no greater than the maximal number of subchannel interfaces.

Figure 5.8
Needed software organization at front-end level

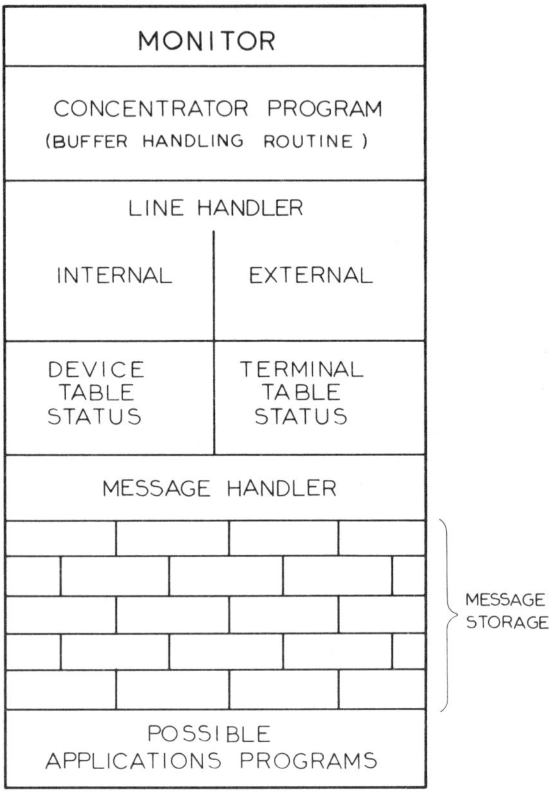

```
┌─────────────────────────────────┐
│           MONITOR               │
│  ┌───────────────────────────┐  │
│  │   CONCENTRATOR PROGRAM    │  │
│  │  (BUFFER HANDLING ROUTINE)│  │
│  ├───────────────────────────┤  │
│  │        LINE HANDLER       │  │
│  │  INTERNAL  │   EXTERNAL   │  │
│  ├────────────┼──────────────┤  │
│  │   DEVICE   │   TERMINAL   │  │
│  │   TABLE    │    TABLE     │  │
│  │   STATUS   │    STATUS    │  │
│  ├────────────┴──────────────┤  │
│  │      MESSAGE HANDLER      │  │
│  │  ┌──┬──┬──┬──┐            │  │
│  │  ├──┴─┬┴─┬┴──┤  } MESSAGE │  │
│  │  ├──┬─┴┬─┴┬──┤    STORAGE │  │
│  │  └──┴──┴──┴──┘            │  │
│  │       POSSIBLE            │  │
│  │  APPLICATIONS PROGRAMS    │  │
│  └───────────────────────────┘  │
└─────────────────────────────────┘
```

With front-ending

The central processing unit spends less time servicing the teleprocessing network; its resources are available for more applications processing.

The access method has few line-handling responsibilities; it can devote more time to message processing.

The access method communicates with all stations through a single interface.

The front end has both logical and physical control over the teleprocessing network; it also can process data.

Since the front end requires only a single interface with the central processor, the size of the teleprocessing network is increased.

As we pointed out, front-ending becomes more limited as the number of terminals to be served increases. With the very complex networks of the coming decade the nodal (horizontal) approaches rather than the vertical will be the solution.

Breaking Down the Front-End Tasks

Whether hierarchical (star) or nodal (horizontal) solutions are adopted, it is advisable to review and evaluate critically the concept of front-ending and to break down the earlier approaches into a layered solution, making use of specialization. We have said that the original front-ending was intended to relieve the central processor of most or all of the overhead responsibilities related to communications, but that the communications requirements kept on growing, so that the work load, overwhelming the capabilities of the front end, was turned back to the host. It became evident with practice that this was not efficient, and something had to be done about it. Channel control programs, for example, were created to be self-standing and microprocessor-implemented. They were given functions, such as the transfer of communications characters from data blocks in main memory programs, message delimiting, some editing, and control character deletion.

This separation of functions at the communications end followed a broader view of the system. The tendency has been to divide the computer architecture, not into a host and a front end, but into the data base machine, the main processor (host), and the front-end machine. Each was subsequently subdivided into component parts, and those into smaller elements. Figures 5.9 and 5.10 outline the component functions of the data base machine, of the main processor, and of the front-end machine. Specialization is the modern approach to system design, whether we talk of the front-end equipment or of the system as a whole: The data base machine is specialized in rear-end operations consisting of four groups of three elements each. The host also has four groups of operations to perform. But, as will be appreciated, the front-end machine is the most functionally intense in terms of assessments. As the requirements increase, so do its duties.

The division is far from conclusive. It depends on the applications programming (AP), the operating environment, and the optimization we wish to accomplish, and this is true of the more detailed levels of breakdown, in particular the division between the line functions and the main supervisory activities of the network. There is a real division between overall communications control, line control, and character control. Each level is answerable to a specific group of functions driven by specialized tables for communications control. Together with the control programs these tables must be transferred to the appropriate control device, usually through a downline-loading procedure.

Specialization and functionalization have both preceded and followed this process. In a specialized channel controller, for example, space exists (for each channel) for a list of consecutive control words. Each is used to store main-memory address information. It indicates the area to which data are to be delivered in a "receive" process or from which data are to be obtained in a "transmit" process.

A channel control program directs the movements of each character. It can cause the character to be processed in a simple manner within a minimum of time

Figure 5.9

Data base machine

A. Information elements (items)
    Files
    Data descriptions

B. Codes
    Data formats
    Edits

C. Access requests
    Integrity
    Security

D. Add
    Delete
    Upkeep

↕

Host

A. AP and utilities library management

B. Character transforming, encrypting, decrypting, compacting, expanding

C. Session supervision
    Get messages
    Process them
    Return them

D. Process handling
    Queue requests for resources
    Interpret AP
    Execute AP

Don't deal with the terminal, but with the function of the system and the way the AP work together.

Division depends on AP, environment and optimization.

Figure 5.10

Front-end machine
(works on block/message level)

A. Addressing work stations (polling decisions)
   Queueing for distribution (downstream)
   Editing and sending data

B. Receiving requests (polling decisions)
   Addressing host
   Delimiting data enclosures (segmenting and blocking)

C. Handling sessions
   Establishment
   Maintenance
   Validation

D. Assuring network status
   Turning DTE and lines on/off
   Changing assignments

E. Protecting data
   Buffering FE level
   Quarantining

F. Journaling
   Statistics (traffic, failures)
   Checkpoint and recovery (Generally, data traffic regulation)

Front-end machine executes top-level functions

Typically handles only 10% of the data communications work load, particularly if journaling is moved to DC machine and upper level.

Its operations are customer oriented (here lie the differences between banks, airlines, and commercial and industrial companies).

Tables at the front-end level are on a total network basis. Functional tables are moving downstream and become specialized and more primitive.

or to conduct extensive checking and editing functions. This has been done at the original front-end level in most cases, but character handling beyond the basic operations of message delimiting and block checking developed at the expense of throughput speed. More powerful algorithms, such as cyclic redundancy checks (CRC), though they improve data integrity, aggravate the throughput situation. Therefore, the separation of functions and dedication of a microprocessor to a homogeneous functional group is technically valid and operationally efficient.

The Data Communications Machine

Figure 5.10 demonstrates how the principles we have outlined are put into practice. Notice that the low-level functions, now assigned to the data communications (DC) machine, represent some 90 percent of the total communications load, which is not only an elegant design but also a necessary one, now that terminals do not number 50, 100, or 200, but 2,000, 8,000, and 12,000.

Notice also that in this structure care has been taken to divide the functions unevenly, the greater part being brought toward the lower levels. The 5, 20, and 75 percent distribution of load is not a superficially arrived at division of labor but a carefully thought out approach. While the upper level is unified, the middle level can be divided into a discrete number of components. Further, the lower level is divided into a larger number of homogeneous processors each implemented by a microprocessor. This lower (character) level of the data communications machine is in essence a "microline controller." The design depends on individual protocols, and that fact underlines its flexibility.

As we have said, the statistically uneven division of assigned labor is intentional. For an example of handling at the lower level we have considered the character-oriented tasks. At the lower levels the functions are simpler, and a multiplicity of more primitive devices can be dedicated to them. This tends to create a hierarchical structure within the data communications machine.

Let us now briefly look at the line control tables, which belong to the higher level. The line control table is logically divided into two halves. The first 32 bytes, say, are dedicated to the receiving channel of the line and the next 32 to the transmitting channel. Both input data and programming work space are critical elements. A change in configuration is implemented through a change in table, which in turn changes the procedures to be followed. Microprocessors handle several of the table's functions, and parts of the table are moving down stream. Code, line speed, and numbers of lines handled are critical factors in the design.

Typically, the microprocessor has random-access memory and is downline-loaded by the front end. Reliability is easily assured at that level. One idea is to have one backup microprocessor for each four in action, with hot-standby capability.

The microline controller depends on the individual protocols. Program-supplied input data provide information required for character configuration, interruption control, status, error conditions, and the like. The programming work space may be used in any manner needed by the communications-handling program. Figures 5.11 and 5.12 give an idea of how the functions are assigned to the upper, middle, and lower levels of the data communications machine.

Figure 5.11
Data Communications Machine

Front-end machine (works on block/message level)

Data communications machine handles 5% of DC work load

Upper level: can be handled by the FE machine; matter of choice, environment, software.

1. Queueing
2. Communicating to FE (e.g., inform terminal has failed)
3. Acknowledgments
4. Status (line, DTE), decision, restoration
5. Routing decisions
6. Load splitting
7. Message editing

Data communications machine handles 20% of DC work load

Middle level: standardized product specific per line discipline—not AP.

1. Execution level routing: poll, call/send
2. Send blocks to low level; receive same
3. Error recovery
4. Error detection on protocol basis (e.g., missing header)

Software or microprocessor at middle level is data link control oriented.

Data communications machine handles 65% of DC work load

Low Level: also a standardized product

1. Character handling: input, conversion, output. The issue here is specialization by protocols: BSC, HDLC, TTY
2. Status (character basis)
3. Error detection (character basis)

---

72   *Data Communications for Distributed Information Systems*

Figure 5.12

10% / Front-end machine (works on block/message level)
↕
90% / Data communications machine—Upper Level

Management by software
    Set of tables able to maintain line management
    ACK, NAK, EOT, ERP

Data communications machine—Middle (line) Level

To be implemented by microprocessor
    Will encompass a group of lines and involve
        1. Procedure/line discipline (BSC, XDLC, S/S)
        2. ID
        3. Line speed; number of lines
        4. Work space (data storage on temporary basis)
        5. Microprocessor-implemented tables

Data communications machine—Lower (character) Level

All character-oriented tasks
    Code (6 of 8 bit ID a factor)
    Code conversion (if needed)
    Basic level of ACK
To be implemented by microprocessor for a single line or small group of lines.

↕
Electrical interface to the line (DCE)   Line(s)
Front-end machine middle and lower levels
Microprocessors have RAM, and are down-line loaded by FE (need for hot stand-by: 1 per 4)

6
From Data Processing to Data Communications

Having covered some of the broader perspectives in telecommunications, the time has come to clarify the boundary between data communications and data processing.

Data communications concerns the transmission and distribution functions, in which the data are unaltered, the network control (and on-line maintenance), and the link establishment, routing, virtual circuit and Datagram, flow control, store-and-forward, and error detection and correction.

Data processing concerns the use of computers for processing information, in which the semantic content, or meaning, of input data is transferred, the storage and retrieval take place for purposes other than those of store-and-forward and error detection and control, and the output data constitute a programmed response to the input data.

The unit of output in data processing may include such diverse variables as the following:

Tons of paper printed per day*

Number of jobs multiprocessed

Number of on-line terminals allowed in data processing access

Megabytes (usually in the hundreds) available on-line (random access)

Throughput

Turnaround

Uptime

Availability

*Barclays Bank, for instance, prints two tons of paper per day and Scandia Insurance prints a ton and a half per day.

The unit of output in telecommunications may be just as diverse:

Channel facility

Transmission characteristics

Number of terminals managed by the system

Response time

Size of DTE memory and access methods

Allowed protocols

Switching characteristics

Line dependability

System reliability (including concentrators, front end, and terminals)

Bandwidth

Distance

Assurance that data going out of the link are the same as the data entering the link

Regarding the overall systems in data communications, we talk of physical resources and logical resources, and we refer in data processing, correspondingly, to hardware and software.

User Levels in Data Communications

It is wise to separate the computing function from the communicating function so that each may be optimized. Data communications systems must accommodate a wide variety of lines, devices, and geographically dispersed facilities for handling in an expandable network. The structure of the system must meet diverse and constantly evolving needs.

ITT's new network distinguishes five levels of service:

>Facsimile to facsimile
>
>Terminal to facsimile
>
>Terminal to terminal
>
>Terminal to computer
>
>Computer to computer

Rockwell Collins, too, proposes five general levels, but with a different classification:

Host to host (particularly oriented to bulk data transfer)

Terminal to host (switching message and data)

Terminal to terminal (specifically for message-switching)

Terminal to data base (for inquiry–response; this is terminal to host at "disc level")

Data collection (if host has time out)

The functions to be performed at these levels are composed of the following elements: real-time update, remote batch data transmission, remote concentration, and test systems (loopbacks, downline loading, upline dumping). This approach emphasizes connectability, expandability, improved utilization, and reliability.

IBM proposes three basic levels for the electronic office:

Terminal to terminal, for the distribution of priority messages and batches of routine correspondence

Terminal to computer, including the terminal-to-terminal functions and adding on-line processing and on-line merging of file and text

Computer to computer, implementing a protected message-switching system, storing, screening, and transmitting information to and from remote locations.

These are increased levels of sophistication which, like every data communications network, require software modules, protocols, hardware, and support services for overall design and construction of distributed computer networks.

Different levels of sophistication offer options in organizing a network to meet specific communication requirements. We must start with the study of our requirements, both qualitative and quantitative. The more complex they are, the higher the level needed. The services such solutions can offer are valuable: timely documents and messages, improved pace of information flow, reduced paper-handling, increased efficiency in written communication, remote revision capability, and faster response time. Some typical applications are letters, memos, specifications, contracts, confirmation, personnel data, spares and inventories, schedules, and progress reports.

A higher level of sophistication can go further, for instance, by merging electronic mail and point-of-sales equipment (POS) and by creating and maintaining support files, which will eventually be transferred to low-cost media as computer output to microfilm, or microform (COM).

To appreciate the reach of such applications, note that there are about 350,000 word processors in the United States today, less than 10 percent on-line. The number is expected to grow at the rate of 35 to 40 percent per year; by 1985, 90 percent will be on-line. The United States Postal Service alone will be spending $180 million per year by 1982 for research and development on computerized mass mail service. And mail in the form of communications of all sorts is one of the great frontiers of tomorrow.

System Perspectives

Data processing and data communications need thorough studies. Not only do they interact with and complement each other, but also they influence the solutions to be given to the other side by presenting both requirements and limitations. Data processing and data communications come together in a variety of on-line applications, which may be divided into two groups, current and future:

Current	*Future*
Direct delivery (to host)	Correspondence
Data collection	Reports
Inquiry and response	Message broadcast
On-line update	

The services may be installed at the same time or sequentially, if the project takes them into account in the first place and so avoids mistakes of the past.

To understand some of the requirements we are faced with today, we ought to look at the way data processing has developed. Let us consider the branch office of a typical bank as an example; see Figure 6.1.

In the first phase, in the early 1950s, service to the client (an audit, for example) was done by means of a classic electromechanical device installed on the branch-office premises. The balance was registered black-on-white on a personal card and could be consulted and updated at any time. Then in the late 1950s came the central computers and associated machinery. The electromechanical audit at the branch office disappeared, and the data were carried to the data processing center. Delays developed, and with them, errors. This phase left something to be wanted. The third phase promised to correct all that. By the middle and late 1960s the starlike real-time network appeared. The central computer remained king, but the branch office got its equipment back in the form of a terminal.

On paper, it looked wonderful, as if we could eat the pie and have it, too. But snags were cropping up. The terminal, usually unintelligent, would not perform if the line was "down." Sometimes it cuts off fifteen terminals. Worse yet, the central computer's down time made for networkwide blackouts. That was the third phase. Now we are at the point of a new era; see Figure 6.2. Immediate availability of needed information at the branch office is one aspect, but there are others. We must redefine the topology and all devices, support, facilities, native commands, applications, growth potential, restart and recovery, error rates, and maintainability.

The logical support should handle the DTE characteristics, which involves mainframes, front ends, rear ends—in general, minicomputers operating as nodes and hosts.

From Data Processing to Data Communications   77

Figure 6.1
Data processing from the 1950s to now

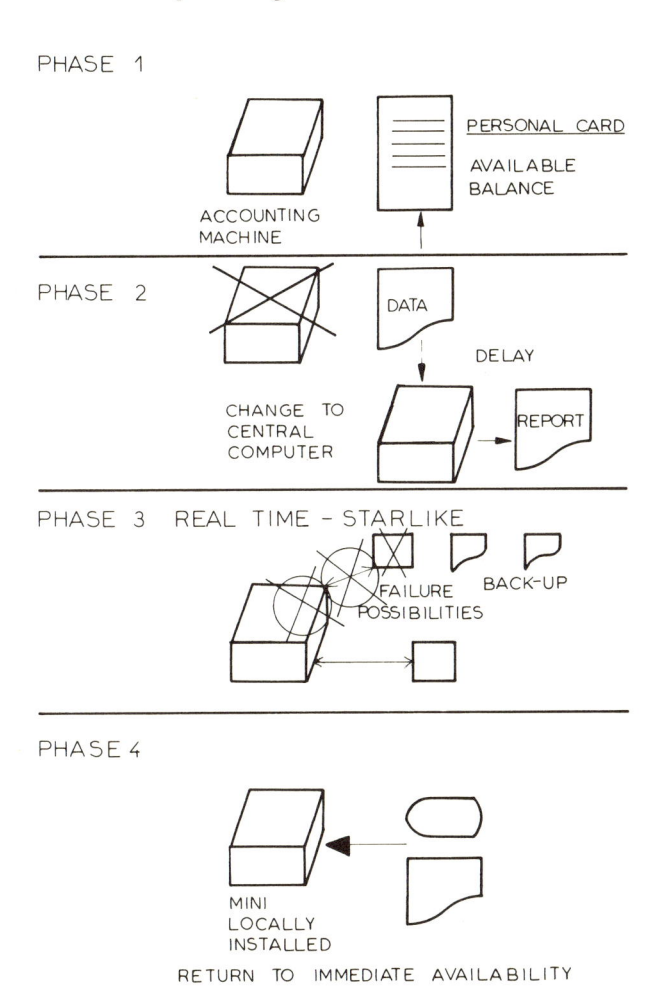

PHASE 1

PERSONAL CARD
AVAILABLE BALANCE
ACCOUNTING MACHINE

PHASE 2

DATA
DELAY
CHANGE TO CENTRAL COMPUTER
REPORT

PHASE 3 REAL TIME - STARLIKE

FAILURE POSSIBILITIES
BACK-UP

PHASE 4

MINI LOCALLY INSTALLED
RETURN TO IMMEDIATE AVAILABILITY

Figure 6.2
History of systems

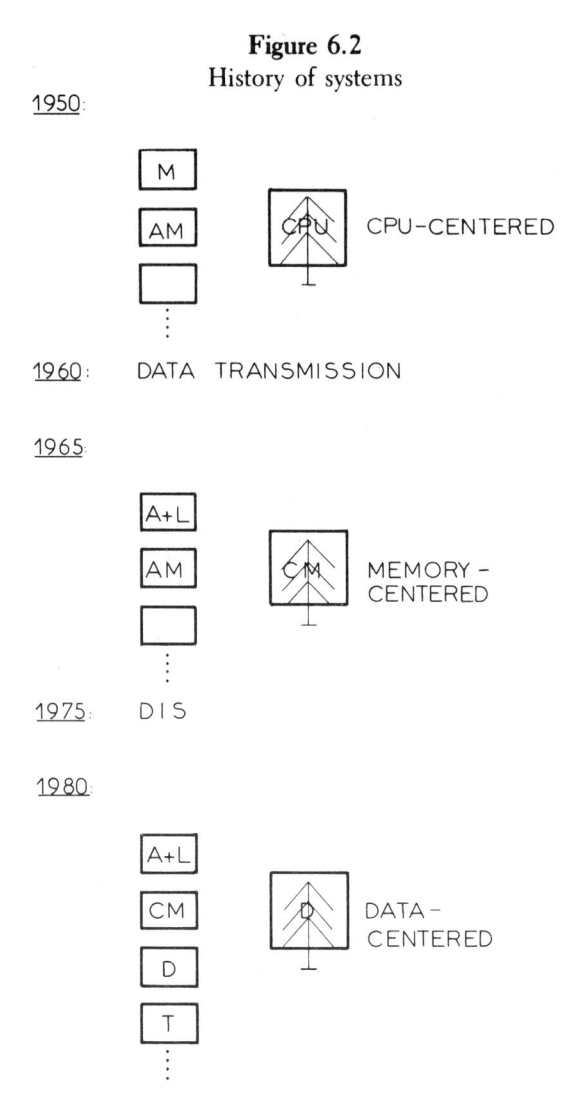

1950:

M
AM
☐
⋮

CPU — CPU-CENTERED

1960: DATA TRANSMISSION

1965:

A+L
AM
☐
⋮

CM — MEMORY-CENTERED

1975: DIS

1980:

A+L
CM
D
T
⋮

D — DATA-CENTERED

Another matter to study is traffic as it relates to communications and networking (Table 6.1). The object here is dimensioning, and this necessarily involves both topology and the design of lines, modems, DTEs, and nodes and switches. Decisions on design parameters are vital, as Table 6.2 shows.

The user's needs must be studied. This usually involves data bases, file access, user access, tracing of mailbox, sender, and author, protection and security, and the ever important applied-programming library.

All this is in terms of facilities. There is another prerequisite: know-how: an understanding of the great steps we have taken over the last twenty-five years and of the horizons that have been opened by the new tools themselves.

Table 6.1
Traffic Description

Application Type	Message Requirements							Priority	Editing Requirements
	Average Length in Characters		Arrival Rate				
	Input	Output	Monthly	Daily	Peak Hour		

Table 6.2
Design Parameters

1. Format
2. Acknowledgment Procedure
3. Growth Rate per Year (by application)
4. Data Link
5. Routing
6. Flow Control
7. Communications Procedures
   Core switch
   Store and forward
   Data-base access
   Message multiplication factor (number of output messages per input message)

Application Type	Multiplication Factor

8. Bit Error Rate
9. Security/Encryption
10. Journaling of All Messages
    Retention Time
        On-line
        Off-line
11. Objectives
    Hosts
    Terminals
        Message switch capability
    Broadcasting
12. Response Time Requirements (by application)

From the central processing unit of the 1950s, we have moved to the memory-centered computer system of the mid-1960s, and we are going on to the data-centered system of the 1980s. The faculties we have at our disposition have changed and, with them, the outlook.

The Three Main Classes of Communications

Currently there are three main classes of communications systems used in business. The telephone is by far the most frequently used means of communicating. The postal service is the second class, consisting of private couriers and intercompany mail-delivery networks that carry messages physically instead of electronically. Finally there is the electrical message system, such as facsimile, Telex, and telegrams, and, more recently, the electronic extensions of these.

About 90 billion pieces of mail move per year in the United States. About 9 billion are writer-to-reader correspondence, of which 4 billion are business mail; interoffice correspondence in the form of letters and memos is estimated at 12 to 15 billion. In addition, there are 220 to 250 billion telephone calls per year and 50 million Telex messages.

Interesting is the question of the lengths of messages. One study shows that 58 percent of management's messages are one page or less, 28 percent are two or four pages, and 14 percent are five pages or more. Electronic message systems (EMS) carry much shorter texts; some 73 percent are less than 100 characters each. Of all messages sent, 45 percent are addressed to one person, 35 percent to more than one, 18 percent to groups, and 2 percent to a combination of groups and individuals. Electronic mail finds its strength in these statistics.

An educated guess is that within a few years electronic mail, including processes assimilated into it, will grow enormously from the 10 percent share it has today of voice and data communications. Estimates range from a 50 percent share of the combined resources to a 90 percent share, and this before the year 1990; see Figure 6.3.

A study found that 40 percent of a manager's time is spent on mail, telephone, and business travel and 12 to 35 percent on writing and reading. Another study identified the percentage of working time some professionals spent handling paper. Statistics show that 550 kilograms of paper are printed each year for every man, woman, and child in the United States, of these a good share being computer output. Other statistics show that a given technical article is read by an average of six readers. The computer was originally thought to be a means of reducing the paper jungle; it has increased it. It is now hoped that data communications will turn the trick.

Electronic Message Systems

Electronic message systems can carry two types of message, hard copy and soft copy, but still the telephone and postal service dwarf other message systems in size. If the telephone is excluded and only intercompany and intracompany hard-copy messages are considered, the picture that emerges is like Figure 6.4. The United States Postal Service revenues break down in this manner: $5.5 billion

82 *Data Communications for Distributed Information Systems*

Figure 6.3
Growth of electronic mail systems

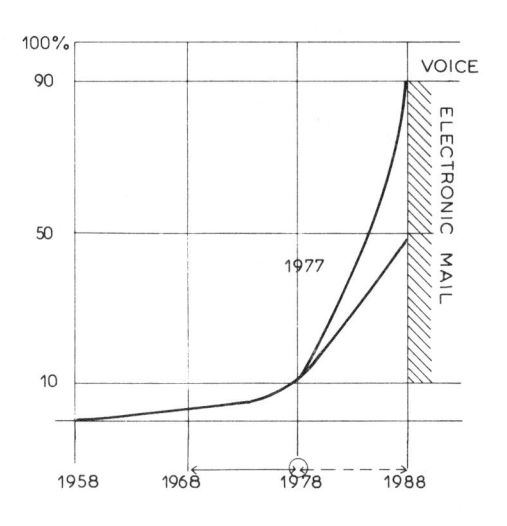

Figure 6.4
Classic hard-copy costs today

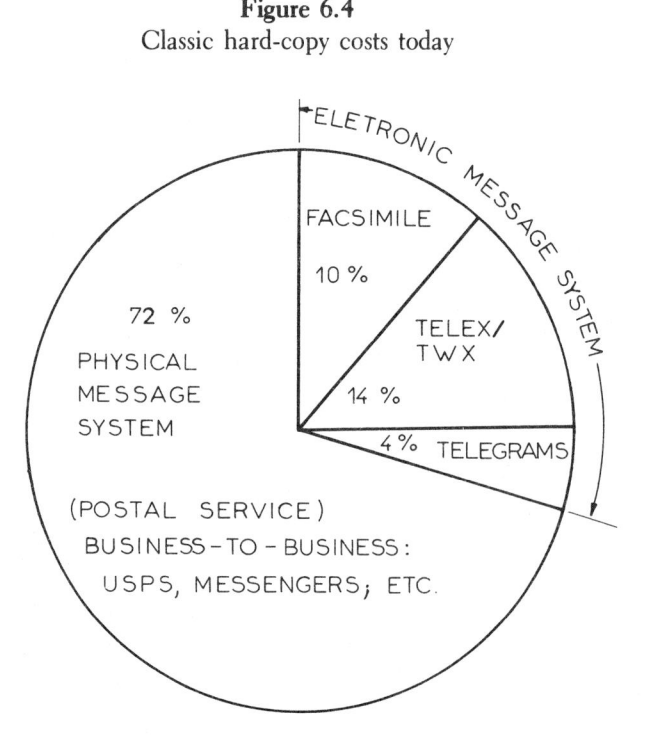

from first-class mail and $5 billion from other mail (magazines, advertising, and packages, etc.). It must all be delivered by hand.

If these statistics are looked at from another angle, data communications revenues have already surpassed those that the postal service receives as a business-to-business message carrier of first-class mail (44 percent of $5.5 billion); in fact, they are about $3.2 billion for 1978.

Further, we observe that electronic messages usually want a higher priority than do others and that they may be delivered in many different ways.

Data communications networks are used for financial transactions, order entry, and associated teleprocessing applications. Formerly quite separate from administrative message systems, data communications networks are now developing at a rapid pace.

Facsimile systems have also found their way into environments that are not computer oriented. About 160,000 units are now in operation in the United States, including 100,000 or more low-speed transceivers that send a page in four to six minutes. Virtually every major company uses facsimile for sending advertising, engineering, and legal documents. Some firms, like Bethlehem Steel, use a few hundred facsimile units for order entry.

One of the early ventures in electronic mail is Mailgram, a message-switching service. It is jointly operated by the United States Postal Service and Western Union. It still has a long way to go before it can compete with the regular postal service's rates or the electronic mail products now in development. Britain, for instance, is planning to implement a full-scale electronic mail system over the next few years. The key advantage that the British PTT has over the U.S. Postal Service is its enormous investment in telephone networks to transmit facsimile via wideband. The system will be operating when the network is not used, from late at night to early morning. The British also are investigating the idea of electronic mail via home television sets.

If first-class mail could be delivered, then so could third-class mail, such as mail advertising. Receivers of such material could identify it and, if not interested, easily destroy it, while reviewing their incoming messages. Otherwise, it can be displayed in color on the television set.

Future Developments

Among many possibilities for the future is voice store-and-forward capability for use on the telephone and, maybe, the television network. The sender directs a verbal message to the recipient's "in-box," and the recipient calls the in-box from any telephone and gets the message waiting for him. Hotels might provide a means of coupling the telephone and the television set, to offer terminal capabilities to the guests for receiving and sending messages.

The merging of written and oral messages on the principles of packet switching will offer the following advantages: decoupling of sender and receiver, so that there is no need of both to be present, electronic speeds and geographic independence, and better composition, storage, retrieval, and reading. Such solutions can operate within different environments: exclusive station-to-station calls, primary addressing with copies to other stations, broadcasts, with messages sent from one station to a distribution list, and teleconferencing (group participation).

At present, experience pinpoints several problems: explaining to users what to do in time out, helping users having difficulties, training the end user on all modifications as they appear, and expanding the topology without increasing the costs. Equipment that now is in development will be able to meet such needs. What is missing are the procedural and end-user studies to help in projecting, evaluating, implementing, and maintaining the systems to come.

Here are some examples. Wideband communications would allow a copier to produce a remote image at the same speed at which it produces a copy locally. This would make facsimile an adjunct of copying. The unit would be reserved for local copying during the day, and it would receive only when it was being used locally. At night a single copier would receive a few thousand pages. Data compression units can receive at best about eight hundred pages in eight hours. A facsimile transmission that now takes six minutes will, by means of wideband, take only about eight seconds.

Considering the speed at which facsimile images can be carried, it is likely that electronic mail networks will be springing up and will be installed first by the top two hundred or so companies in the United States. By being connected to major operating centers those companies will be able to work in a communications environment of unprecedented magnitude and speed.

A Message Service: Ontyme

For an example of current developments we shall consider Ontyme, a carrier service projected as an alternative to other message-switching systems. It is designed to appeal to geographically dispersed organizations that wish to converse rapidly and economically in forms readable by either a machine or a person, including interoffice correspondence and other data to be collected or disseminated. It would also incorporate separate technologies: store and forward, on-line computers, packet data communications, and terminal independence and error control transmission. The following is a list of its functions:

 Verifies authorized use at log-in.

 Allows user inquiry of message status.

 Provides optional on-line message preparation and editing.

 Adds time and date to all messages.

 Assigns a unique master message number.

 Holds or dials out for delivery at the user's option.

Assigns an output sequence number at time of delivery.

Delivers to group-coded destinations.

Responds with error messages to users.

Provides on-line file storage for frequently used messages or data.

Holds all messages three days for on-line retrieval.

Saves archive messages on tape for 90 days.

Provides data on traffic for management control.

Store and forward has given experience in stamping of time and date on all messages and in master control numbering, output sequence, and on-line retrieval of recently sent messages. Further extensive traffic data are captured and made available to users so that they may have the information necessary to control their own costs. From on-line systems have come the following features:

Verification of authorized access

User's inquiry about message status

A straightforward appearance to users, complemented by error messages to assist in application

An optional on-line message-preparation facility that allows messages to be economically prepared and edited at the user's terminal

Optional on-line file storage that allows users to store the text of anything that might be useful to them

An example of the last is a message that may be sent often but with minor modifications each time; it may be stored on-line and then easily retrieved whenever needed.

Packet technology as applied to message-switching brings to the user a heightened reliability. Errors in transmission are detected within the network, and the affected data are retransmitted until they are received accurately. Alternate routing enhances reliability by providing more than one path between nearly all points in the network.

A packet system is designed around a few simple operations common to all users: entering, sending, and reading messages. By customizing the documentation and training the users, the system can take on a variety of forms. In other words, user organizations can shape even a public service to their own needs.

Another freedom has been introduced in the form of terminal independence. Virtually all terminals in the range of 110 to 1,200 bits per second are supported by Ontyme, and any type of terminal can send and receive messages from any other type. Low-volume stations can be served by inexpensive low-speed terminals, while high-volume locations can use video displays for preparation and higher-speed printers for receiving. Moreover, the terminals do not have to be dedicated to the network but may be employed for any other application a user wishes.

Ontyme can be used either for dialing in or dialing out or both; that is, some locations may install dial-in terminal equipment and use the system as a sort of mail box, while others, equipped with the proper terminals, may be called by the system for message pickup and delivery. The choice is up to the user. The sender of a message does not need to know this or any other characteristic of the recipient's terminal. It will generally be less expensive to use dial-in terminals, but some conditions may be better served by a dial-out system.

Finally, messages may be prepared on-line with computer assistance or off-line, as has frequently been the case in the past. At present the on-line preparation facilities are limited to correction of the line being entered.

7
Transaction-Based Systems

A large number of the new computer systems being installed are transaction-based, that is, they are characterized by a fast response to a limited type of inquiry. Some typical ones are the financial, retail, and airline-reservation networks. Transaction systems are human-driven, for mobile users and customers, based on a fixed set of transaction models, highly decentralized, and locally demand-intensive. They must respond to user distribution, a profile of requirements, and a range of facilities offered (e.g., credit and debit cards) and have the dual faculty of being oriented toward both customer and management.

Figure 7.1 dramatizes the difference between a batch and real-time computer environment and a data communications one. In the former the machines and data operate independently of one another. The network idea is of a different sort, and the data communications system is a network. Instead of distinct equipment there are "processes," which are files, programs, and so on. Each process is accessible to each point of the network, by means of either sophisticated or very simple units. Simplicity should be an aim of any project. Indeed, much of the value of transaction systems is that they use the DTE facilities of the most widespread carrier, the voice-grade telephone lines.

The Transaction Network Service

An example of transaction-based networks is Bell System's Transaction Network Service, TNS. This service is largely used for credit approval (it was started in a small bank in Seattle, Washington). It is a new, switched, common-user service designed to meet the needs of high volume, short messages, and inquiry–response applications, with attention to reliability, maintainability, and error-free performance. Its inquiry–response applications include credit verification, cheque au-

Figure 7.1

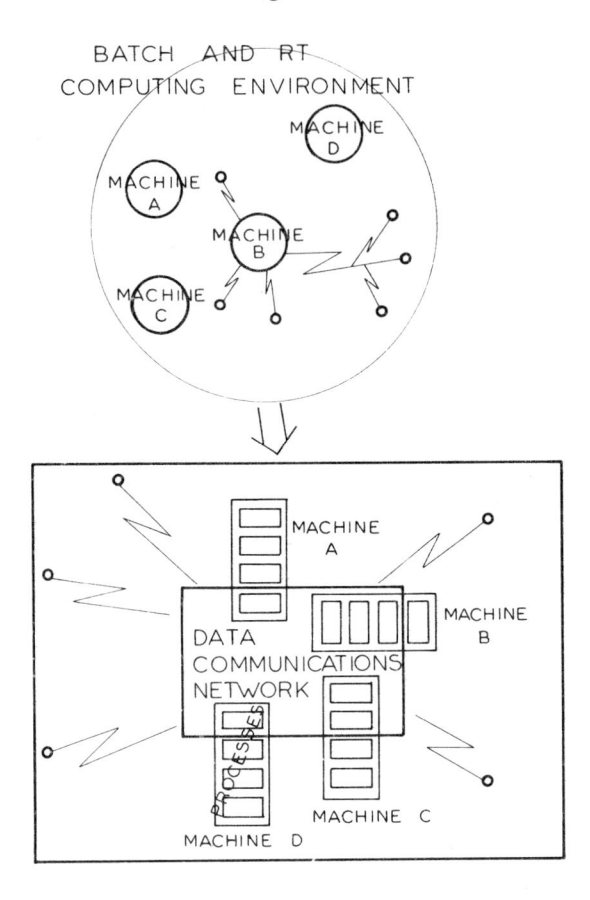

thorization, order entry, and inventory control and quotations. Customer-transaction text sizes of up to 128 characters can be accommodated.

The service has both polled and dial terminals for high-volume and low-volume customer locations. On both, customers have the advantage of a cost-effective communications delivery system with network and message control, high reliability, and low undetected-error rates. The system also has a "voice-answerback" with TNS vocabulary. Customers may select line speeds of 2,400, 4,800, or 9,600 bits per second and message flow options that allow for effective communications with traffic loads.

Service may be between terminals and host computer (data centers), or between data centers. Access to host computers from the network service is provided by synchronous data links, with a specified line control procedure and message format.

The most important aspects of this service may be listed as the following:

Fast and easy startup and expansion

Switching time at the millisecond level

Simpler system and software design, hence less development time

High reliability achieved by total system; redundancy within the common-user network

Good-quality maintenance ensuring maximal network uptime

Network management of the entire communications system, effecting savings in resources

Single-vendor interface for a total-system solution

No private lines, hence inexpensive

Chiefly offered to large customers

Very economical, no major investment needed

Users connected to data bases

A newly introduced data termination equipment has a one-number repertory for repeated calls to the same number. It can dial out from a private branch exchange or on a foreign exchange line. The system contains an automatic facility that tests for proper operation. It may be equipped with an auxiliary manual-entry card, so that the customer at a bank or store can enter a personal identification number when required.

The present-day transaction systems still have limitations. For instance, when the local switched network is seized, a dial tone is recognized, which results in the automatic dialing of the local telephone number. Once this connection is made, a second dial tone occurs, which permits the dialing of the security or billing number. But today's computerized private branch exchanges cannot recognize this second dial tone.

The Choice of Facilities

The foregoing section outlined the capabilities and limitations of a transaction-based system. By and large, the choice of facilities will depend on four basic factors: frequency (bandwidth), medium (cables, radio, satellite), analog or digital signals, and supplier. For instance, satellite carriers will offer digital services at very low cost and very high frequency (12 to 14 gigahertz), and when such services become available, a great many companies will have to reexamine their network design.

The data communications networks of the future will offer many services that today are now obtainable only through private, sophisticated arrangements. Four trends may be observed: digital networks (the existing voice networks no longer are sufficient), value-added networks (VAN), which offer more than the carrier facility (store-and-forward procedures, error detection and correction, routing, and so on), large private networks (probably using types of value-added solutions and, possibly, value-added backbone facilities), and new tariff structures for the mass requirements expected in the next decade.

The technical requirements to be observed in all future solutions quite definitely include full error detection, error correction, recovery, fast selection, two-way simultaneous transmission, interaction (dialogue), store-and-forward procedures, and bit-oriented protocols. The last (which is beyond the scope of this book) needs more capabilities from terminals, such as new operating codes, buffered data transmission, synchronous mode of operation, error detection and correction, and address and command fields framed in a unique way. Most terminals do not meet these criteria. Other technical requirements are standardization (hope of), an extensive topology, complete code independence, and device independence. Standardization, topology, and code and device independence are suggested by the sheer size and diversity of the data communications systems to come. The following example presents an order-of-magnitude calculation of the data loads to be applied on data communications systems during the next decade.

First-class mail and interoffice memos represent 16 to 19 billion pieces, say, 17 billion; see Table 7.1. Some 54 trillion characters are the estimated annual exchange of information in United States business, with about 4.5 trillion characters a month. A typical minicomputer today holds 10 megabytes. Hence, under current conditions the aforementioned statistics would represent 450,000 minicomputers.

Table 7.1
Estimated Annual Exchange of First Class and Interoffice Mail in the United States

Mail	Number of Characters per Page	Annual Total of Characters per Page (billions)	Annual Total of Characters (trillions)
1 page	1,000	9.86	9.86
2 to 4 pages	4,000	4.76	19.00
5 pages	10,500	2.48	24.99
			53.85

Types of Communications Link

The choice of communications facilities will necessarily be influenced by the type of link. The links may be analog or digital and may use sub-voice-grade, voice-grade, or wideband speeds.

Analog facilities transmit analog signals that have been converted by modems at each end of the link; modems convert the digital signals from terminals and computers to analog signals. Typically the facilities follow the late-nineteenth century principle of transmitting voice over wire. The circuits transmit a continuous range of frequencies; the information being transmitted bears an exact relationship to the original. Analog repeaters amplify the signal and noise. The transmitted frequencies are susceptible to distortion from resistance, thermal noise, fading, and so on.

Digital facilities are relatively recent. They transmit digital signals without conversion to analog signals and with no need of modems. In this case voice (the analog signals) is converted into digital signals for transmission. Digital circuits transmit discrete signals, and digital repeaters detect the precise signals (or bits) being transmitted and retransmit them at their original strength. That is why we said that modems (digital data sets) are required for interfacing between the circuit and the terminal (central processing unit). Digital repeater stations reduce the error rate significantly below that of analog circuits.

The speeds fall into three categories:

Sub-voice-grade, or narrowband, is used for telegraph and typewriter terminals; the channel can carry up to 600 bits per second.

Voice-grade speeds are 1,200 to 9,600 bits per second; the channels have a bandwidth of 3,000 to 4,000 Hertz.

Wideband is for speeds in excess of 20,000 bits per second; originally up to 240,000 bits per second, it now is in excess of 1,000,000 bits per second, with a bandwidth of 48,000 Hertz.

The modes of operation may be one of three types:

Simplex, which allows transmission in one direction only.

Half-duplex, or two-wire, which allows transmission in two directions but not at the same time.

Full duplex, or four-wire, which allows transmission in two directions simultaneously.

These differences have their origin in design, but their impact on applications is very substantial. Furthermore, the wires, or the radio band, may be leased, switched public, dial-up, or value-added.

Leased, or private, lines are used only by the subscriber and are available at all times; the lines are in an established routing pattern that does not change.

Switched public lines are used by many subscribers, but only one at a time. They are part of the carrier's network and are not dedicated to any single subscriber, though they guarantee access time (usually minimal) to each subscriber.

Dial-up connections are often used for temporary and relatively short periods of time. The connections are established by calling numbers, as in a regular telephone service. Inbound and outbound WATS is often used with this type of facility.

Finally, the newer packet-switching and value-added networks are private services supplied by vendors that use one or more of the above-mentioned facilities. Figure 7.2 integrates the characteristics we have been discussing.

Further factors govern choices:

1. Number of messages (or interactive sessions)
2. Distribution of message length (or holding time)
3. Urgency, allowed response time, lags, priorities
4. Peak versus off-peak volume
5. Geographical points of origin and destination of traffic (distance between points, clustering)
6. Location and access nodes on a common-carrier network
7. Pricing classification (e.g., high or low density)
8. Adaptability of network to widely varying traffic loads, both short-term fluctuations and long-term trends, without apparently affecting the response time and without maintaining excess capacity
9. Ability to take advantage of technological development in communications and switching without maintaining a large expert staff
10. Ability to link a large variety of terminals of low to intermediate speed with a number of different host computers
11. Types of terminal and host computer that must be connected through the network
12. Reliability
13. Security and privacy
14. Vendor dispersion and support (whether from one vendor or many vendors)
15. Expected changes in traffic patterns (e.g., a steady growth in traffic)
16. The fairly high cost of modifying a host computer's operating system or front-end processor, or the possible use of microprocessors
17. Terminal-to-host traffic (which many value-added carriers apparently see as the bulk of its potential market) or host-to-host connections

Notions of networks are subject to widely varying definitions, which largely depend on the subscriber's viewpoint, the service objectives per se, and the thrust

Figure 7.2

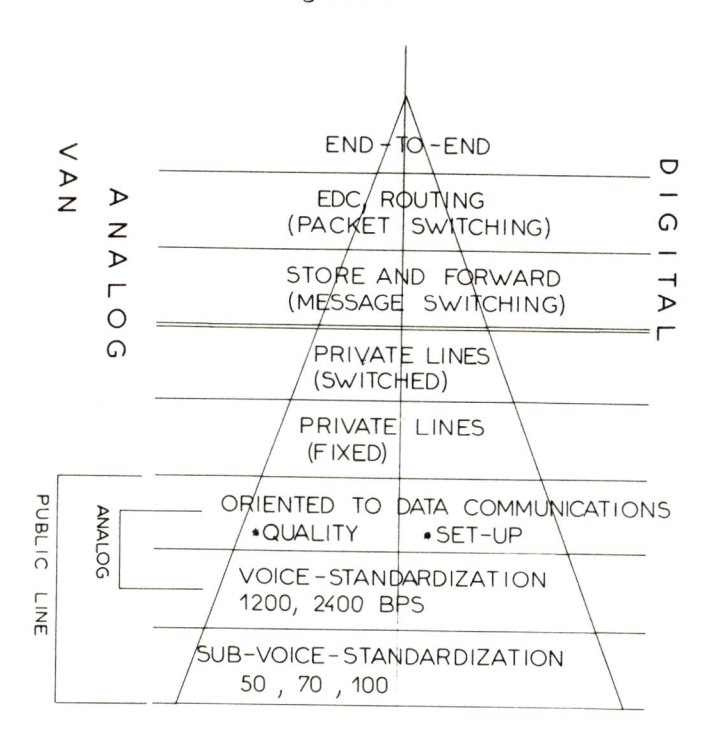

```
                          END-TO-END
         V                ─────────────              D
         A     A          EDC/ROUTING                I
         N     N          (PACKET SWITCHING)         G
               A          ─────────────              I
               L          STORE AND FORWARD          T
               O          (MESSAGE SWITCHING)        A
               G          ═════════════              L
                          PRIVATE LINES
                          (SWITCHED)
                          ─────────────
                          PRIVATE LINES
                          (FIXED)
     P         A          ─────────────
     U         N          ORIENTED TO DATA COMMUNICATIONS
     B         A          •QUALITY    •SET-UP
     L         L          ─────────────
     I         O          VOICE-STANDARDIZATION
     C         G          1200, 2400 BPS
                          ─────────────
     L                    SUB-VOICE-STANDARDIZATION
     I                    50, 70, 100
     N
     E
```

of the vendor. The designer concerns himself primarily with function, and this concern tends to mask certain physical details or questions of implementation. Such characterstics as the type of service provided by the network (switched or dedicated, point-to-point, or multipoint), the mechanisms required to invoke the service (circuit setup, addressing, or other conventions), the procedures required or available to manage the service (flow control, sequencing) and, finally, the overall reliability of the service—these are the crucial variables that define the nature, structure, and cost of the service.

Change in Structure

In the animal kingdom some reptiles change their skin when their body has outgrown the skin's boundaries; something similar is happening with transaction systems. Originally designed to serve a limited number of users, the starlike networks, with point-to-point or multidrop lines, have long passed their usefulness.

The expansion in terminal installations since 1970 has been fantastic. International Business Machines, for example, saw the 100,000 terminals it had in 1970 multiply to 350,000 by 1975. The pace is steadily accelerating; we now forecast 5 million terminals in the mid-1980s. The increase implies a corresponding one in other facilities: what often escapes attention is the fact that teleprocessing tends to produce a twofold to fourfold increment in main-memory use and a threefold to sixfold one in disc storage. More significantly, on-line terminals are giving rise to requirements of unprecedented proportions; we shall outline them in the following section.

First let us quantify the tremendous growth of teleprocessing. The following assumptions are being made. By 1981 an estimated 280 American users will have 2,000 terminals each, which, worldwide, can easily represent 500 organizations; of all the terminals 85 percent will be located at remote sites; the population of large teleprocessing networks will double by 1985. Banks, telephone companies, airlines, large manufacturers, oil companies, merchandising firms, and government institutions will be heading the list (see tables 7.2 and 7.3). This colossal investment is still below the current level of cumulative capital investments at AT&T. Besides, it is worldwide; telephone companies in the United States alone have invested $130 billion. For every 16 terminals there will be an average of one minicomputer; some 412,000 minicomputers will be needed. Probably there will be one maxicomputer (or its equivalent) for every 10 minicomputers, or a total of 40,000 maxicomputers. Finally, the number of earth stations will equal the number of maxicomputers; this means about 40 per organization. As to earth stations, we should count not only the dedicated installations but also those used by business, industry, and the public at large.

Eventually the investments in computers and data communications will exceed those in telephony. To appreciate this potential market we must remember that by mid-1978 about 500 of IBM's Series 1 computers were delivered, yet IBM had an estimated 14,000 in backlog orders, and orders were building up rapidly.

Table 7.2
Estimated Increase in Number of Teleprocessing Networks in the United States between 1981 and 1985

Number of Firms	Terminals per Firm	Total Terminals (millions)
200	12,000	2.4
200	9,000	1.8
200	6,000	1.2
200	4,000	0.8
200	2,000	0.4
		6.6

Table 7.3
Market Estimated for 1985

	Number of Units (thousands)	Dollars per Unit (thousands)	Total Dollar Business (billions)
Terminals	6,600	3	19.8
Minicomputers	412	50	20.6
Maxicomputers	40	1,000	40.0
Earth stations	40	300	12.0
			92.4

This colossal investment is still below the current level of cummulative capital investments at AT&T. Besides, it is worldwide; telephone companies in the United States alone have invested $130 billion.

To see beyond statistics, we should note that the typical Series 1 has a raw computer power of 370/135. The use of such power at local sites will revolutionize computers and data communications.

System Requirements

The specific objectives to be reached by the implementation of a generalized architecture include the following. The terms are defined elsewhere in this book; here we merely have a list for a bird's-eye view.

Task-to-task, job-to-job, and process-to-process: We would not need to know the precise characteristics of the topology and hardware or software.

Device-sharing: One machine must be able to run the devices of one or more other machines.

File-sharing: On a distributed basis and with a dependable security and protection mechanism.

Downline loading, upline dumping, and loopbacks: With the use of facilities in the network, such as data, programs, and systems commands.

Fail-soft: For meeting the requirements networkwide, the topology and management facility must be kept dynamic.

Route-through: Neither the architect nor the applications programmer should need to know how the network routes the messages to each destination, but he must know how the mechanism works.

Virtual devices and virtual programs: Resources would be shared by operating virtual-level DTEs so that several programs might have access to dispersed devices *as if* they were local; provision would be made for optimization of resources and avoidance of duplication.

On-line network and device maintenance: Through on-line tests, histories and diagnostics of good quality would be available.

Network response: Microscopically small decisions are made, second by second, which condition the response of the network.

The network: In its overall operation it *must be immune* to noise, error, and failure; it must detect and correct errors and automatically retransmit correctly; the user must not have to be concerned whatsoever with these processes.

The accomplishment of these functions is an involved, demanding job. It is the best practical example of how far the more advanced systems may be developed.

8
Message Theory

A message is any datum that is communicated. Messages encompass exchange of information, financial documents, cheques, sales orders, billing, personnel data, advertising, and engineering documents. Messages are carried by diverse communication systems, all of which are neutral concerning the content of the information. Some, like circuit switching and packet switching, are also neutral regarding the structure of the messages, that is, they are applications independent. Other kinds of message switching are applications oriented. We shall return to these notions.

Communications theory provides one important perspective: the channel is far more significant than the device. The capacity of a communications channel limits, for the most part, the speed of the device; rarely has the opposite been the case. Channel capacity, security, and speed recently have been profoundly influenced by the convergence of communications and computer technologies. This, and developments in applications, have brought message-processing from the world of accounting and order-entry into the mainstream of business, and the developments are far-reaching. It is possible that the entire organization chart will be altered to make way for new structural relations and also positions. The trend has been developing for several years and should be accelerated by the influence of the new technologies.

Message Technology

A surprising aspect of so-called message technology is the unanticipated and unsupported nature of its birth and early growth. In the beginning messages were discrete events spaced in time; telegrams are an example. Voice communications changed this; particularly important has been the question of continuity. Some messages exchanged by voice were converted to hard copy. Then the flow of messages grew, organizations were heavily affected, and shifts were made from the postal service to the telephone to the Telex. Communication took place at electronic speed. Records of the communications were kept, and the sender and receiver were decoupled, eliminating the need for real-time channels.

The message technologies followed rather than preceded these structural changes, and they suffer from that historical fact: they evolved without planning, and they were obliged to integrate codes and equipment from different manufacturers lacking common standards. Message technology "just happened," and its early history has been more the unconscious evolution of a phenomenon than the deliberate development of a scientific discipline.

This state of affairs changed, however, as the potentials of the new media began to reveal themselves. While the procedural developments followed the new media, they took on certain characteristics. Initially messages were a simple text, but then came message-manipulation programs, in which structure was imposed, and structure meant header fields. A header field includes recipient, sender, number of copies going to recipient, time of sending, and keywords. For a while the early approaches continued to view the nonheader part as an unbroken text, but now we see that messages ought to include other information: in addition to text as such, messages ought to consist of numerical data, pictures, and other matter. In general, arbitrary objects of many types ought to be transmittable as the text of a message.

Functional layers are needed, and so is software. The logical support necessary at the terminal and host levels is presented in Figure 8.1. Conventions for interpreting the structure now permit senders to generate and recipients to distinguish the components of a message and to interpret its contents.

Other necessary information is the author, the sender, and the person to reply to, besides annotations, if any. A message is composed by an author, sent by a sender, and received by a recipient. The recipients are usually people, but they may be "roles" or computers or terminals. The author of a message has in mind one or more recipients. Among the tasks of the sender, who may be the same person as the author, is that of determining what conventions must be followed to guarantee that the message will reach the recipients. He must first select a mechanism of delivery and then determine what information and action will effect that delivery.

All this goes beyond the nineteenth-century attitude toward message-handling, which still characterizes telegrams. If a total path is to be assured automatically, every facet of the operation must be studied and detailed and the proper procedures implemented.

Principles of Message Systems

During the next ten years computer-based message systems will have as great an influence on business practices in our society as that which the telephone had

Figure 8.1
Message handling involves (1) functional layers, and (2) subsystems: data base, applications programs, terminals, hosts, network management

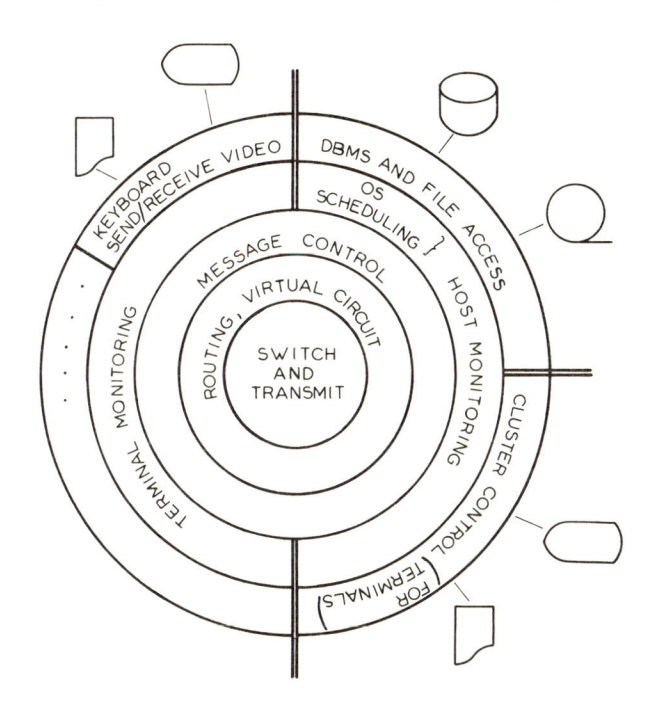

during the last hundred years. Applications usually are the factor that determines a data communications system. Some prominent applications are the following:

- Credit inquiries
- Banking operations
- Electronic fund-transfer
- Electronic mail
- Stock-brokerage information
- Travel reservations and scheduling
- Point-of-sale data collection
- Sales order and inquiry
- Inventory control and reordering
- Production monitoring and control
- Accounting and finance
- Management information

Document cataloguing and retrieval
Hospital and medical information
Home-sector applications

Since exchanging messages is the chief objective of data communications systems, the processing capability of the computer has been applied at both ends of the communication path. Computer-run can offer geographic independence to both sender and receiver; either can transmit messages or have access to the other's files, from any point to any other point on the network.

A sophisticated use of the computer's capability emerged for the network Arpanet, when it was realized that a network could be exploited in more than one way as a medium of intercommunication. Workable software support was needed, and it became available in the form of service programs that supported an exchange of information between host computers. The development of software took advantage of an underlying network file transfer protocol and its associated "server" processes for the distribution of messages to users of the same or other host computers. As we have pointed out in the preceding section, the next step was to view the message as a whole structured object. Besides distinguishing the components of a message, manipulation programs were designed to interpret the contents of those components.

Necessity being the mother of invention, and a message program being needed for carrying out such operations as sorts and searches on "user fields," the data type of each such field had to be made known to the program; consequently, the agreed-upon structure of a message was defined as one rich enough to support the existence of user fields and to allow the inclusion, in each such field, of the data type of its contents. The development and operation of networks dedicated to message-handling underlined a great many requirements. Some basic principles were promoted in answer.

To create a message is to insert a record into a data base.

A message is a field in the data base and as such affects design of the data base, the methods of access, and the choice of communications.

To send a message is to provide a set of recipients with access to the records.

Problems are created by the fact that addresses indicate, not recipients, but mailboxes.

Like the telephone companies, we need a sort of directory and a real-time algorithm for updating it.

Message systems designed on the concept of data bases are especially suited to collaborating groups and teleconferencing.

If technology can be mustered to support this approach, some rather powerful effects may be achieved.

Conventions

A message may be viewed as a device by which an author grants a recipient or recipients access to certain information. A message system must therefore ensure that access—and ensure that it be granted only to designated recipients and denied to all others. Message systems have an additional problem: A recipient may wish to know with some certainty the identity of the author and perhaps also of its sender. Identification facilitates the creation and distribution of information, the reference of one message to another, and the replying to or forwarding of a message. These activities are supported by the presence of appropriate information in specified message fields:

The identification of a message is given in the message-identification field.
The form field indicates the author of the message.
The sender field identifies the actual sender.
The reply field gives the address to be used in replying.

Messages generally are of three formats. The author sends a message in one format, the sender transmits it in another, and the receiver gets it in yet another. The first and last of these formats depend more or less on human preference, as whether the message shall be written or spoken, and consequently cannot be decided on a purely technical basis, but no such choice is allowed for the transmission; communications must perfectly agree on the format of transmission. The transmission format is affected by such pragmatic considerations as the writing code and the need to convert to and from a given format during the act of sending and receiving.

A basic question is whether the movement of data and messages for communication is most important, or whether making any movement apparent to the users is.

One view is to consider the message system in its entirety, including the delivery subsystem and all the manipulation tools, as a data base management system. Another concerns the recipient. If we look closely at addresses, we see that they indicate not recipients, but logical entities to which messages are addressed; we call them "mailboxes." The fact that mailboxes are not the same as recipients causes problems. Some way must be provided for the sender of a message to determine what set of mailbox addresses will reach the intended human recipients. One way is to use each recipient's name as the address associated with his mailbox. This can work reasonably well when the recipients are people, but it may not work as well with programs, because such entities may not have distinctive names associated with them. This suggests a central agency that is responsible for keeping order among addresses, in particular for preventing identical mailboxes and names.

Protection and accountability also must be considered.

Accountability may be handled in either of two ways. One is to build into the systems a means of determining who is accountable for what parts of each message; this information may be placed in a message in a form apparent to the recipient. The other is to give authors and recipients a means of encoding, in the text, keys by which they may recognize one another.

Protection of access to mailing lists also may be handled in either of two ways. One is to control the access to mailing lists wherever they may be kept, whether in private files or in an information service. The other is to replace the mailing list with a program which, upon receipt of a message, sends that message to the recipients named in the mailing list. A difficulty with this is that, when one redistribution program transmits to another, which in turn transmits back to the first, an unending recycling of messages may result.

Performance Criteria

The mechanisms of a message-handling system must be evaluated in regard not only to technical and financial aspects but also to operating performance. Performance criteria may be grouped in three distinct categories:

Delay

Throughput

Error

Delay is a function of the following time intervals:

Call setup

Call clearing

Network transit

The call setup time is the time interval from the correct receipt of the last bit of a "call request" packet at a source node to the completed reception (including all processing) of an internal "accept" at that same node, but excluding all queueing, transmission, propagation, and processing time at the called terminal end.

The call-clearing time is the time interval from the correct receipt of the last bit of a "clear request" packet at a source node to the completed reception (including all processing) of an internal "clear" at that node.

The network transit delay is the time interval from the correct receipt of the last bit of a packet at a source node to its completed reception (including processing) at the destination node.

Throughput is the number of bytes (or bits) per second that can be maintained continuously on a circuit. The objective is that the throughput of, say, a virtual circuit (with full data packets) is limited only by the attainable throughput of the slower of the access lines of the two communicating terminals.

Error, the last of our criteria of performance, involves the following:

Bit error (due to burst or white noise)

Circuit disruptions detected by data link control procedures but recoverable at higher levels

Probability of network reset

Probability of loss of data integrity

The last two are virtual-circuit errors; we shall be talking of virtual circuits in chapter 13.

Bit errors are generally recovered through error detection and correction by retransmission; such schemes are governed by data link control procedures, some of which are standardized, like the X.25.

Circuit disruptions also are detected by data link control procedures but are usually recovered only at high levels.

Virtual circuits introduce virtual-circuit errors. The probability of network reset is the probability that a virtual circuit will be reset because the network has detected the unrecoverable loss of a packet. The probability of loss of data integrity is the probability that the network is not detecting, and, therefore, not delivering, a packet with a mutilated data field, a duplicate of a packet, an out-of-sequence packet, or a lost packet.

The User's Requirements

By and large, the user's requirements will fall into one of three classes, and users will be well advised to establish into which one their interests fall.

The first class of requirement is high volume, remote deadlines, low-cost operation, and long messages. This class today is implemented through circuit switching. Generally speaking, the users are satisfied with the service but not with the cost. Their needs are best served through remote batch operation. Accumulation can be at the source point, for instance, the branch office, and then the line used for four or five hours per day, *as if* there were one long message being sent.

The second class is small volume, medium deadlines (a "stack" of them can be made, as in the SWIFT system), and medium-sized messages. Money transfers fall in this class. Deadlines are important, but the time intervals are not in fractions of a second. A dedicated DTE with a local memory can best carry out this job.

The third class is interactive service, immediate transactions (access to memory for a small amount of information), small messages, and very near deadlines. Time sharing (inquiry, status, balance, etc.) with its demanding deadline is an example of this class. Cost is a key issue; near deadlines can get very expensive, and therefore they require a network approach. Packet switching is the answer, although intelligent terminals may turn the tide back to message switching. (The virtual circuit may be expensive; a Datagram is probably better adapted to transaction-oriented operations.) The important thing is to design networks so that they are open to cost effectiveness as technology evolves.

Network performance must be studied in detail, along with data integrity. It will focus on three factors: speed of transmission, delay (time between transmission and delivery of the first bit of the message), and throughput (number of bits transmitted, divided by time between transmission of the first bit and delivery of the last bit). These factors are independent of each other, and so trade-offs can be made in good service, queues, error control, leaders and the like (Figure 8.2).

The implementation of choices calls for a pronounced flexibility in design. The next generation of communications technologies will be characterized by a modular and growth-oriented approach, and this is feasible. The whole technology and the basic economics behind it are in full swing. The field of data communications is based on a shift in economics that makes it necessary for us to continue to reevaluate where we are and where we wish to go. To use technological developments to our advantage, we need perspective. A single technological event will help to build the framework, but in itself it is not really important. Telephony, for example, was the first commercial use of electricity; it was a physical discovery that remained latent for nearly half a century. What *is* important is the broad view. Many see it, but few have given it expression.

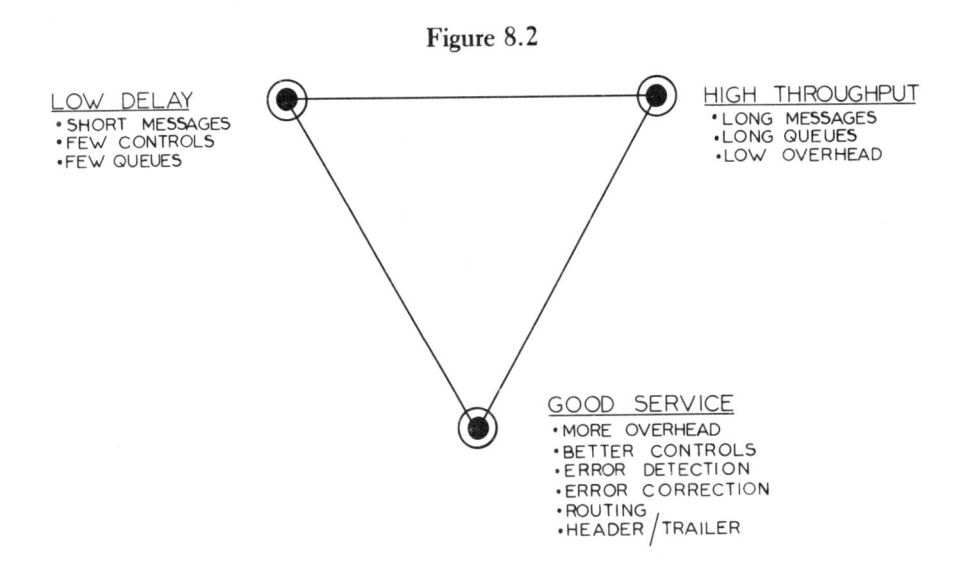

Figure 8.2

LOW DELAY
• SHORT MESSAGES
• FEW CONTROLS
• FEW QUEUES

HIGH THROUGHPUT
• LONG MESSAGES
• LONG QUEUES
• LOW OVERHEAD

GOOD SERVICE
• MORE OVERHEAD
• BETTER CONTROLS
• ERROR DETECTION
• ERROR CORRECTION
• ROUTING
• HEADER / TRAILER

9

What Is a Protocol?

A protocol, also called a line procedure or a line discipline, is a set of conventions governing the format and the control of data (the control covering input, transmission, and output). A protocol is a well-defined procedure that is clearly understood by all parties. It constitutes the logical connection to the physical line of the carrier. It is an orderly exchange of data between computers, terminals, and other communications equipment, a logical setup supplementing and complementing the computer-to-computer or terminal-to-terminal connection. The procedure constitutes a predetermined dialogue scrupulously maintained by both ends of a communications link. At the particular level of the link it consists of an interchange of characters or character sequences that guarantees the control and integrity of the message transfer.

The protocol is a new concept, but it standardizes known, not new, things. Broadly speaking, all protocols have two functions. One is contact, which includes identification and synchronization as, for example, the creation of a virtual channel; synchronization concerns both source and destination. The other is transfer, which comprises not only the transmission functions but also error detection and control and the assurance of delivery of a message the protocol has received; see Figure 9.1.

Network architectures are layered, and so are protocols. In data communications we have protocols addressing themselves to the data link, the routing, and the logical link, but we need them also for error detection and correction, access to the data, and management of the memory; see Figure 9.2. Notice that the protocol level for the management of memory is higher than those for access, and access higher than error detection and correction; still, that last is higher than the data communications protocols.

We distinguish transparent from virtual protocols. A transparent protocol sends data through the system without particular constraints due to low-level details; the

Figure 9.1
Protocols

PHYSICAL SET-UP

COMPUTER — COMMUNICATION PATH — COMPUTER

LOGICAL SET-UP

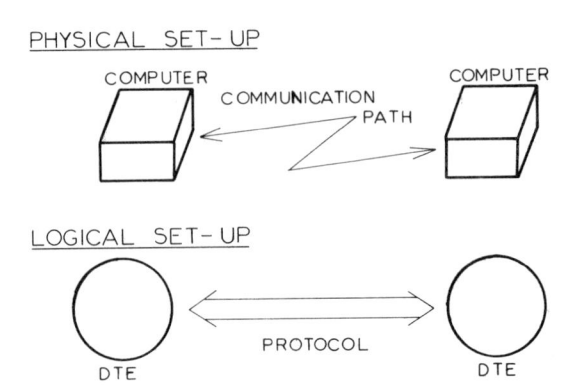

DTE — PROTOCOL — DTE

A PROTOCOL IS THE LOGICAL ABSTRACTION OF THE PHYSICAL PROCESS OF COMMUNICATION

PROTOCOLS ARE ALSO CALLED 'LINE PROCEDURES' OR 'LINE DISCIPLINES'. BUT LAYERED PROTOCOLS ARE MUCH MORE SOPHISTICATED THAN THIS SIMPLE CONCEPT

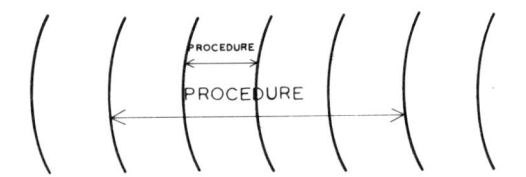

PROCEDURE
PROCEDURE

IF DIFFERENT PROCEDURES ARE USED, WE MUST RECONSTITUTE THE ORIGINAL MESSAGE AT DELIVERY.

user cannot see it, but it is there. A virtual protocol obeys sequence and other constraints. It is, therefore, handy to have transparent protocols, but it is not easy.

The early line disciplines, using the Baudot code, had no inherent control of the link. They relied totally on sequences of data characters to implement supervisory functions. Later work led to protocols with better control. Each manufacturer, however, created protocols that reflected the needs of his particular product, usually optimized for a specific implementation. This is the story of binary synchronous communications. The protocols of the 1960s were character-oriented and generally incompatible with one another.

Protocol Reliability

A protocol is reliable only if it provides end-to-end accountability for flow control, connection management, and delivery of messages. For a message to be delivered,

Figure 9.2

WE MUST DEFINE

PROTOCOLS:

1. MEMORY MANAGEMENT
2. D B
3. A P
4. MESSAGE MANAGEMENT
5. DATA COMMUNICATIONS

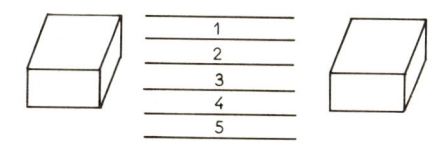

COMPUTER-TO-COMPUTER
TERMINAL-TO-COMPUTER

a number of functions must be carried out, such as packaging, headers, sequencing, acceptance, acknowledgment, and, if necessary, retransmission.

The design study must consider the topology, the network's objectives, the network's characteristics, and the connections to be provided. It must be done with the understanding that processes do not know each other and do not know how to make use of the flow control information and must be instructed.

Reliable protocols support and sustain the communication mechanism, which is structured around the concept of a conversation. Its operational commands are as follows.

Connection: The creation of a data path (the term *data path* may be used for both virtual circuit and dataform solutions).

Transmission: The sending of information over a logical link.

Reception: The information received from a logical link, synchronized with data transmission via a flow control mechanism.

Interruption: The notification of the object at the other end of the logical link, of some unusual condition or event.

.Disconnection: The destruction of a logical link, returning any resources back to the system.

Conversations are established and terminated by means of physical or virtual connection between sender and receiver. Connection is the process of dialing; transmission and reception are the processes of speaking and listening. Message routing, error control, and physical link management are transparent to the users.

Modern protocols extend the functionality of communications processes while reducing the requirements for implementation and the conditions for refusal. The option negotiations of the Telenet system, for instance, are based on four expressions:

Desire	Command
Receiver to begin	DO X
Receiver not to begin	DON'T X
I start	WILL X
I don't start	WON'T X

Echoing is done through the basic commands DO ECHO, WILL ECHO, DON'T ECHO, WON'T ECHO. In Telenet the remote-controlled transmission and the echoing support responsive approaches, which in turn make possible the use of remote and very inexpensive hosts.

The receiving host or other DTE, upon receipt of a message coded at the origin (by the sender), not only uncodes and prints it but also enriches the content (text actuated by codes). This process, controlled by remote hosts, can also enrich data at the source terminal (which gives an idea of the range of modern protocols). In fact, such functions account for much of the difference between the ôlder and better known physical links (twisted wire, coaxial cable, or radio beam) and the new virtual, or logical, links. By the same token, the aforementioned services are some of the assets of a value-added network as opposed to the older telegraph and telephone services.

The Access Method

The "access method" is a protocol. It directly affects response times, reliability, costs, and other problems. Costs are directly related to the ability of one user to share the resources with others. A data communications network most efficiently shares those resources which are allocated only when data are actually being sent. The classical polling protocols are particularly inefficient, for example, since the messages must be sent continually, even when they contain no meaningful data.

What Is a Protocol? 109

A message-by-message protocol is a desirable alternative to polling. (The same arguments may apply to private lines and dial-up connections.)

How can the method of network access affect the response time? The two principal ways in which terminals and computers now have access to each other are through the switched telephone network and through polling over dedicated lines. In the switched network the response times are long because the time needed to make a connection is long. In polling—considering only the more common half-duplex polling for the moment—the response times again are long, because one transaction with one terminal must be completed before a transaction with another can begin.

Full-duplex polling allows for some overlapping of operations, but not enough to alleviate the problem substantially, and a radically different approach is needed. Ideally, messages and responses would be presented to the network in a fashion that would altogether overcome the disadvantages of polling; several transactions would be carried on simultaneously at a single access port. One solution is to distinguish transactions from each other by including identifiers within the messages; then the messages are identifying their sources and destinations, making polling unnecessary. For this to work, the network and its users must recognize and know how to handle the identifiers, which means that a network access protocol must be established, defining the formats of the data messages and control messages and their sequence. The components of such a protocol are the following eight:

1. Configuration: pass-system configuration information between subsystems involved in a network exchange as, for instance, the operating system and the file system
2. User identification: authentication, passwords, and accounting information
3. Attributes: details relative to the representation of the data base and the files being accessed, among others
4. Access proper, specifically:
    a. Type of access or type of operation, as opening a new file
    b. File name and file specifications, in the format required by the remote node
    c. Mode of access, whether sequential, random, or keyed, etc.
    d. User-oriented access operation, as "get," "put," etc.
    e. Optional files and record processing (user exits)
5. Control (device, file): sending of control types of information to a device or file system, which also allows the access mode to be changed from previous settings
6. Continuation of transfer: activation of alternative recovery strategies, as "try again," "skip," "abort"
7. Acknowledgment: acknowledgment of access commands
8. Completion: indentification of the termination of access for remote systems and the recovery procedures, for record transfer

Procedural Requirements

Several demands are posed on the new services. The link control procedure must recover from failures of the computer or circuit and also allow resynchronization of various communications parameters.

A good example of the range of services that protocols and network architecture must provide is the system developed in the late 1960s and early 1970s, the Arpanet, which has been taken as a standard ever since. It is a distributed assurance mechanism, which involves the following:

>   Access rights
>   Retrieval capability
>   Additions
>   Deletions
>   Modifications
>   Batch terminals
>   On-line systems
>   Connective-action mechanism
>   Layered-protocol dependencies
>   Considerations of data base management systems
>   File access
>   Data dictionaries

These are fundamental functions within a distributed data assurance environment, since the services must not only transfer data but also add to them, delete from them, and modify them to and from the data base. This calls for overall design, audit trail and control, error detection and correction, synchronization, testing and logging, and protocol sensitivity.

Performance evaluation, balancing procedures, study, examination, and steady reporting on conditions are organizational responsibilities. They include process unit access, authorization and authentication, query validation, process limits control, and isolation by distribution point (no spreadover). Their mechanizations require a physical sensitivity (to errors created or infiltrated), proper journaling, operating statistics and, as stated, protocol responsibility.

Procedural requirements are a relatively new problem in protocols; we shall return to them in the next chapter. First we must look at the fundamentals, which afford exceptional insight into the way the system works.

Synchronous and Asynchronous Transmission

We have said that the exchange of data between two units requires a protocol. At the level of data link control (communication) protocols are established when the one DTE must speak and then the other (Figure 9.3). This exchange of information may be carried on asynchronously or synchronously.

Figure 9.3

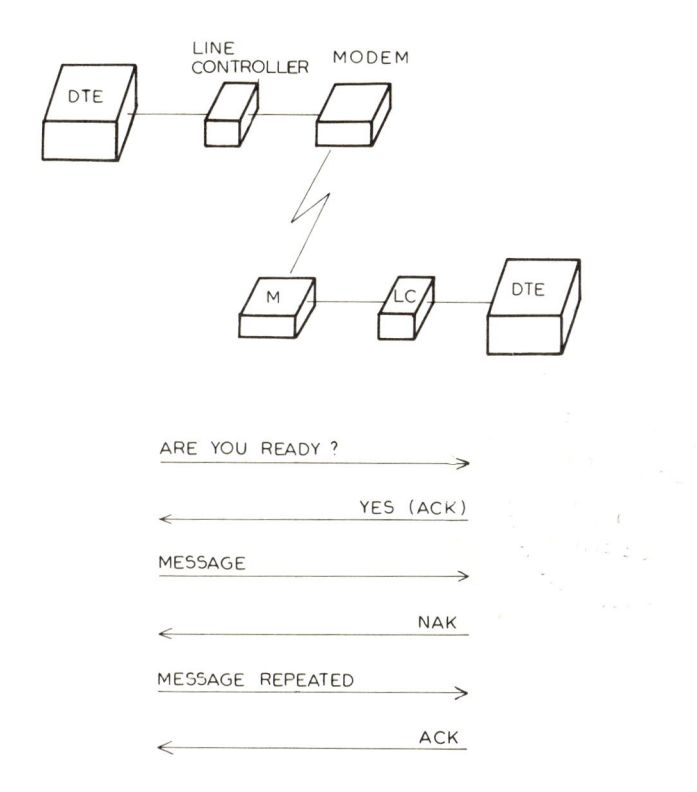

```
         LINE
         CONTROLLER   MODEM
  DTE

                 M        LC        DTE
```

```
ARE YOU READY ?
                        ──────→

                             YES (ACK)
                        ←──────

MESSAGE
                        ──────→

                                  NAK
                        ←──────

MESSAGE REPEATED
                        ──────→

                                  ACK
                        ←──────
```

In a synchronous line discipline a clock always times the transmission, and synchronization bits are sent first, followed by data. In an asynchronous line discipline (the older of the two) there is no clock timing the transmission; instead, start and stop bits "bracket" the character, and transmission is character by character. Teletype line procedures, for example, support only asynchronous transmissions on point-to-point lines; a message of this type contains only text, no header or trailer.

The choice of a synchronous or asynchronous protocol depends on a number of things. The synchronous are the more efficient—a background factor in their development—but it is not possible to mix two disciplines on the same line. Most terminals work in an asynchronous mode. Computer-to-computer communications usually are synchronous; given the amount of data to be transferred, efficiency is quite important. But terminal-to-computer communications or multidrop lines can very well be asynchronous, which is not true of modern, horizontal networks.

Slow speeds, say 50, 200, or 300 bits per second, call for the asynchronous mode, and more than 1,200 bits per second nearly always need the synchronous.

Some terminals are designed to work only synchronously, others only asynchronously. Still others may work in either mode, changing "line management devices" when they switch from the one to the other (line control functions have been discussed in chapter 4).

As we have noted, asynchronous protocols operate largely on a character-by-character basis. Of the many kinds one of the best known and most widely used is the teletype. ITT's Model 35, for example, uses an 11-bit frame for each character: 1 start bit, 7 data bits, 1 parity bit, and 2 stop bits. Thus the start–stop is character by character. The error detection is poor; as in many of the protocols, *no* parity check is performed by the receiving terminal. If a check is made and an error detected, a standard error character is inserted for the data characters by the receiving device. Only when a computer is used will an error check be made, character by character; in case of error, all the characters starting with the word or block in error must be retransmitted.

Asynchronous protocols are important because many of today's terminals use them and because they work on both full-duplex and half-duplex lines and therefore impose no particular restraint in that respect. Networks incapable of handling asynchronous protocols refuse a wealth of new devices, because only the new terminals are compatible with them. Packet-switching protocols have made evident the need of gateways able to handle asynchronous devices, within a network utilizing more advanced disciplines.

Synchronous Protocols

Binary synchronous communications (bisync, BSC) have the best known and probably most widely used synchronous protocols. Because in this mode it sends multiple characters per block, the overhead is less than in the asynchronous mode. It operates, however, only on half-duplex lines, so that for each block transmitted at least two line turnarounds are needed; a turnaround means that after a block has been transmitted the direction of the line must be turned around for sending the acknowledgment, then turned around again for sending the next block. Each turnaround takes 100 to 300 milliseconds; this is a loss in efficiency, except when a "supervisory" wire facility—offered by many telephone companies at no extra cost—is used for indicating which way the message is going. Figure 9.4 presents a typical binary synchronous protocol. The ETX, or end of text, terminates the last block of a message and requires a reply. Preceding any SOH, or start of header, of any block of characters are the synchronization signals, usually referred to as SYN; terminals normally omit 2 to 8 SYN characters.

The procedures are not absolutely standard. For instance, IBM suggests following the SOH with a special character, possibly a dash, that will not be used after the STX. This would help prevent a line error from changing SOH to STX. Other

What Is a Protocol? 113

Figure 9.4
Typical binary synchronous protocol

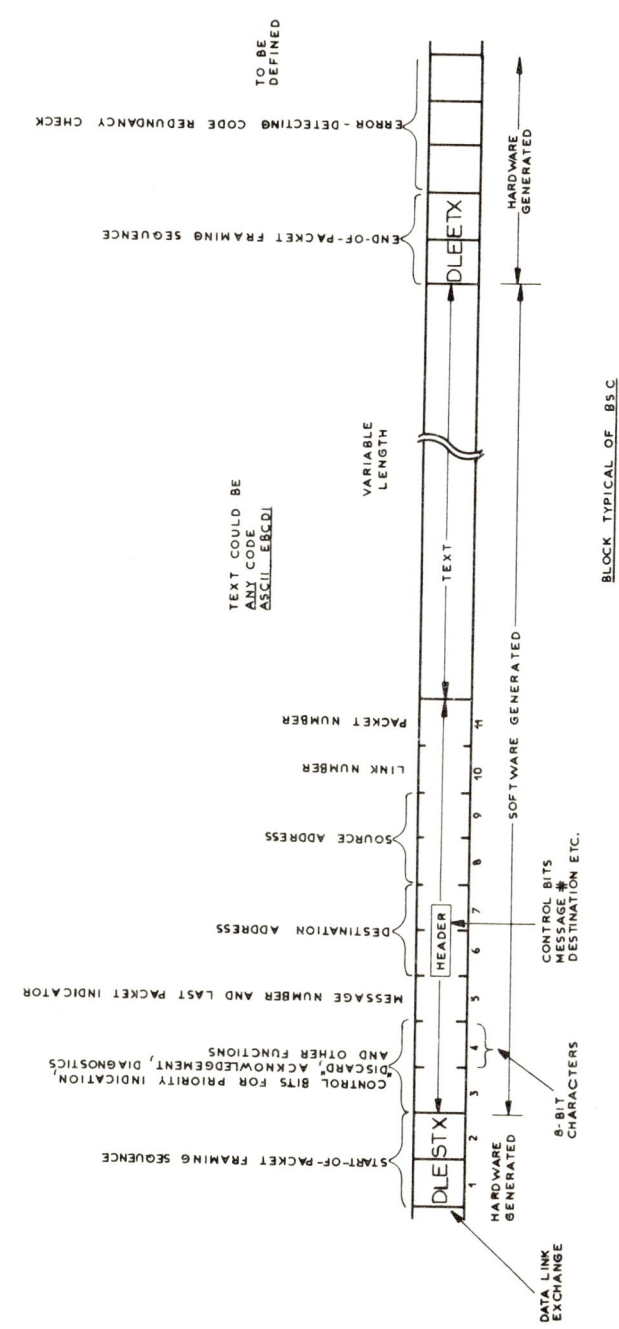

dialects do not follow this procedure. Figure 9.5 presents three binary synchronous dialects. Table 9.1 identifies the most frequently used characters in binary synchronous communications. The protocol is character oriented. Its codes may be ASCII (7 bits plus parity), EBCDIC (8 data bits), or Transcode (6 data bits), and the transparency mode. It uses block-by-block acknowledgments for correct or incorrect receipt; the ACK0 and ACK1 are two forms of positive response employed alternatively in a series of blocks, and NAK is used when a data error in transmission is detected.

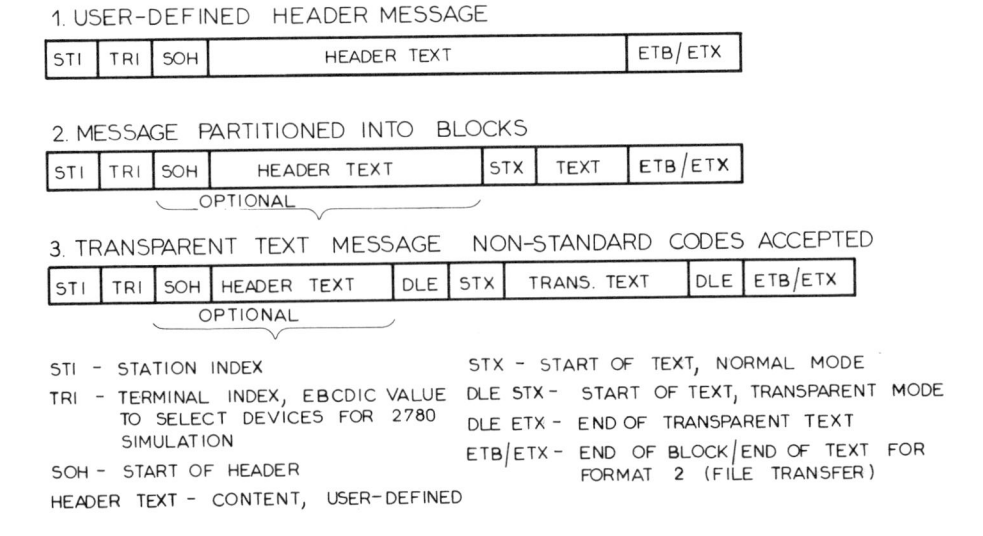

Binary synchronization allows for polling and addressing on multipoint lines. As a discipline, it has a rigorous set of rules for establishing, maintaining, and terminating a communication. It has many variants, though in its origins it belongs to a previous generation of protocols and does not fit the modern model we shall be discussing in the following chapters.

One of the criticisms of BSC is that the different protocol functions, present in a layered approach, have not been separated into independent components. In some of its variants it is not a pure link control protocol but mixes device control of applications functions with communications functions. It does not separate the link-management component from the data-transfer component. Therefore, error recovery, once initiated, must be completed in a given system before other systems may be selected. Moreover, the acknowledgment message is not block checked. This is as much a failure as not block checking the data and can result in undetected duplicate or missing messages. Yet it should not be forgotten that the binary synchronous is one of the two earliest synchronous protocols (the other is

Figure 9.5
Three binary synchronous dialects

1. USER-DEFINED HEADER MESSAGE

STI	TRI	SOH	HEADER TEXT	ETB/ETX

2. MESSAGE PARTITIONED INTO BLOCKS

STI	TRI	SOH	HEADER TEXT	STX	TEXT	ETB/ETX

OPTIONAL

3. TRANSPARENT TEXT MESSAGE NON-STANDARD CODES ACCEPTED

STI	TRI	SOH	HEADER TEXT	DLE	STX	TRANS. TEXT	DLE	ETB/ETX

OPTIONAL

STI – STATION INDEX
TRI – TERMINAL INDEX, EBCDIC VALUE TO SELECT DEVICES FOR 2780 SIMULATION
SOH – START OF HEADER
HEADER TEXT – CONTENT, USER-DEFINED
STX – START OF TEXT, NORMAL MODE
DLE STX – START OF TEXT, TRANSPARENT MODE
DLE ETX – END OF TRANSPARENT TEXT
ETB/ETX – END OF BLOCK/END OF TEXT FOR FORMAT 2 (FILE TRANSFER)

Table 9.1
Frequently Used Characters for Defining and Assuring a Block of Data in Binary Synchronous Communications

ACK0	Acknowledgment
ACK1	
ARQ	Automatic request for transmission
DLEEOT	Data link escape and end of transmission
ENQ	Enquiry: demand for something
EOT	End of transmission: "I give you back the control," "reset"; a necessary in polling and selecting; can force the end of a transmission
ETB	End of transmission block: requires a reply indicating receiving station's status
ETX	End of text
ITB	Intermediate text block: helps divide a data block into sub-blocks; after it the line management automatically adds CRC, CRC.
RVI	Reverse interrupt: modifies a situation, as when the receiving end wants to change direction of transmission, such as transmitting instead of receiving; largely device dependent; chiefly used by IBM
SOH	Start of header: device dependent, used for some types of machine, used in some types of message
STX	Start of text
SYN	Synchronous idle: establishes and maintains synchronization
TTD	Temporary transmit delay: transmitter's ACK; if the time out is exceeded, transmitter uses it; if receiver cannot reply immediately, transmitter, to avoid an error situation, sends WACK
WACK	Wait for acknowledgment: "wait," sent by receiver

General Electric's VIP) and could not possibly contain any potentialities unrevealed by a dozen years of practice.

Terminals for Synchronous and Asynchronous Protocols

Table 9.2 presents a remarkable collection of terminals which, as of mid-1978, were being offered on the market. Three main classes are included: the interactive versus batch, the video (soft copy) versus hard copy, and the synchronous versus the asynchronous. Some of these terminals have become standards; this is true of IBM's 2740 and 2848, among the interactive terminals, and of the famous 2780 among the batch-oriented terminals.

Table 9.2
Terminals

Model	Communications and Imitation

Particularly suited to interactive applications

IBM
- Video 2260 — 1971; 960 char., low-volume applications
- Video 3270 — 1974; now up to 3440 char., compatible with BSC/SDLC; imitates the 2740
- Video 4949, Series/1 — Imitates the 3270; 1920 char.
- HC 2740/41 — BCD, EBCD, S/S, nonbuffered
- HC 2848 — ISO, USASCII, S/S, buffered, polling-selecting
- HC 3270 — BSC, SDLC
- HC 3600 — Terminal system with video; HC, MCR, ATM (banking)
- HC 3790 — Terminal system with video; HC, SNA, SDLC, and BSC (RPQ)
- HC 3767 — SNA, SDLC, and S/S
- HC 3630, 3650, 3660 — Terminal system; manufacturing, supermarkets, cash-and-carry
- HC 5935 — Bank terminal (video, HC, tape), RPQ Europe only

Olivetti
- HC TC 339/349 CB — Imitates IBM 2740; no longer produced
- HC TC 349 BI — Imitates IBM 2848; polling-selecting, no longer produced
- HC TC 380 — Imitates IBM 2848; polling-selecting, no longer produced
- SP 600 — Imitates IBM 2780; BSC 1
  Imitates IBM 3270; BSC 3
- HC TC 800 — Synchronous, S/S, SDLC, programmable
- HC TC 808 — Synchronous, S/S, SDLC
- TC 480 — Contention, ISO, S/S
- Video TCV 270 — S/S (polling-selecting), synchronous (BSC 2/3)
- Video/TCV 280 — BSC 3
- Video TCV 450 — S/S, contention, ISO
- Microcomputer 6060 — BSC, S/S (time-sharing)

Honeywell Information Systems
- Video VIP 7700 — Synchronous
- Video VIP 7100 and Video VIP 7200 — S/S

Table 9.2 (cont.)
Terminals

Model	Communications and Imitation
Video 7800	Synchronous, S/S
HC TTU 1124	Low cost
HC TTU 1126	Low cost
HC TTU 1221	Low cost
GTBH 3074/72	Banking, low cost

Univac
Video Uniscope 100, 200	
UTS 400	
DCT 500 (teletype)	
MTS Micro-based	Imitates Honeywell VIP and TTY. BSC/SDLC. Imitates TC 500; ISO, S/S. DNA, SNA, X.25 (available 1979)
1770 (in collaboration with MTS)	Imitates TC 500; ISO, S/S
7740 MCS (CMC7 encoder) (in collaboration with MTS)	
770 TCU-based	Imitates TC 500; ISO, S/S
796-101 Video	TTY, synchronous
796-201 Video	TTY, synchronous
796-301 Video	Polling-selecting, S/S
796-501 Video	Polling-selecting, S/S
721	Message-switching, store and forward, front end, programmable

Burroughs
Video TD 730	480 char. display, up to 4080 display memory
Video TD 830	2000 char. display (other references as above)

Both half-duplex, S/S, synchronous.
Line procedures: imitate IBM 2260, BSC 3 IBM 3270.

TC 5000, TC 5110	Imitate IBM 2260 and BSC 3 IBM 3270; S/S up to 1800 bps, synchronous up to 4800 bps, BDLC (looks like SDLC). Queued buffer: BSC 3 IBM 2770, IBM 2740 Model 2, Olivetti TC 100, Olivetti TC 349 BI
TU 1700, 1800	Banking terminals, video 256 char. display, memory of 1024 char., passbook reader

Table 9.2 (cont.)
Terminals

Model	Communications and Imitation
Hewlett-Packard	
Video 2640	Up to 4096 char.
Video 2645	Up to 8192 char.
NSF VT52	Upper and lower case ASCII, 24 lines, 80 char.
SF VT55	Graph drawing
SF VT61/t, VT62	Alphanumeric text-editing
HC Decwriter III	DC terminal for 1200-baud lines, 180 char. per sec., upper and lower case ASCII, 128 char. set
Video 2641	Like 2645 plus APL char.
Video 2647	Like 2645 plus graphics, programmable

The 2640 family is both synchronous and S/S.

HC 2631	Bidirectional printer, 180 char. per sec.
HC 2635	Like 2631 plus keyboard

Batch-oriented terminals

IBM	
5100/5110	Portable microprocessor terminal
3741	Data entry terminal
HC 2780	1967; first to use BSC; 1200 to 4800 bps.
377X	RJE
Series/1	Imitates HC 3780
HC 3780	Replacement for 2780 but not programmable; 1972
Series/1 to 370	Connection
Olivetti	
HC A.5	Imitates IBM 2848; BSC
HC A.6	Imitates IBM 2848; BSC
HC A.7	BSC
DE 700	Data entry, synchronous and S/S, programmable
TES 501	Word processor, BSC
Honeywell Information Systems	
HC DN 700	
G 100	
L 6	
L 6	DN 700

What Is a Protocol? 119

Table 9.2 (cont.)
Terminals

Model	Communications and Imitation
Univac	
HC 1004, UTS 700	
UDS 2000	Data entry
National Cash Register	
499 Mini-based	Imitates TC 500; BSC
7750/3000 Mini-based	Imitates TC 500; BSC
8130 Micro-based	BSC
8150 Micro-based	BSC
8230 Mini-based	BSC
8250 Mini-based	BSC
7200/7500 Micro-based	TTY, BSC, SDLC
Burroughs	
DC 125	Low-cost terminal concentrator (few units), 12-kilobyte microprogram, 32-kilobyte data or program memory
DC 140	64 kilobytes (COBOL or assembler), up to 9600 bits per sec., BSC 1/2 EBCDIC, BSC 1/2 ASCII. Imitates BSC 3 IBM 2972-8, BSC 3 IBM 3270, BSC 3 IBM 2770, IBM 2740 Model 2, IBM 3940, IBM 2260. Queued buffer: Olivetti TC 100, Olivetti TC 380
B 80	Up to 128 kilobytes (COBOL or RPG), BSC, BDLC (SDLC)
Digital Equipment	
HC Decprinter I	Medium-speed HC, 132 columns, 180 Hertz
HC Decwriter II	16 char. buffer, 7 x 7 dot matrix, 30 Hertz, 60 Hertz catch-up mode, cassette option
SF/HT VT 100, VT 150	Intelligent terminals, accept BASIC, FORTRAN, and Macro-II
Nixdorf	
HC/SC 8820	Programmable, up to 3 floppy discs, cassette, tapes, badge, OCR. Imitates IBM 2740, 3740, 3270, and Uniscope 100, VIP 770

10
Circuit Switching and Polling and Selecting

Protocols are necessary for shared, switched data communications services. Conceptually the services are like the dial telephone network, except that the interconnected subscriber equipment consists of computers and computer terminals instead of telephone handsets.

Communication circuits and switching centers are shared in the sense that all users have access to the same facilities on demand. A network is switched in the sense that calls can be routed via a series of switches or nodes to user points. The facilities are leased often with a fixed charge for the basic connection to the network and then monthly usage charges.

Recent services, such as the Advanced Communications Service, ACS, of AT&T, offer two basic types of transmission service: a call service and a message service. The call service gives the customer a two-way path between the originating and the terminating stations, which facilitates applications that require real-time communications, such as time-sharing and inquiry–response systems. The message service is a variety of functions for the presentation and handling of messages and for directing their movement through the network; it is needed for applications that require only one-way transmission. Data entry and remote batch are examples.

The understructure of the services reveals the differences between switching techniques. They are all based on simple principles. Switches may be intelligent or unintelligent. If intelligent, they receive data from a DTE, interpret the dispatching instructions, store the data for some period, and send them on to a destination; packet switching and message switching perform intelligent functions. If the switches are unintelligent, they are subject to circuit-switching disciplines, although, as we shall see, new developments might radically change all this.

Circuit-Switching Principles

For voice-grade traffic the telephone network is invaluable. For data communications, too, it brings computers and terminals together wherever there is a telephone line. The problem with it is the fact that it was originally designed for voice-grade traffic, not data. The question of noise will make our point clear. The human ear filters extraneous sounds, accepting only the relevant information. Terminals cannot do this, and noise is often read as meaningful data, with resulting errors. The first circuit-switching networks were analog and thus incapable of affording the accuracy inherent in digital transmission. Table 10.1 outlines the chief differences between circuit switching, message switching, and packet switching.

The earliest service designed for data was based on point-to-point private lines. It used the analog system available, with a circuit that connected each terminal to its host. The costs of analog point-to-point private lines were, however, a major limitation, and as distances grew, they became more prohibitive. The solution, with batch-type operations (requiring the sender to have access to more than one computer or terminal), has been circuit switching. It takes place through a dedicated data switch that is in use only for the duration of the communication. The user shares the network facilities, including transmission lines and switches, with other users, buying only the transmission speed or bandwidth needed and paying accordingly.

The best example of circuit switching is the dial telephone network. A user dials the desired telephone number. The switches assign a circuit from source to destination, and, if answered, communication is established. A difficulty was that a line may be busy and delays in setup might result. So, instead of point-to-point connections, a multipoint arrangement was devised whereby a primary station authorizes a secondary station to transmit, in this way assigning a circuit. The circuit remains assigned to this particular operation until the call is terminated, during which time the circuit is dedicated to this particular operation, whether data are being transmitted or not.

The basic characteristics of circuit switching may be outlined in the following terms. First, circuit switching involves the establishment of a total path, at all initiations; this results in a serious inflexibility, given the way in which current voice-grade networks are implemented. Second, the circuit is established by a special signaling message, which threads its way through different switching centers. Third, the circuit, being a total path, is subject to the speed, and the code, limitation of the slowest link. As stated, the total path remains allocated for the transmission, regardless of utilization. When a call is terminated, the circuit is dropped, each line and switch returning to the "pool."

Three advantages of circuit switching are that the routing is simpler, the method is quite widespread today, and it is possible to attach terminals having differing characteristics. Among the disadvantages are the bit error rate, the relatively long call-setup times, the lack of automatic retransmission, an inefficient use of the circuits, and switching failures that are fatal to the communications. The greatest disadvantage is that the facilities are really built for voice-grade traffic.

Many of the problems in circuit switching are part and parcel of today's networks, the connection times, bandwidth, conditioning, and incompatibility between voice and data being examples. With the new technologies the entire way of handling the traffic will change, and circuit-switching may stage a comeback. The present-day disadvantages essentially mean that sharing common resources in a circuit switching function has its price. A protocol-based solution, designed to meet the needs of inquiry–response systems, has been the development of multipoint and multidrop networks. Multipoint networks have terminals in several locations, which communicate with a computer along a single communications line Multidrop networks have several terminals in one region, which are connected to a remote computer through one communication channel. Usually networks are exclusively neither multipoint nor multidrop, but a combination of both.

Multipoint networks use the facilities of the circuit-switching voice-grade network provided by the telephone company. The line is either "fixed" (dedicated to the user) or it is preferentially handled at the switching centers with a minimal setup time. Once the user is on a multipoint line, he must apply a protocol, a control procedure, which permits the central computer to manage a number of terminals operating on the line in question. The exact number of terminals depends on the length of the message, whether the terminal is intelligent or unintelligent, and the speed of the line. Twelve or fifteen terminals are usual. The most generally employed control procedure is the subject of the following sections.

Control Procedures: Fixed, Switched, and Multipoint

Control procedures, or protocols, should depend on the nature of the communications link, the technical characteristics of the terminal equipment, the software support, the user topology, and the applications requirements. The connections between two stations, whether terminal to terminal, terminal to computer, or computer to computer, may be one of three kinds: fixed point-to-point, multipoint, or switched point-to-point. This has been the essence of the discussion we have presented so far. We have said that the control procedures, the protocols, are most relevant to multipoint and switched point-to-point communications. In the general case we distinguish five basic phases:

Connection: A dial-up operation most relevant in switched end-to-end communications.

Establishment: Identification of sender and receiver DTEs.

Message handling: Transfer and delivery of message from sender DTE to receiver DTE.

Termination: Return of the system to its initial state, releasing the resources from their temporary assignment.

Table 10.1
Comparison of Three Disciplines

Circuit Switching	Message Switching	Packet Switching
1. Uses classical electromechanical (or computerized) switching centers	A fairly intelligent message switch center is needed, with storage facilities	Switching computers are used at the nodes; they can be micromini, mini, or midi
2. Wire circuit (or its equivalent radio link) connects the parties	No direct wire connection.	No direct wire connection
3. Point-to-point transmission	Permits broadcast and multiaddress of messages	Can permit broadcast and multiaddress of messages
4. Transmission is fixed bandwidth on voice-grade lines.	Usually low-speed transmission (sub-voice)	Users effectively employ small or large bandwidth according to need
5. Network cannot perform speed or code conversion	Network can perform speed or code conversion	Network can perform speed or code conversion
6. No delayed delivery possible	Delayed delivery is feasible if recipient is not available or lines are busy	Delayed delivery is possible as a special network facility
7. Network and its facilities are of a generalized type	Network and its facilities are applications oriented	Network and its facilities are of a generalized type
8. No particular optimization of speed of transmission or throughput	Optimization is made in terms of throughput	Optimization is primarily for speed of transmission
9. No store and forward	Store and forward capability	Store and forward is possible
10. Switched path is established for entire conversation	Route is originated for each message	Route is established dynamically for each packet

Circuit Switching	Message Switching	Packet Switching
11. Time delay in setting up the call	Call setup is reasonable	Negligible delay in setting up the call, usually the least of the three alternatives
12. Negligible transmission delay	Delay in message delivery can be substantial	Negligible delay in packet delivery
13. Busy signal if called party is occupied	No busy signal, store and forward solution	Packet returned to sender if undeliverable
14. Increased probability of blocking because of overload	Increased delivery delay because of overload	Overload results in increased delivery delay, but delivery time is short
15. No effect on transmission once connection is made	Saturation has a great impact on delay	Blocking when saturation is reached
16. Old type of real time between the parties	Too slow for conversational interaction	Old real time unnecessary, since conversational interaction is assured through modern technology
17. Messages are not filed at the nodes	Messages can be filed at the nodes	Messages are not filed except for journaling purposes
18. Protection against loss of messages is responsibility of the end user	Protection against loss of messages is responsibility of the network	Protection against loss of packets is responsibility of network with virtual circuits, of user with datagrams
19. Any length of transmission is permitted	Lengthy messages can be transmitted directly	Lengthy messages are divided into packets (1,000 to 8,000 bits each)
20. Economical with low traffic volumes, if public lines are employed, but very expensive with private lines	Economical with moderate traffic volumes	Reasonably high traffic volumes needed for economic justification, but less expensive than private lines

126   *Data Communications for Distributed Information Systems*

Disconnection: Corresponding to hanging up in a voice network; particularly relevant in switched end-to-end communications.

Let us now examine the basic characteristics of each type of connection, i.e., the fixed point-to-point, the multipoint, and the switched point-to-point, along with an outline of the procedures.

In a fixed point-to-point arrangement (Figure 10.1) a DTE needing to send a message to another can initiate its action with ENQ (enquiry). The receiving DTE responds with ACK (positive acknowledgment), which indicates that the destination is ready to receive a message. The sender then sends the message, and the receiver responds with another ACK, if it accepts the message. It is up to the sender to terminate the communication; this is done with an EOT (end of transmission), which returns the system to the idle state. Either station may be the primary one. Notice that a NAK (negative acknowledgment) may indicate that the destination DTE is not ready to receive or that the received message is in error. The NAK depends on the phase in which it is emitted. The two alternatives correspond respectively to the establishment and the message handling.

In a multipoint or a multidrop connection the control is rather complex, since more than two stations are on the same link. For this reason a choice is made between whether one DTE masters the communications link, acting as the control

Figure 10.1
Fixed point-to-point connection. (I/NR, invalid or no reply; ERP, error recovery procedure; EOT, end of transmission)

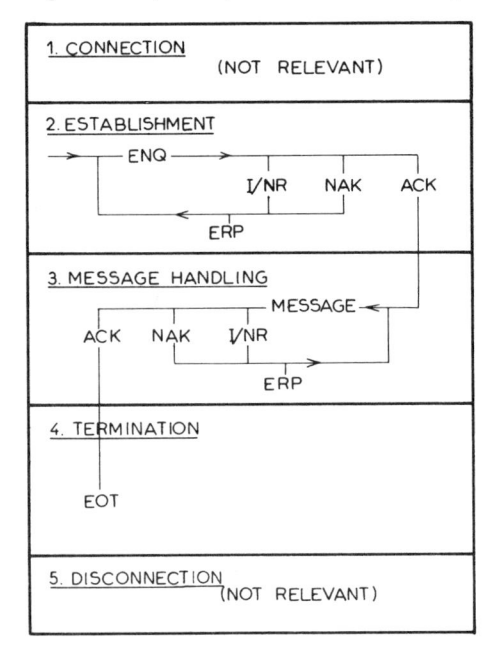

```
┌─────────────────────────────────────────────┐
│ 1. CONNECTION                               │
│                    (NOT RELEVANT)           │
├─────────────────────────────────────────────┤
│ 2. ESTABLISHMENT                            │
│         ──── ENQ ────                       │
│                    I/NR   NAK    ACK        │
│                                             │
│               ERP                           │
├─────────────────────────────────────────────┤
│ 3. MESSAGE HANDLING                         │
│                       ── MESSAGE ──         │
│        ACK   NAK    I/NR                    │
│                                             │
│                    ERP                      │
├─────────────────────────────────────────────┤
│ 4. TERMINATION                              │
│                                             │
│        EOT                                  │
├─────────────────────────────────────────────┤
│ 5. DISCONNECTION                            │
│                 (NOT RELEVANT)              │
└─────────────────────────────────────────────┘
```

station, or whether all the stations talk to one another at the same time; the latter is the case of contention.

When a master station is responsible for polling and selecting, one of two hypotheses must be made. The first is that the control station wished to send a message, and the second is that, not the control station, but one of the tributaries did.

When the master station starts a communication (Figure 10.2), it sends a SEL (selection) command. The DTE being addressed responds with an ACK, if it is ready to receive the message; a NAK brings up procedural choices that we have already discussed. When the master station is being spoken to (Figure 10.3), a tributary DTE waits for a POLL (polling) command. Then it replies with an EOT, if it has nothing to send, or with an ACK if it wishes to forward a message. The transfer procedure that follows resembles that of the preceding examples.

A basic difference between the foregoing cases and the switched end-to-end connection is that in point-to-point and multipoint the channel is a physical one, but in the switched end-to-end the channel is a logical one (Figure 10.4). In the first phase, connection, dialing is done by the DTE. After the link is established, the procedure is much like the one we have just described, except for the need to initiate and to break the connection (disconnection).

First of all, a discipline must ensure connection. This is the job of data link

Figure 10.2
Multipoint connection, master DTE sending. (SEL, selection; I/NR, invalid or no reply; ERP, error recovery procedure; EOT, end of transmission)

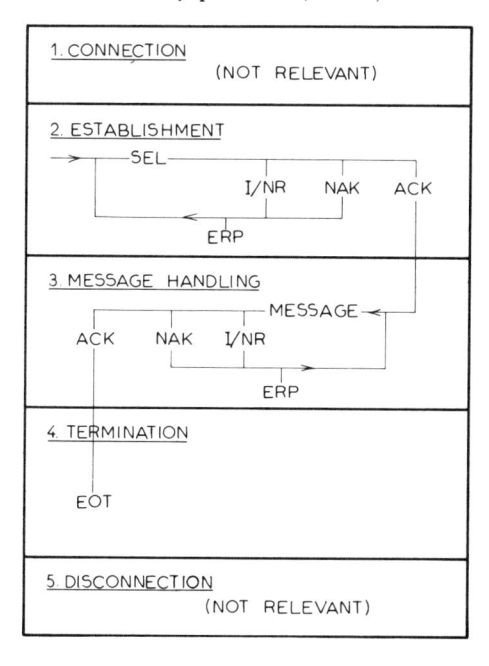

1. CONNECTION (NOT RELEVANT)
2. ESTABLISHMENT → SEL → I/NR   NAK   ACK ← ERP
3. MESSAGE HANDLING MESSAGE ← ACK   NAK   I/NR → ERP
4. TERMINATION EOT
5. DISCONNECTION (NOT RELEVANT)

Figure 10.3
Multipoint connection, master DTE receiving. (I/NR, invalid or no reply;
EOT, end of transmission; ERP, error recovery procedure)

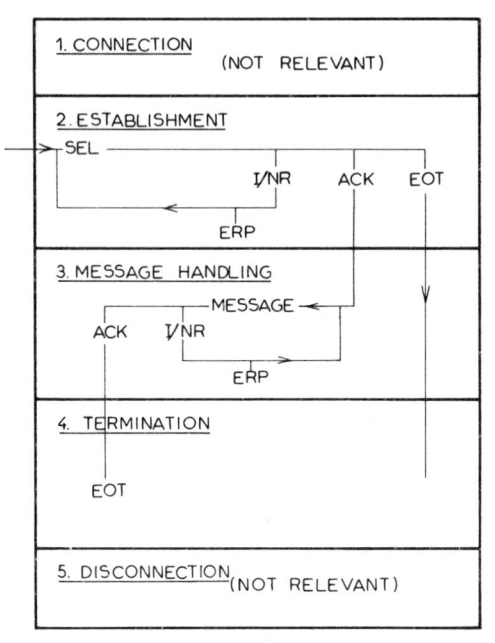

```
┌─────────────────────────────────────────────┐
│ 1. CONNECTION                               │
│                   (NOT RELEVANT)            │
├─────────────────────────────────────────────┤
│ 2. ESTABLISHMENT                            │
│  ┌─► SEL ─────────────────────────────      │
│  │             I/NR    ACK    EOT           │
│  └──────◄──────                             │
│                ERP                          │
├─────────────────────────────────────────────┤
│ 3. MESSAGE HANDLING                         │
│         ┌──── MESSAGE ◄──┐        ▼         │
│       ACK    I/NR                           │
│              └────►                         │
│                  ERP                        │
├─────────────────────────────────────────────┤
│ 4. TERMINATION                              │
│                                             │
│    EOT                                      │
├─────────────────────────────────────────────┤
│ 5. DISCONNECTION                            │
│                  (NOT RELEVANT)             │
└─────────────────────────────────────────────┘
```

control (discussed in the following chapter). Quite simply, the DTE that dialed the connection sends an identification command, which includes its own identity and a request to reply. The reply includes the identifying symbols of the called station together with an ACK or a NAK. When the identification is successful (ACK), the communications process is established; a NAK, no reply, or an invalid reply, leads to a restart of the identification procedure or to an error recovery routine. A communication process will be terminated by an EOT. If either station sends a DEOT (disconnect), the channel is released, a procedure assured by the protocol we have just explained.

The Coming Possibilities

Polling and selecting is by now an old discipline, yet it is still around and will continue, probably, to characterize a large number of networks, which is why we include it in this text.

We have made frequent reference to planning for the future. Optical fibers and satellite communications are the solution for the physical media, and efficient end-to-end protocols are the solution for their logical understructure.

The lightwave communications system under downtown Chicago exemplifies the use of optical fibers. For more than a year of test service, it performed even

Circuit Switching and Polling and Selecting 129

Figure 10.4
Switching end-to-end connection. (I/NR, invalid or no reply; ERP, error recovery procedure; EOT, end of transmission)

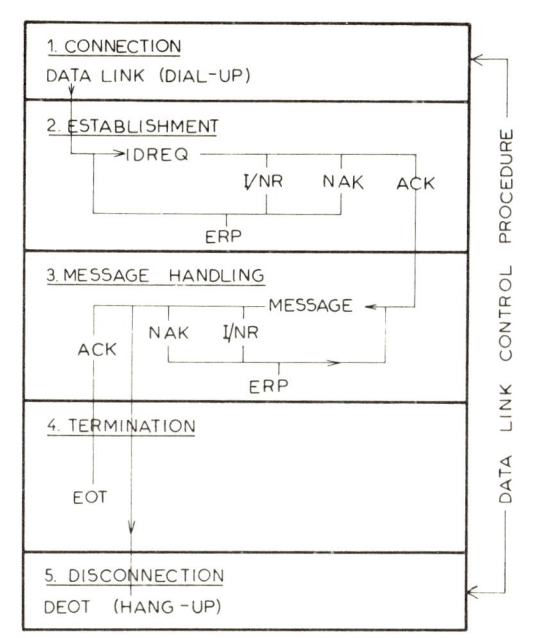

```
┌─────────────────────────────────────────┐
│  1. CONNECTION                          │ ←┐
│  DATA LINK (DIAL-UP)                    │  │
│      ↓                                  │  │
├─────────────────────────────────────────┤  │
│  2. ESTABLISHMENT                       │  │
│      └→IDREQ ─────────┬─────────────    │  │
│                       │                 │  │
│                     I/NR    NAK    ACK  │  │
│                                         │  │
│              ERP                        │  │
├─────────────────────────────────────────┤  │
│  3. MESSAGE HANDLING                    │  │
│                          ┌─ MESSAGE ←   │  │
│            NAK    I/NR                  │  │
│      ACK                                │  │
│                                         │  │
│              ERP                        │  │
├─────────────────────────────────────────┤  │
│  4. TERMINATION                         │  │
│                                         │  │
│      EOT                                │  │
│       ↓                                 │  │
├─────────────────────────────────────────┤  │
│  5. DISCONNECTION                       │ ←┘
│  DEOT  (HANG-UP)                        │
└─────────────────────────────────────────┘
    ── DATA LINK CONTROL PROCEDURE ──
```

better than expected, with virtually no downtime, surpassing stringent performance objectives.*

The current domestic and international satellite systems are efficient and economically competitive. Digital data have been transmitted at rates in excess of 56 kilobits per second, and projected rates are in excess of 400 megabits. Earth stations have reached a level where sharp reductions in cost are in sight. The data systems operating by satellite are achieving bit error rates of 1×10^{-8} and better; their reliability is better than 99.99 percent.

Switching, we said, is the key component in a circuit-switching network, and efficient switching is very important because the nodes represent about 40 percent of the total cost of the large telephone networks. A good approach lies in the use of two-dimensional, time-and-space technologies that handle digital signals directly and share in the time of switching paths through nodes.

Because for many years from now no network can be envisioned that is totally based on the new technologies, the ability to transform data is a must. This can be enhanced by microprocessors attached to the switching equipment. Something similar might be said about built-in diagnostics.

---

*That there is virtually no downtime refers to the system's projected annual outage rate of 0.0001 percent, about 30 seconds per year. The accuracy of digital transmission averaged less than 1 second per day of transmission error; the 1-second intervals that were error-free stood at 99.999 percent.

In a modern, powerful, extensive data and voice network, automatic diagnostics must allow for easy trouble-shooting, not only of failures within the system itself, but also of failures in the external devices being monitored and controlled. Although field repairs may be made by replacing modules, a complete on-line maintenance is necessary for quickly locating a faulty one.

With respect to protocols a lot of work has been done for data but not much for voice—a missed opportunity, considering that technology offers a means of developing protocol chips. Voice and data protocols must complement and support, not contradict or defy, each other. The "flag" in current data protocols is not long enough for voice traffic, and there are buffering problems with voice stations and similar ones for encrypted traffic. These are vital issues in establishing, implementing, and maintaining circuit services.

Let us now look into the sort of facilities a user requires for end-to-end data communications. They must accommodate different users, different uses, and different equipment, and they could do so through the adoption of a standard format and a few well defined protocols. Although many types of terminal and computer, built by different manufacturers, can communicate with one another, virtual configurations may have to be defined, as the DTEs proliferate and too many combinations of terminal and computer make integrating dissimilar equipment too complex. In other words, the logical understructure must support the attachment of the terminals. It will be easy to branch DTEs that are "plug-compatible" with the network's specifications and to leave it to the software and the protocols to define the functional capabilities.

Packet switching is an example of a discipline able to handle computers and terminals of many vendors who observe established specifications. The switching nodes accept streams from many sources and dynamically interleave the packets of digital, high-capacity, internodal trunks. This seems a better use of transmission facilities and eventually reduces investment and lowers cost.

Already applied in a number of advanced networks, packet switching presents a significant potential. The protocols discussed in the following chapters split up a series of packets from one terminal and send them along various routes, depending on the volume of traffic, the error conditions, and other factors. At the receiving node they are reassembled in their correct sequence and delivered to the destination.

Since the switching nodes are essentially programmable minicomputers, they can be instructed for a variety of communications-processing functions that normally either are undertaken by the host computer or are not feasible at all. The intelligence inherent in a packet network provides users with several kinds of operation, from fully switched ones to closed user groups.

Such are the solutions of the 1980s. As the cost of communications continues to decline, and microcomputer technology offers features never imagined before, new concepts, functions, and services may be expected to change radically the services now offered.

11
Bit-Oriented Protocols

Bit-oriented procedures are recognized as intrinsically more efficient in utilization of resources, even though character-oriented protocols are vastly more in use today, but before microcomputer technology had matured, their computations were felt to be too demanding for widespread use. After several years of research, carried out primarily by the American National Standards Institute, ANSI, and the International Standards Organization, ISO, the new bit-oriented data link control procedures reached a reasonable level of development. The ANSI standard is the Advanced Communications Control Procedure, ADCCP. The original ISO standard was the "high-level data link control," HDLC, which in its original version, was fairly similar to IBM's "synchronous data link control," SDLC. Both ANSI and ISO started working on this subject in 1969, but IBM made one of the first announcements in 1973.

The SDLC and HDLC were initially designed as unbalanced—or asymmetric, or vertical—structures. This means they presupposed a master control. The HDLC is now referred to as the line access protocol A, LAP A. In the last couple of years it has been superceded by LAP B, which supports a balanced—or symmetric, or horizontal—structure.

The ADCCP, CDCCP, SDLC, BDLC, UDLC, HDLC, and LAP B are all "dialects" of a bit-oriented protocol. Together we shall call them XDLC. Flag sequences at the beginning and end of a frame effect synchronization (a 0 bit followed by six 1 bits and then another 0 bit). The frame includes address, user data (information) and control fields.

The Data Link

In the short twenty years of its existence the data communications industry has steadily searched for an efficient use of its resources, and the bit-oriented protocols are the latest development. Like any other line discipline, they are the content and sequencing procedures for transmission between terminal and computer, but they do so on a higher level than that of a physical medium. The communications medium concerns itself with the physical transmission of bits over a channel; the bit-oriented protocol addresses itself to the logical transmission of data. The data, in logical transmission, are grouped into physical blocks, the packets (Figure 11.1). Packets must be transmitted over a link, so some form of control is necessary. The lowest level of protocol is the "communication level," which provides the physical data link. A packet consists of a "frame" bracketed between an opening and a closing flag; we shall discuss the structures of the frame and the flag in the next sections. The frame is the vehicle for every command, every response, and all information that is transmitted by use of a protocol. It is the basic grouping. A higher grouping, called a frame sequence, is checked for missing or duplicated frames. A DTE transmitting sequenced frames counts and numbers each; the counting is referred to as N(S). A station receiving sequenced frames counts each error-free sequenced frame received; the receiver count is known as N(R). Upon receipt of an error-free frame an N(R) is incremented, indicating the next expected frame. All information frames are designated by four parameters:

    I: "this is an information frame"

    N(S): "send sequence count"

    N(R): "receive sequence count"

    P/F: "poll" or "final" bit

Supervisory frames are designated by type, such as "receive ready," "receive not ready," and "reject," followed by N(R); unnumbered frames have a command–response structure; management frames provide the data needed for activating, initializing, and controlling the response mode of the DTE in the network and also for reporting errors in transmission procedures. The time base is horizontal: left to right.

Bit orientation permits the use of positionally located control fields rather than code set combinations for link control. Framing flags and control fields divorce the link control from the pattern or code structure of the information content. This makes the bit-oriented protocols inherently transparent.

Bit orientation provides error checking of both control and text information. (It will be recalled that binary synchronous communications control only the text.) Furthermore, it is versatile in its applications and with respect to communications facilities.

Being a third-generation protocol (after the synchronous and binary synchronous protocols), the XDLC takes advantage of full-duplex lines while being able to operate efficiently on half-duplex, if need be. It also separates the lower link controls of the physical communications media from the higher controls, such as packet format control (which we shall be discussing).

Figure 11.1

Data transparency is provided by each of the three structures. SYN, synchronous; DLE, data link escape; STX, start of text; ETX, end of text; BSC, binary synchronous communications; PAD, packet assembler–disassembler

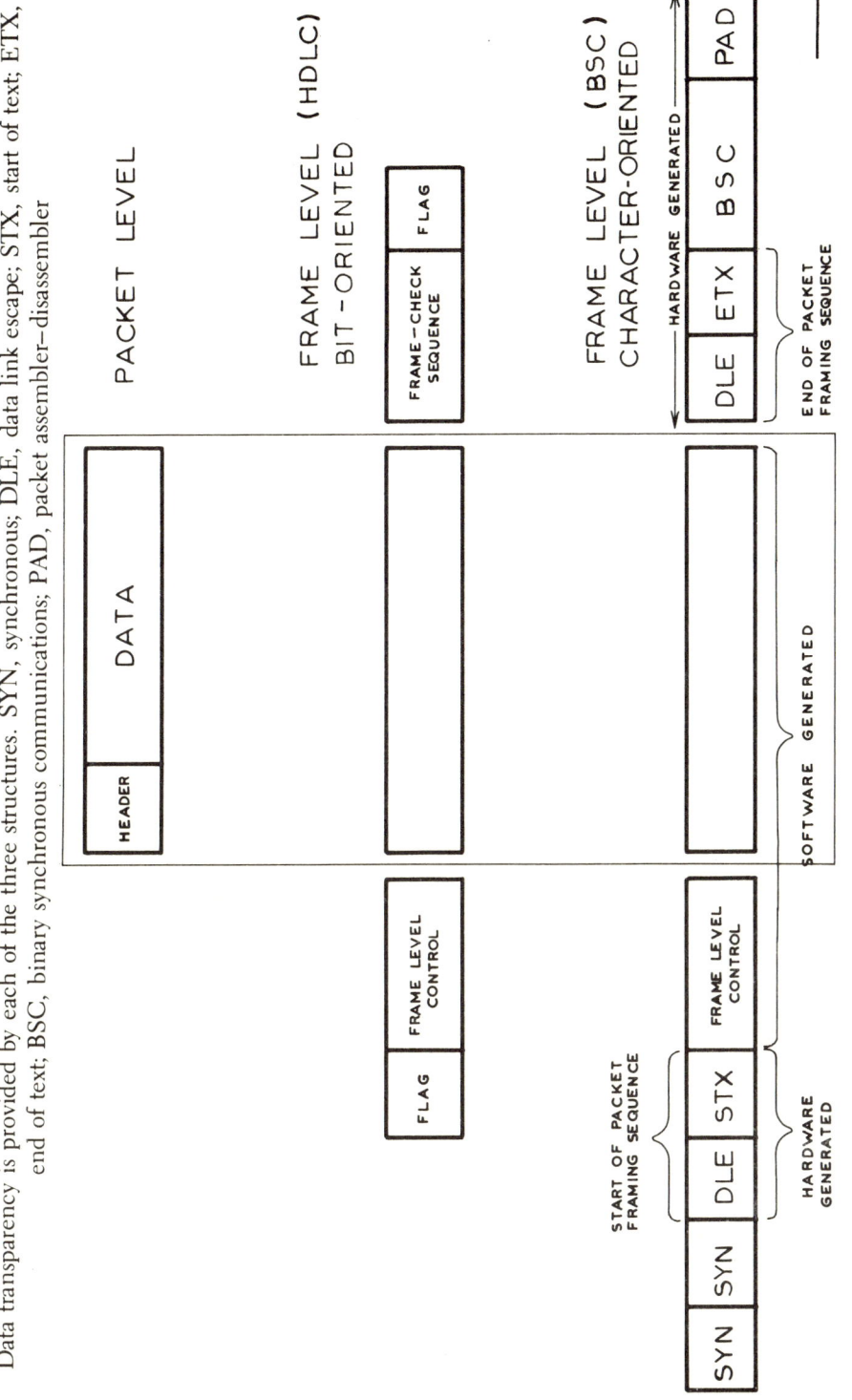

The XDLC is evolutionary, and in its present form it is not the whole answer to the communications problem. It is merely a link-level mechanism, concerned solely with the transfer of data at that level. Moreover, it is, quite definitely, not a network architecture: it was not designed to control the flow of information between users in a multinodal network. It can, however, be applied between nodes or between a node and a user. The relationship of XDLC to a network architecture is straightforward if we consider their respective functions. The purpose of architecture is to transfer data between applications, or "processes"—a user program, a line printer and its software, a file system, etc.—on different systems, which systems use links between them to support the processes. The links need the assistance of a bit-oriented line access protocol.

The data being transferred should not influence, nor be influenced by, the XDLC. They may be a single character, parts of a data base, or a program to be executed. The XDLC must also be device independent, since the terminals or computers may belong to different families, and have different operating systems, different data bases, and so on. The links between systems may be temporary (dial-up) or permanent and stable. They may work at different speeds, and that, too, should be transparent to the XDLC.

The XDLC has its price. The need to distinguish between data and control characters places a burden on the implementation of software and requires a high intelligence of the hardware. Further, transparency has been achieved only in complicated ways.

Figure 11.2 shows the LAP A protocol, as an example. All the XDLC protocols have in common a number of basic characteristics:

All are synchronous protocols, though different from the binary synchronous protocols.
All are similar but not completely compatible among themselves.
All work on half-duplex and full-duplex transmission.
All may be used in loop (ring) or multidrop configurations.
All have fixed length of header, but among themselves and within their own dialects this length can vary.
All have a fixed trailer length (cyclic redundancy check).
All are bit oriented.
All in their original forms were asymmetric (new forms tend to be symmetric, like LAP B).

The difference between a symmetric and an asymmetric structure is, of course, fundamental in the development of systems with user exits and significant possibilities of growth. Table 11.1 compares some of the differences among the dialects of XDLC.

The XDLC is *not* designed for certain things, listed below. Note that the information carried by the supervisory signals, item 8, can serve for item 7, and that the data at the bit level may be information or commands.

Figure 11.2
SDLC protocol (LAP "A")

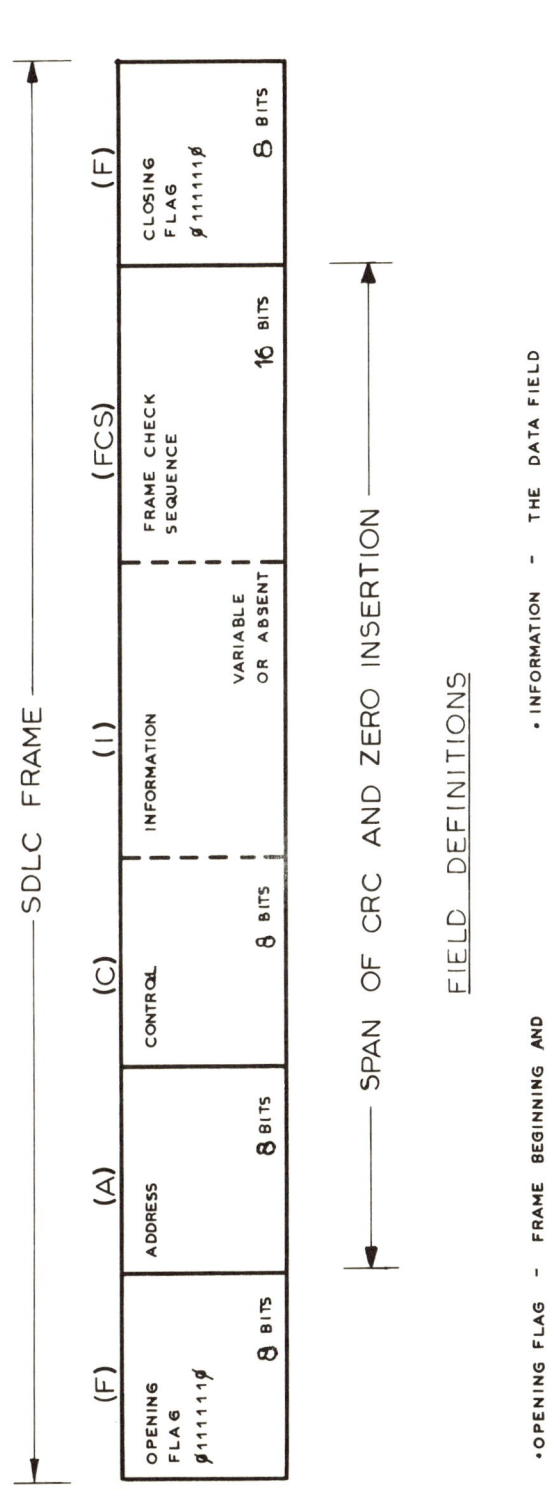

(F)	(A)	(C)	(I)	(FCS)	(F)
OPENING FLAG ∅111111∅	ADDRESS	CONTROL	INFORMATION	FRAME CHECK SEQUENCE	CLOSING FLAG ∅111111∅
8 BITS	8 BITS	8 BITS	VARIABLE OR ABSENT	16 BITS	8 BITS

──────── SDLC FRAME ────────

──── SPAN OF CRC AND ZERO INSERTION ────

FIELD DEFINITIONS

- **OPENING FLAG** – FRAME BEGINNING AND FRAME SYNCHRONIZATION

- **ADDRESS** – SECONDARY STATION
  WITH 8 BITS WE CAN ONLY ADDRESS 256 TERMINALS BANK OF AMERICA ADOPTED A VARIATION

- **CONTROL** – DEFINES FRAME TYPE AND INCLUDES SUPERVISION COMMANDS INCLUDING SHUT DOWN OF TERMINALS; SEND/RECEIVE INFORMATION; NO MESSAGE COUNT WITH 8 BITS.

- **INFORMATION** – THE DATA FIELD

- **FRAME CHECK** – ERROR DETECTION
  CRC 16 COVERS BOTH DATA FIELD AND HEADER PREVIOUS PROTOCOLS CHECKED ONLY THE DATA

- **CLOSING FLAG** – FRAME TERMINATION AND LINE FILL

136 Data Communications for Distributed Information Systems

Table 11.1
Comparative Table for XDLC*

	ADCCP		HDLC		SDLC (IBM)		SDLC (BOA)†	
Criteria	C	R	C	R	C	R	C	R
Frame structure								
1. Basic format	Y	Y	Y	Y	Y	Y	Y	Y
2. Extended format	Y	Y	Y	Y	N	N	Y	Y
Control field								
3. Selective reject	Y	Y	Y	Y	N	N	N	N
4. Unnumbered information	Y	Y	N	N	N	N	N	N
5. Disconnect	Y	N	Y	N	Y	N	Y	N
6. Request disconnect	—	Y	—	N	—	N	—	N
7. Check pattern in information field	N	N	N	N	Y	Y	Y	Y
8. System tailoring	Y	Y	N	N	N	N	N	N
9. Station-off disconnect line	—	Y	—	N	—	N	—	N
10. Asynchronous response	Y	Y	Y	Y	N	N	N	N
11. Balanced-mode capability	Y	Y	N	N	N	N	N	N
12. Exchange identification	Y	Y	N	N	Y	Y	Y	Y

*C, command; R, response; Y and N, yes and no.
†The version implemented by the Bank of America.

Asynchronous transmission

Either grouping or breaking of messages

Queries about device status

Device control

End-to-end control

Integrating of voice packets

Establishment, maintenance, and termination of a communication session

Exchange of supervisory signals

These functions are taken care of by the network architecture. That is why it is important to select an architecture—and the right one.

The Fields of XDLC

The first XDLC is the opening flag. In the SDLC and other dialects it is an 8-bit sequence generated at the transmitter. The flag indicates the beginning of a frame,

Bit-Oriented Protocols 137

is a synchronizing reference for the position of subsequent fields, and triggers a transmission-checking algorithm. All terminals monitor the network in an idle state; they become active when they detect an opening flag. The 8-bit flag is also an integral part of the trailer; by being repeated at the end of the block, it provides synchronization, part of which is indicating beginning and end.

The frame thus closes with a flag. Both the opening and the closing flags have the binary configuration 01111110, that is, a 0 bit, followed by six 1 bits, followed by a 0 bit. Senders send complete 8-bit flags; receivers search continuously, on a bit-by-bit basis, for the frame synchronization.

For transparency throughout the frame (Figure 11.3), and to avoid duplicating the flag, the transmitter inserts a 0 bit after five successive bits anywhere between the beginning and the ending flags, which bit is then detected and removed at the receiving end; see Figure 11.4. That is to say, in order to safeguard the 8-bit flag, *if* the same bit pattern appears in the information field, it is sensed by the transmitting equipment, and an extra 0 bit is inserted after the fifth 1 bit (one more bit is thus added to the information field). At the receiving end the equipment feels for a string of 1 bits and, when it finds the 5-bit string, it deletes the extra 0; in this way the message is restored. This so-called bit stuffing is one of the reasons that SDLC cannot be used for asynchronous transmission.

The address field immediately follows the opening flag. It identifies one or more secondary stations on the link. Each secondary station normally has an individual and a group address, the latter being shared with other secondary stations. The address field is useful when messages must be accepted from, or go to, several terminals. In the SDLC dialect the field is 8 bits long, a length which allows identification of as many as 128 terminals—clearly a hierarchical structure for systems that may have several thousands of terminals. In other dialects the address is a multiple of n octets. In this extended mode the secondary link address field is a sequence of 8 bits, which constitute a single secondary station address when the least significant bit is 0; the following octet is an extension of the address field.

Figure 11.3
Data transparency. The Problem: how to tell where a packet begins, and still be able to send any data pattern. The Solution: sender adds special bytes or bits which receiver removes, preserving original data pattern.

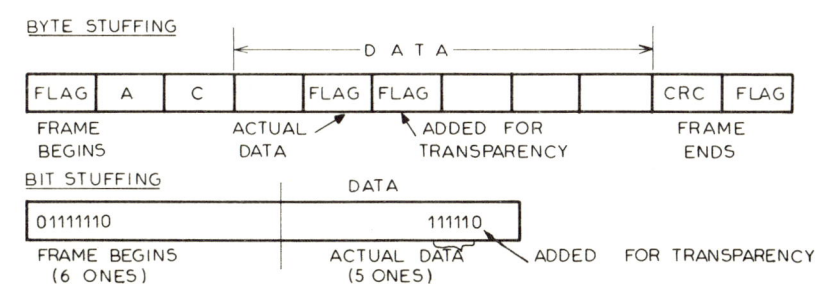

BYTE STUFFING

FLAG	A	C		FLAG	FLAG			CRC	FLAG

FRAME BEGINS — ACTUAL DATA — ADDED FOR TRANSPARENCY — FRAME ENDS

BIT STUFFING

| 01111110 | | 111110 |

FRAME BEGINS (6 ONES) — ACTUAL DATA (5 ONES) — ADDED FOR TRANSPARENCY

138 *Data Communications for Distributed Information Systems*

Figure 11.4
Bit stuffing. Procedural steps: (1) Transmitter examines frame content for five consecutive 1's; (2) Inserts a 0 after the fifth; (3) This breaks the *possible* sequence 01111.11110; (4) The message is then transmitted; (5) Receiver examines frame content for five consecutive 1's; (6) If the sixth bit is 1, flag is assumed; (7) If the sixth bit is 0, the bit is discarded; (8) Message takes original form again.

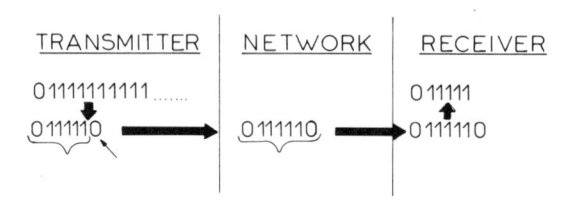

```
    TRANSMITTER   |   NETWORK   |   RECEIVER
    0111111111....|             |   011111
         ↓        |             |      ↑
      011111̣0 ───▶│   0111110 ──▶│   0111110
```

The address field is terminated by an octet having a 1 in the least-significant-bit position. Figure 11.5 compares the address fields of SDLC and two other protocols.

The XDLC control field identifies the type of frame, whether informational, supervisory, or nonsequenced; see Figure 11.6. It includes the frame acknowledgment and the poll and final fields and generally provides the signals needed to operate the data links. Its bits identify the frame type, the sequence numbers, and the command or the response mode.

If the leading bit in a frame's control field is a 0, the transmission constitutes an information frame.

One 3-bit value is a count stored at the transmitter, N(S); it designates the number of frames already sent in a sequence.

A second 3-bit value, the total stored at the receiver, N(R), gives the number of error-free frames previously accepted in the sequence.

The remaining bit in the control field acts as a send or receive indicator, such as poll (primary) and final (secondary).

If the leading bit in a frame's control field is a 1, then the protocol examines the second bit, to distinguish between a supervisory and a management frame. A supervisory frame initiates and controls subsequent message transfers. It has six additional bits: three for the receiver count, two for a command or response code, and one for a poll or final indicator. It is utilized for acknowledgment, polling, temporary interruptions, and error recovery. A management frame, on the other hand, is a means of operating communications devices; its six additional bits include 3-bit and 2-bit command and response codes and a 1-bit poll or final indicator (Figure 11.7).

The nonsequenced management frame is utilized for data link management: an opening flag, an address field, and a control field, which form the header.

Bit-Oriented Protocols   139

Figure 11.5

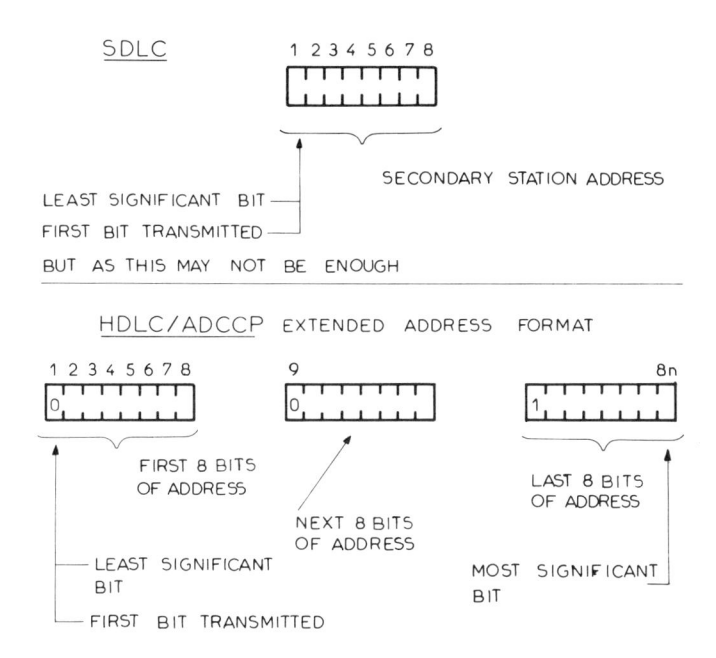

SDLC   1 2 3 4 5 6 7 8

LEAST SIGNIFICANT BIT
FIRST BIT TRANSMITTED
SECONDARY STATION ADDRESS

BUT AS THIS MAY NOT BE ENOUGH

HDLC/ADCCP EXTENDED ADDRESS FORMAT

1 2 3 4 5 6 7 8   9   8n
0...........   0...........   1...........

FIRST 8 BITS OF ADDRESS
NEXT 8 BITS OF ADDRESS
LAST 8 BITS OF ADDRESS

LEAST SIGNIFICANT BIT
FIRST BIT TRANSMITTED
MOST SIGNIFICANT BIT

Figure 11.6

- INFORMATION FRAME (UTILIZED FOR THE TRANSFER OF DATA, ACKNOWLEDGMENT)

| 0 | N(S) | P/F | N(R) |

N(S) : SEND SEQUENCE COUNT
P/F : POLL (PRIMARY)/FINAL (SECONDARY)
N(R) : RECEIVE SEQUENCE COUNT

- SUPERVISORY FRAME (CONTAINS NO I FIELD). UTILIZED FOR ACKNOWLEDGMENT, POLLING, TEMPORARY INTERRUPTIONS, OR ERROR RECOVERY.

| 1 1 0 | S S | P/F | N(R) |

SS	SIGNAL NAME	DEFINITION
00	RR	RECEIVE READY
01	REJ	REJECT
10	RNR	RECEIVE NOT READY
11	SREJ	SELECTIVE REJECT

- NON-SEQUENCED FRAME (CONTAINS NO I FIELD EXCEPT FOR CMDR). UTILIZED FOR DATA LINK MANAGEMENT.

| 1 1 1 | VARIABLE |

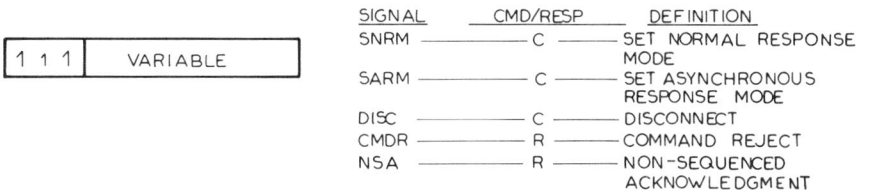

MAJOR SIGNALS

SIGNAL	CMD/RESP	DEFINITION
SNRM	C	SET NORMAL RESPONSE MODE
SARM	C	SET ASYNCHRONOUS RESPONSE MODE
DISC	C	DISCONNECT
CMDR	R	COMMAND REJECT
NSA	R	NON-SEQUENCED ACKNOWLEDGMENT

140 Data Communications for Distributed Information Systems

Figure 11.7

(a) Basic mode control field, where N(s) = transmitting station send sequence number, bit 2 is low-order bit; N(R) = transmitting station receive sequence number, bit 6 is low-order bit; S = supervisory function bits; M = management bits; P/F = poll/final bit (1 = poll/final). (b) Where X bits are reserved and set to 0. Bits 2 and 10 are the low-order bits of the sequence numbers.

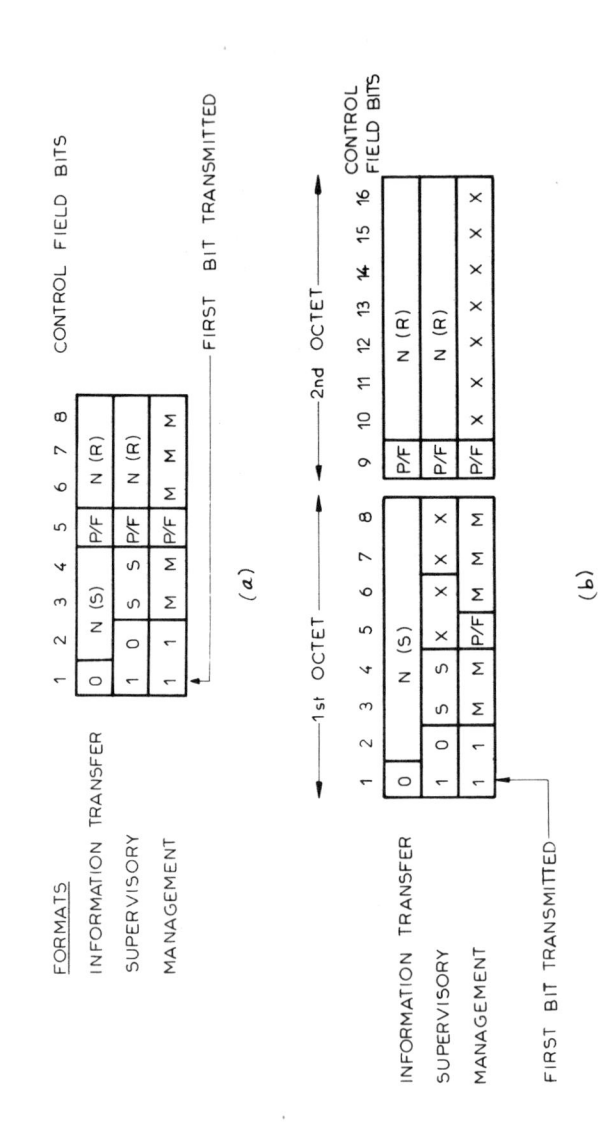

	1	2	3	4	5	6	7	8
FORMATS								
INFORMATION TRANSFER	0	N (S)			P/F	N (R)		
SUPERVISORY	1	0	S	S	P/F	N (R)		
MANAGEMENT	1	1	M	M	P/F	M	M	M

CONTROL FIELD BITS

⟵ FIRST BIT TRANSMITTED

(a)

	1	2	3	4	5	6	7	8	9	10	11	12	13	14	15	16
INFORMATION TRANSFER	0		N (S)			X	X	X	P/F			N (R)				
SUPERVISORY	1	0	S	S	X	X	X	X	P/F			N (R)				
MANAGEMENT	1	1	M	M	P/F	M	M	M	P/F	X	X	X	X	X	X	X

⟵ 1st OCTET ⟶ ⟵ 2nd OCTET ⟶ CONTROL FIELD BITS

FIRST BIT TRANSMITTED ⟵

(b)

The information field, variable in length, has upper limits that depend on the implementation (factors limiting the length are channel-error characteristics, logical properties of data, and node or station buffer sizes). Under current standards, the limits are 1,000, 2,000, and 8,000 bits minus the header and trailer. The data link control is completely transparent to the contents of the information (I) field.

The header and information fields are followed by the frame-check sequence for error control. This is 16 bits long and precedes the closing flag; its object is to validate the accuracy of transmission. A 16-bit cyclic redundancy check (CRC) also controls errors. It uses a generator polynominal, $x^{16} + x^{12} + x^5 + 1$. The transmitter's 16-bit remainder value is initialized to all 1's before a frame is transmitted, and the binary value of the transmission is premultiplied by x^{16} and then divided by the generator polynomial. Integer quotient values are ignored, and the transmitter sends the complement of the resulting remainder value, high-order bit first, as the field of the frame-check sequence. The frame-check sequence, the cyclic redundancy check, and the closing flag constitute the trailer.

Frame Sequence and Acknowledgment

The following statements put in a nutshell the bit-oriented procedure we described in the preceding sections.

Information transfer is in the form of a frame.
Each frame is sequenced to allow for duplication or loss detection.
The field of the frame-check sequence provides for error control.
A transmitting station sequences and counts its frames in the N(S) field.
A receiving station counts each error-free sequenced frame it receives (the receiver count, N(R), is the count of the next expected frame).
Arriving frames whose N(S) field does not equal the receiver's N(R) field (out of sequence or duplicate) are rejected.

As many as seven frames may be transmitted before receipt of the N(R) field from the receiver. The transmitter, detecting that the receiver's N(R) has fallen behind his N(S), must retransmit consecutively, starting at the receiver's N(R) (the selective reject is optional in SDLC); this is called the "go back N" technique. Hence, when the poll frame contains the receive sequence number N(R), it permits a specific solicitation (for the station) to send I frames numbered N(S) = N(R) and following sequential I frames. This also serves as an acknowledgment to the station for all I frames by means of send sequence number N(S) = N(R) − 1. In case a terminal has no I frames to send, it responds with a supervisory frame with the F bit set to 1.

Two response modes may be distinguished: the normal response mode (NRM) and the asynchronous response mode (ARM). In the normal mode the P bit is set to 1 in command frames, to solicit response frames from the other terminal. The DTE (secondary) cannot transmit until a common frame with the P bit set to 1 is received. The originating DTE can also restrict the receiving station from transmitting I frames by sending a "receive not ready" (RNR) supervisory frame. In the asynchronous mode the frames may be transmitted by the receiving DTE on an asynchronous basis. The P bit is set to 1 when this becomes possible. If the originating DTE wants a positive acknowledgment that a particular frame has been received, it may set the P bit in the command to 1, which will force a response from the receiving DTE.

The fact that P and F bits are exchanged, one to one, and that only one P bit can be outstanding at a time, helps the N(R) count of a frame (containing a P or F bit set to 1) to detect sequence errors in the I frame. This acts as a checkpoint; it is helpful in detecting frame sequence errors and in indicating the frame sequence number for beginning retransmission.

Another important matter is the selective reject technique for frame acknowledgment.

Selective reject allows the transmitter to retransmit only the frame that has been rejected by the receiver.

After retransmission of the selectively rejected frame the transmission continues where it had left off.

This is more efficient than the "go back N" technique because all frames following the rejected one need not be retransmitted.

The selective reject technique has disadvantages in certain applications. For instance, the receiver must be able to reshuffle received frames, and efficiency may be reduced below the level of the "go back N" technique if successive frames are rejected, and the automatic handling of selective reject is fairly complex. Figures 11.8 and 11.9 compare the two techniques.

Using a Bit-Oriented Protocol in a Loop

The original protocol developed by IBM for primary and secondary stations in a loop may be seen as the predecessor of the XDLC. The IBM loop operation as applied, for instance, with the 3600 series is asymmetric. There are a primary and several secondary stations. The secondary station originates transmission only when it receives the go-ahead pattern 01111111. If the secondary DTE wishes to transmit, it must change the seventh 1 to a 0. This change produces the flag byte, which becomes the start of the message. Notice the similarity of this pattern to the opening and closing flags of XDLC.

For an example of a loop application with SDLC we shall follow an environment based on central control; see Figure 11.10.

1. Each link has an assigned primary station and one or more secondary stations.
2. A secondary station can transmit to the primary only when authorized by it.

Figure 11.8
Go back to acknowledgment. N(S) denotes the sequence number of a transmitted frame. N(A) denotes the acceptance of this and all previous frames. N(R) denotes the sequence number of the oldest rejected receive frame.

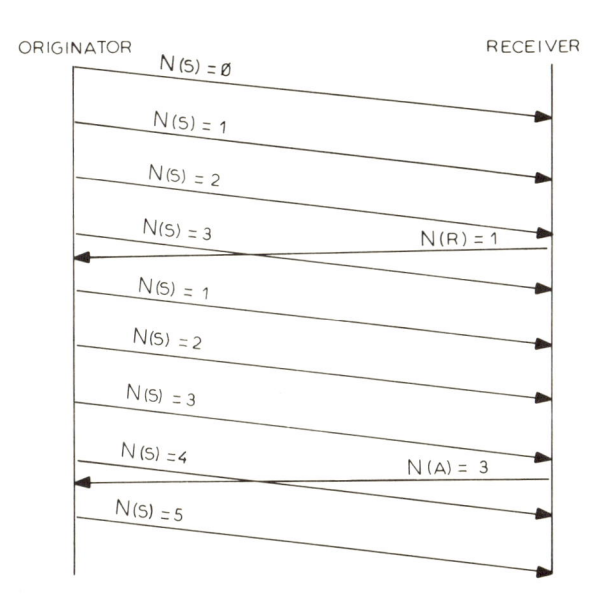

```
ORIGINATOR                                    RECEIVER
       N(S) = 0
       N(S) = 1
       N(S) = 2
       N(S) = 3
                                   N(R) = 1
       N(S) = 1
       N(S) = 2
       N(S) = 3
       N(S) = 4
                                   N(A) = 3
       N(S) = 5
```

3. All secondary stations are repeaters.
4. The loop controller initiates by transmitting a specific poll to a unique secondary and an optional response poll (ORP) to a common loop address.
5. The loop controller transmits the go-ahead signal.
6. The secondary station captures the loop by converting the go-ahead to a transmit frame.
7. Eventually the secondary station releases the loop by returning to the repeater operation.

In different terms, the primary station polls the secondary for status. It sets the secondary to an initialization mode. The secondary acknowledges.

The SDLC allows transmission of up to 7 packets before an acknowledgment is required. Each block has its own header and trailer. The objective is to reduce line turnarounds in half-duplex. Furthermore, satellite transmission imposes severe earth-to-satellite and satellite-to-earth delays, which make such a procedure advisable (the 7-packet limit is indeed too low). The delay from earth to satellite and back is 0.24 second, which is the least amount of time before the receiving station gets the first packet. Acknowledgment, one per packet, would take another 0.24 second. This delay could be cut by using terrestrial circuits, which would speed the operation but complicate the system. If transmission were 50 kilobits per

Figure 11.9
Selective reject acknowledgment. N(S) denotes the sequence number of a transmitted frame. N(RS) denotes the number of a received frame which is being selectively rejected. N(A) denotes the acceptance of frames up to and including the frame specified.

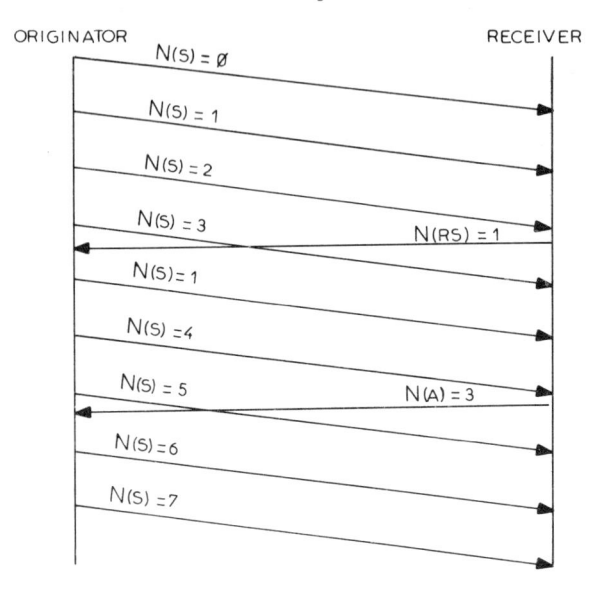

Figure 11.10
A loop application. Loop propagation time is 1 msec per 15 miles of loop length plus the sum of secondary-DTE relay times.

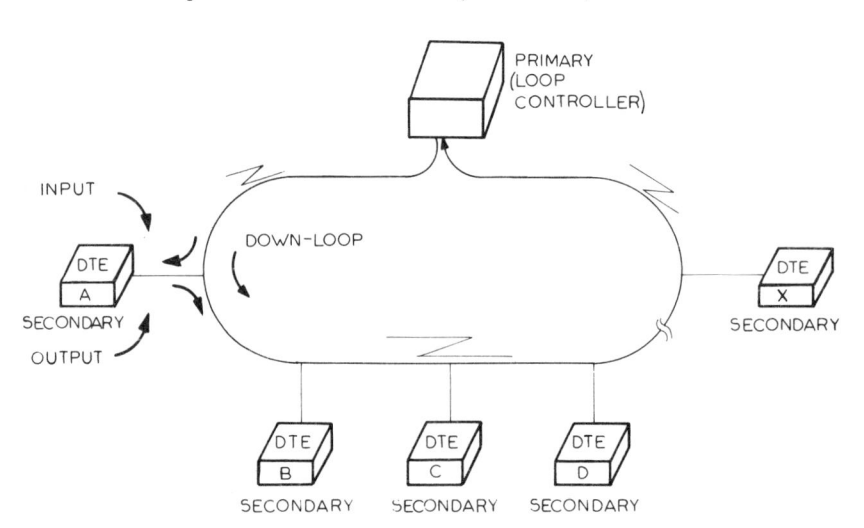

second with packets of, say, 5 kilobits in length, 10 would be transmitted before the first acknowledgment were received. Moreover, a good deal of packets would need to be kept in transit at any one time. The SDLC, however, does provide for acknowledgment in multiple packets, the acknowledgments being included in the header of a message going in the "other" direction (piggy-backing).

Detected errors do not launch a response; the receiving station does nothing. When the sending station gets no ACK within a specific time, it automatically retransmits the packet or packets in question. Packets are numbered sequentially; those that are out of sequence are detected, and the receiving station sends a NAK.

This brings us to incarnation numbers. An incarnation number, or name, is unique for an instance of the protocol module. The incarnation number, or name, is sent in each packet and is used by the receiver to filter out packets from old connections caused by a "crash" and restart. It is helpful in conjunction with sequence numbers for uniquely identifying an octet of data or control. The uniqueness of the incarnation number allows the resetting of the sequence number space to 0 at the initialization of each new path (first connection between two users).

Objectives of XDLC

The XDLC is designed to operate at the physical link, or communications, level. Its procedures should unify the standards for all distributed networks and offer new features to the user, such as file transparency, downline loading, four-wire simultaneous operations, and security. The five following functions must be performed by the data link control procedures.

The XDLC must create error-free sequential links. Practically speaking, this means two things: no bit error and observance of sequence (also provision of data necessary at the higher level of networking).

The XDLC must manage the physical link; simply, it must mask from both the user and the nested higher level the functions of the physical link. Let us recall the functions of the physical link: link turnaround, modem interface, control action, device interfaces, and others necessary for data transmission.

The XDLC must perform efficiently; essentially, this means to add as little overhead as possible, to take advantage of the performance features of the physical link, and to observe the synchronization requirements (transmitter–receiver).

The XDLC must be widely applicable. To answer this requirement, it must operate over links with different physical characteristics. It must also be available for differing applications, that is, applications independent.

The XDLC must be easy to implement. Therefore it must consist of a minimal number of states, be variable, and have processing algorithms. It must also be implementable on small systems; this is a fundamental DIS requirement.

Table 11.2 lists the chief XDLC commands and their definitions, which are helpful to keep in mind.

Table 11.2
Abbreviations and Definitions of the XDLC Commands

Abbreviation	Definition
CMDR	A DTE's indication that it received a nonvalid command
DISC	Disconnect, used for performing a logical disconnection
DM	Disconnect-mode response, used for reporting a nonoperational status
I	Sequenced information frame
NSA	Affirmative response to an SNRM, DISC or SIM
NSI	Nonsequence numbered information
NSP	Used for providing an optional response from a DTE
RD	Request-disconnect response
REJ	Reject supervisory frame, used by a station for requesting retransmission of information
RIM	Request-for-initialization mode
RNR	Receive-not-ready supervisory frame, used by a station for indicating temporary inability to accept additional incoming information
ROL	A DTE's indication that it is disconnected
RR	Receive-ready supervisory frame, used by a DTE to indicate that it is ready to receive an information frame and to acknowledge previously received ones
RSPR	Response reject, used for reporting exceptional conditions not recoverable by link-level action

Bit-Oriented Protocols   147

Table 11.2 (cont.)
Abbreviations and Definitions of the XDLC Commands

Abbreviation	Definition
SABM	Set asynchronous-balanced mode
SARM	Set asynchronous-response mode
SARME SABME SNRME	Extended mode commands for placing the addressed DTE in the extended mode
SIM	Set initialization mode
SNRM	Set normal mode, used for placing the addressed DTE in the NRM
SREJ	Selective-reject supervisory frame
TEST	TEST frame sent to a DTE to solicit a TEST response
UA	Unnumbered acknowledge, acknowledging receipt and acceptance of the SNRM, SARM, etc.
UI	Unnumbered information, command and response, used for transferring NSI across a link
UP	Unnumbered poll command used for soliciting response frames from a single DTE
USR 0 USR 1 USR 2 USR 3	Commands and responses (user 0, 1, 2, 3) permitting the definition of special system-dependent functions not having general applicability
XID	Exchange identification, causing the addressed station to report its station identification.

12

The Nesting of Protocols

We have spoken often of the need of layering in network architectures and in the protocols supporting it. Figure 12.1 recapitulates the different levels, or layers, to which we have been making reference.

The first level, the physical interface, concerns the data circuit terminating equipment, which we have also called the modem, or data set; it has been standardized by the CCITT. The physical interface specifies a four-wire point-to-point synchronous circuit, for a transmission path between the terminals and hosts on one side and the network on the other. The CCITT standard ensures that no changes in the interface hardware of the DTE are required; the modem is on the network side of this interface.

The second level, the frame level, is oriented to communications; it is concerned with synchronous and asynchronous transmission modes and with the XDLC. We should remember that the SDLC is a type of protocol, not a specific one, and that neither it nor the other dialects of bit-oriented protocols (HDLC, ADCCP, etc.) have been standardized by the CCITT.

The third level, the packet level, has two purposes: the routing of packets from node to node and the provision of a data path (virtual circuit or Datagram service); the two functions are broadly known as networking. Performance in this area is the goal of Proposition X.25 adopted by the CCITT; it will be discussed in chapter 14.

The higher levels address themselves to the user. Here the end-to-end connection is important. This may involve only communications, as identified in Figure 12.1, levels 1, 2, and 3, to be precise; but an end-to-end structure might also be carried into the user's own environment. Figure 12.2 indicates ten different end-to-end sublevels, which are defined and qualified by the user's viewpoint.

Having discussed the bit-oriented protocols and the data link control mechanism, let us see what other functions are necessary in the services of a network.

Figure 12.1

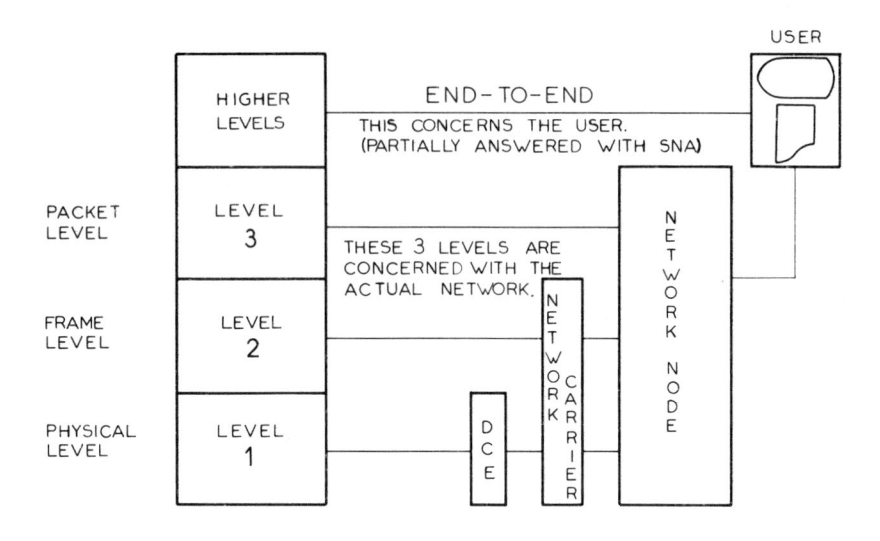

Standards for the Physical Circuit

The modem is hardware, standardized by the CCITT. Broadly, it is any communications processor, or even line, which serves as a terminal's point of entry to a network. The physical standards deal mostly with pins, signals, voltage levels and, generally, the setting up of physical connections through circuit-switching networks.

Until now the modem and DTE have had no effect on the messages; hence, there has been no incentive for the development of logical protocols for them. Electronic signals control the modem, but modems can be made intelligent. What we worry about today is what moves between the computers, namely, the message moving on the wire, which we must study and standardize, and the services offered by the host operating system. To repeat, modems can be made intelligent, and it is therefore worthwhile to review briefly the functions at the modem level and see what exactly is done.

The physical-circuit standards include both electrical characteristics and any others necessary for physically connecting to a network. At present, the American and international physical standards are adhered to by manufacturers of computers and terminals and by distributors of data communications equipment and network services. The two most important bodies setting the standards are the Electronic Industries Association, EIA, in the United States and the CCITT, already mentioned.

Typical of the standards of these organizations are the EIA's RS232, for data circuit interchange and the CCITT V.24, which is essentially equivalent. These standards define the data, the clocking, and the control leads (including the number of pins in a plug) that are used for passing data between DTEs and DECs.

Much effort has been expended in the last few years on defining new standards, which has resulted in a simpler interface. They are called the X series, and they are expected to displace, over the years, the older V series.

The principal new data interchange standard is the X.21. Agreement on it has been obtained, on the whole, between the common carriers and a number of manufacturers, but since it calls for a significant change, an interim recommendation, X.21bis, will be used first. The latter is for implementing the X.21 but retaining the V.24 physical interface. Both the X.21 and X.21bis define physical circuits for three types of service: the leased circuit (private line), direct-call switching, and address-call switching. The leased circuit is intended for continuous connection between a terminal and a network switch processor (such as a packet switcher) or between two terminals. The direct call and address call both involve circuit switching, but a direct call is one that is always switched to the same destination whenever a connection is requested, like a "hot line," and an address call is one in which the destination is designated by the terminal, like a dial-up call but without a phone dial.

Over the next several years the X.21 type of standard will be more and more prevalent. It will give the user a simpler physical interface and also more flexible and faster call-setup procedures.

Second-Level Protocols

We have described the second level of protocols, communications, through the examples of asynchronous, bisynchronous, and XDLC protocols, and we have said that it is a data link control that includes data flow initialization, control termination, and error recovery. The goal is to transfer data over the link sequentially and without error. Once the framing and link management are established, then a set of sequencing rules for exchanging messages and ensuring their correct receipt takes over.

Framing basically is executed at the receiving end of the link. It consists of locating the beginning and end of the bit stream sent over the link. Link management is the process of controlling transmission and reception over links where two or more sources and two or more destinations are active, i.e., connected to the channel in a given direction. The transfer of data is the transmission, sequentially and without error, of user data over the link. Among its features are pipelining, piggybacking, and ACK and NAK.

Data transfer mechanisms or, when they exist, the higher levels, must ensure that the data going out of a link are the same as the data entering. Assuming unintelligent lines, for this to happen at the node it is necessary to have routines for detecting missing or duplicated packets, to give identification numbers to each packet, and to maintain information on and for senders and receivers. The XDLC protocols have a mechanism for this purpose, which is that for each message correctly received a positive acknowledgment is returned, notifying the transmitter of the correct receipt of the message.

A timer helps the system to recover from either messages or acknowledgments received in error; in the latter case recovery can be initiated. This procedure makes for an independence of the data transfer mechanism from the link management mechanism, which permits specific response-time limits to be set.

Framing and Link Management

Framing is performed at the receiving end of the link. It calls for the synchronization of bits (and packets) in the signal being received on a link. The process of synchronization, however, is carried out by the modems (and other interface components) and, as such, is outside the logical aspects of data link control.

In bit-oriented protocols, as we have seen, the bits are grouped in meaningful patterns. This is fundamental for an understanding of control of information by the protocol and for storage into and retrieval from computer memory. These mechanisms make sure of operation over single physical channels with a short delivery time and of sequential transmission such that one message cannot "hop" over another—exactly the property of physical communication channels. They also guarantee sequential delivery from the time of protocol initialization until the failure of either system. Since failures cause a loss of synchronization, sequential delivery is not guaranteed until reinitialization.

Positive-acknowledgment retransmission calls for a block check for bit errors, a unique message-identification number, an acknowledgment (based on the message number), and a timer to recover from outages and unreceived messages, for the purpose of retransmission. The message number is set up along with the initialization procedure. It is then incremented, modulo a constant value (8 for SDLC) for each new message sent. In fact, this constant value minus 1 determines the maximal number of data messages that may be transmitted before acknowledgment is required.

Since the early 1960s and IBM's "byte" standard, the most used common group has been the 8-bit group which finds widespread acceptance from the 16-bit minicomputers to the 32-bit maxicomputers. The byte is a building block and, after byte synchronization has been established, the beginning and end of a message may be located. The key, then, is to achieve byte synchronization, and that is based on the characteristics of the data channel and the desired properties of the user data.

We have spoken of the search for a unique 8-bit sequence and the reason for bit-stuffing and how it operates. Identification of the starting flag marks the begin-

The Nesting of Protocols   153

ning of a message. The end of the message may be found in different ways, through the closing flag with XDLC (hence the need for bit stuffing), or a count of bytes based on a fixed message length (control messages are of fixed length).

Again, the second layer establishes the physical link, conventions handle control of the physical link, and error recovery—and that is data link control. The conventions relating to communications links usually are designed to operate with existing hardware interfaces over full-duplex and half-duplex links and with synchronous, asynchronous, and parallel circuits.

For both multiple access and error control a data link control, or frame-level, protocol must offer a means of exchanging data across the terminal–network interface (once physical connection is made), assuring effective synchronization, controlling errors on a communication link, and operating on circuits with long propagation delays (satellite circuits).

The protocol XDLC does all this and allows two different modes of operations handling, one called asymmetric and the other symmetric. In the asymmetric (unbalanced) mode one DTE acts as the primary, or control, station. Because this particular mode does not go very far in overcoming the queueing problems of polled multipoint operation, an alternative may be used: the symmetric (balanced) mode, with two DTEs. In the latter only two-point operations are considered. Each of the two stations involved acts as primary and secondary at the same time, for which reason this mode is called "symmetric."

Communications protocols are not concerned with the content or routing of messages, nor with how the messages are physically transmitted and received; the higher ones, levels 3 and up, take care of that, and they are the subject of the next section.

The Higher Levels

We have often stated that a network architecture is based on a set of network protocols, each of which is designed to fulfill specific functions. Collectively, they present a layered aspect. The left side of Figure 12.2 repeats the four-way breakdown of Figure 12.1 and is the usual depiction in the literature. It lacks, however, the needed detail. For instance, the third level performs two functions, routing and virtual link (data path), which were better depicted as two layers themselves. A ten-level picture is on the right side of Figure 12.2. Networking now becomes the third and fourth levels, network management, of which packet structure and message format are part. As we shall see in the next two chapters, such considerations deal with call setup and clearing, data transfer and interruption, flow control and reset, congestion control, and restart procedures.

At the user levels the picture becomes less definite, and work is just starting. Not even is there a commonly accepted terminology or a proper division into distinct layers. A given level may deal, for instance, with system protocol; it might

Figure 12.2
Breakdown into layers

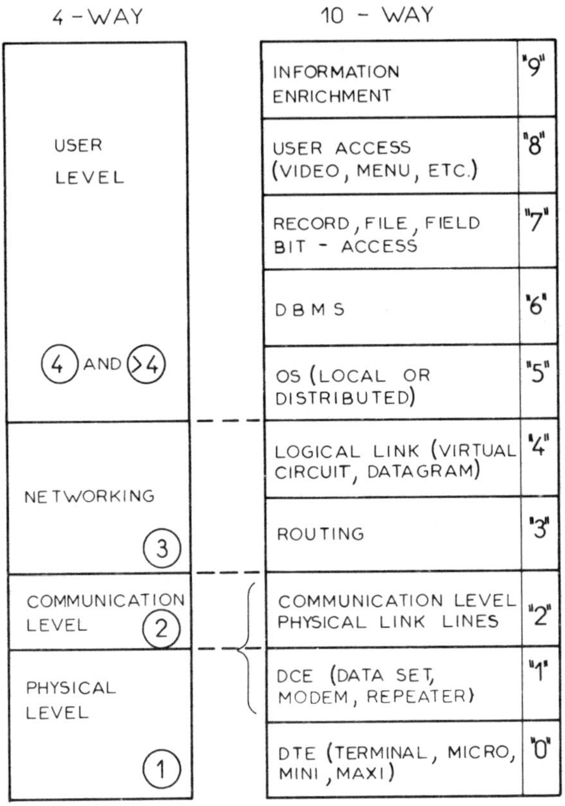

4 - WAY	10 - WAY	
USER LEVEL	INFORMATION ENRICHMENT	"9"
	USER ACCESS (VIDEO, MENU, ETC.)	"8"
	RECORD, FILE, FIELD BIT - ACCESS	"7"
	DBMS	"6"
(4) AND (>4)	OS (LOCAL OR DISTRIBUTED)	"5"
NETWORKING (3)	LOGICAL LINK (VIRTUAL CIRCUIT, DATAGRAM)	"4"
	ROUTING	"3"
COMMUNICATION LEVEL (2)	COMMUNICATION LEVEL PHYSICAL LINK LINES	"2"
PHYSICAL LEVEL (1)	DCE (DATA SET, MODEM, REPEATER)	"1"
	DTE (TERMINAL, MICRO, MINI, MAXI)	"0"

include packet or message assembly and disassembly, priorities, and code definitions and structures. Another, higher up, might deal with users' applications, such as programs, memory access, and device independence; see Figure 12.3.

Some of the reasons that make the higher levels difficult to define are historical: practice grew like weeds. Other reasons are functional: the transition from data processing to data communications has not yet become clear. The functional reasons are fundamental. The problems posed by the development and use of distributed data bases must be taken into account.

A possible structure is shown in Figure 12.4. It separates the user's operations—file access, process, and receiver at window—from the networking and communications. The same user operations might be separated into data transfer, file transfer, and remote job entry, and these might be further divided

Figure 12.3
User environment level(s)

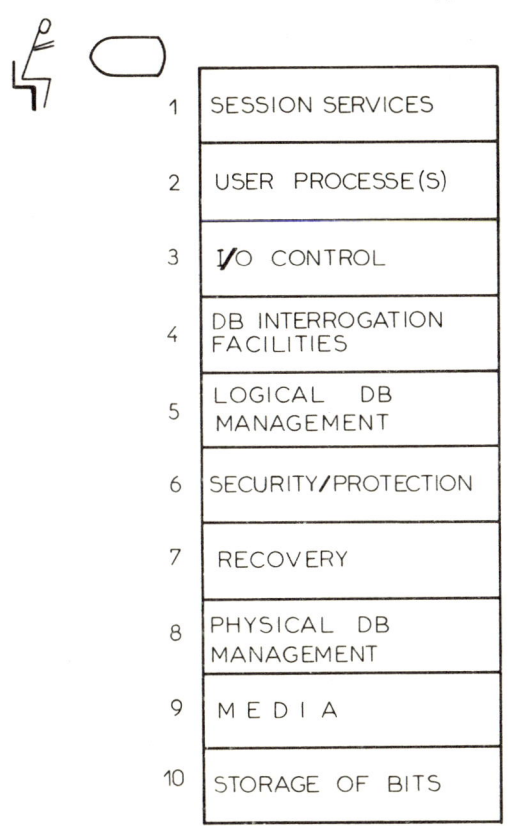

1	SESSION SERVICES
2	USER PROCESSE(S)
3	I/O CONTROL
4	DB INTERROGATION FACILITIES
5	LOGICAL DB MANAGEMENT
6	SECURITY/PROTECTION
7	RECOVERY
8	PHYSICAL DB MANAGEMENT
9	MEDIA
10	STORAGE OF BITS

into graphics and other applications. Subdivisions such as these might benefit the private networks, but they have not been considered by any formal standards organization. One reason is that the people most actively working on standards for data communications do not consider such protocols to be their province, and those working on standards for data processing have not yet recognized the need.

The question of the duplication of functions is also interesting. It may well be that, in the zeal to identify independent levels that might be standardized separately, some duplication is sneaking in. If this is so, experience with implementation should reveal the necessity for change. It is perfectly true that the progress in standards that we appreciate so well today was not achieved easily. Each standard was arrived at a step at a time, after much analysis, review, conversation, and revision. It is remarkable, in fact, how much progress has been made, considering the wide divergence of opinion when work began.

Figure 12.4
(VC, virtual circuit, R, routing—on the basis of this information ID (identification), logical channel, control—the node will calculate, route and establish the virtual circuit; FA, file access; W, window; CRC, cyclic redundancy check; P, process)

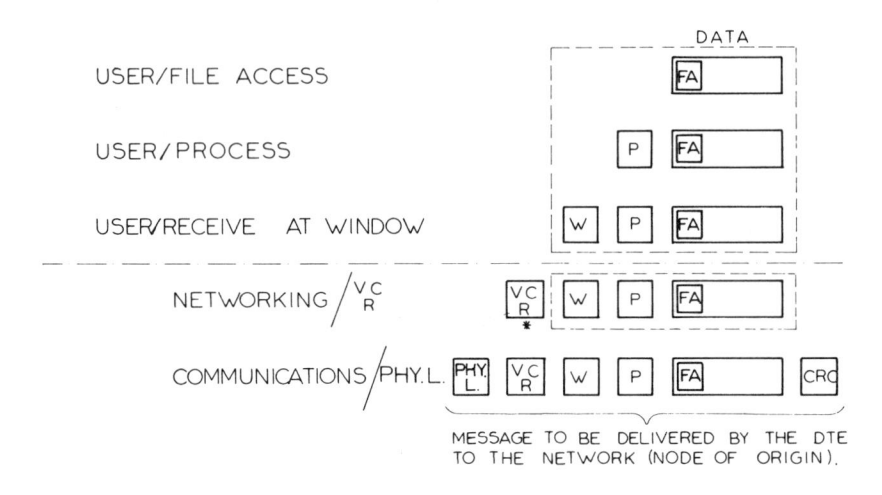

Applications Protocols

Having said that there exist no standards, but only individual solutions, for applications-level protocols, we can now take a constructive view and search to define the component parts in a typical case.

Like the communications protocols, user-level protocols may be broadly subdivided, in this case into a systems level, a data base management level, and an applications level. Each function or mechanism will consist of dialogue (the exchange of information) procedures. The objective will be to perform a specific function oriented toward data bases. The dialogues must conform to a set of rules and have definite message formats. There is nothing new in this approach; protocols have been designed for obtaining access, within the network, to input–output devices and to file services. User-level systems, however, are of many varieties, and therefore the protocols must be designed for efficiency between user systems, within different operating environments.

The routines must have general-purpose file-handling capabilities. They must allow written applications programs to create and maintain data files that may be accessed in different ways. This is difficult, because the exact structure of the information field has not been standardized. (As terminals perform more and more data processing functions, reaching agreements on standards so that different DTEs may work together becomes more urgent and, as time passes by, more complex.) One way of solving the problem of applications standards has been to introduce the concept of a "virtual terminal," which is an imaginary, logically defined terminal with all the attributes of real terminals. Within the context of a virtual terminal, character strings are defined which have a one-to-one correspondence with the features offered by specific real terminals, although the character strings may not be the same as those used by any specific terminal. There are two ways to use the virtual terminals. In one the network operator supplies a translation that transforms the applications protocol of some specific real terminals to that of the network's imaginary standard terminal. In the other the users attach real terminals that have been programmed to operate directly in network virtual-terminal protocols.

At the systems level the logical protocols necessarily deal with data exchange on a totally end-to-end basis, from operating system to applications program or from applications program to applications program. An example of a pending user-level protocol (not always recognized as such) is the so-called packet assembly function and its associated support, the packet assembler, for unintelligent, character-mode terminals. Such terminals are capable of sending only one character at a time, and they have no local processing power to implement protocols of any sort. In Arpanet this support is called a minihost. It is implemented in the terminal interface message processor (TIP), a kind of terminal concentrator, which also serves as a network switch. The network, the user, or a third party also may provide support through a separate terminal-support device such as a front end or a terminal controller that connects with the processor, which in this case is a node, acting only as a switch.

The packet assembler supports the standard networking protocol (in order to communicate through the network). In addition, a higher protocol must deal with terminal support between the packet assembler and the destination host. The host may need to be informed of, or be able to set, such terminal parameters as duplex, code, speed, and packet termination conditions.

In short, layering covers all aspects of communication between system components. Major roles are played by file access and data transfer.

Connecting a user process to a file constitutes access to the information. Depending on its internal structure and the device in which it resides, this connection takes different forms. Hence, the virtual file-access protocol was conceived to define a standard file-access method within the operating system that makes all files accessible to any processes, no matter where they might reside.

Gaining access to remote files may be described as proceeding in three phases: setup, transfer, and termination. Setup involves establishing the connection, exchanging the information necessary to authenticate the user, and addressing the file. We shall speak more about these issues.

13
Networking Functions

As a network architecture has been discussed (and documented), it must offer two levels of visibility, first to the systems expert and, second, to the user, and it includes the following:

>Overall design
>
>Protocols
>
>Message control
>
>Line control
>
>Systems management for communications
>
>Systems management for data base
>
>Systems management for operating system
>
>Applications interfaces
>
>Software standards and supports
>
>On-line maintenance

Networking is the performance of the functions assigned to the network level, level 3 of Figure 12.2. A view of these functions, including the DTE (terminal and host), the operating system, the data base, and the applications programs, is given in Figure 13.1, which identifies the characteristics of the services and also the user and network functions. Properly speaking, the networking functions are two: routing and the establishment of the logical (data) path. Yet these involve a number of faculties to be provided through network commands. We distinguish native commands, those native to the particular set, subset, etc., of an operating system, which are supported by the operating system and are nominally visible instruc-

160   *Data Communications for Distributed Information Systems*

Figure 13.1
Networking functions

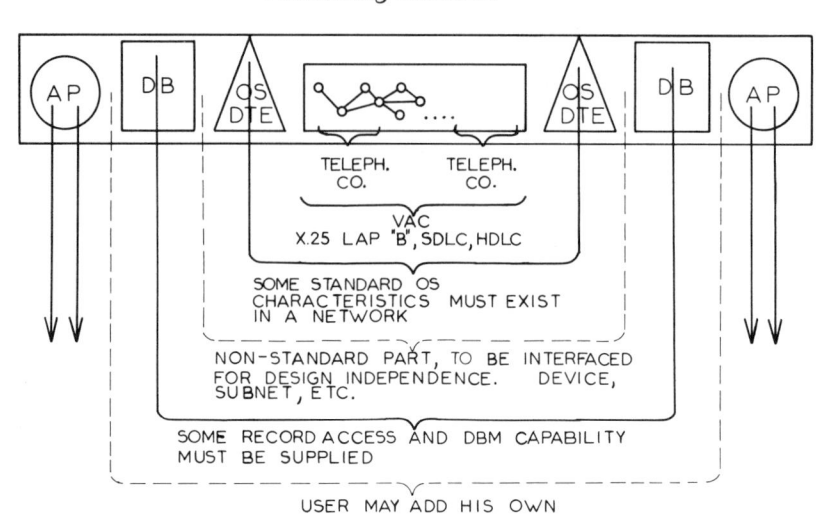

```
┌─────┐ ┌──┐ ┌────┐                              ┌────┐ ┌──┐ ┌─────┐
│ A P │ │DB│ │ OS │    ～～～～                    │ OS │ │DB│ │ A P │
│     │ │  │ │DTE │   o   o  ....                │DTE │ │  │ │     │
└─────┘ └──┘ └────┘                              └────┘ └──┘ └─────┘
                    TELEPH.        TELEPH.
                      CO.            CO.
                           VAC
                    X.25 LAP 'B', SDLC, HDLC
                    ┌────────────────────────────┐
                    │ SOME STANDARD OS           │
                    │ CHARACTERISTICS MUST EXIST │
                    │ IN A NETWORK               │
                    └────────────────────────────┘
                    NON-STANDARD PART, TO BE INTERFACED
                    FOR DESIGN INDEPENDENCE.   DEVICE,
                    SUBNET, ETC.
                    ┌────────────────────────────┐
                    │ SOME RECORD ACCESS AND DBM CAPABILITY │
                    │ MUST BE SUPPLIED                      │
                    └────────────────────────────┘
                         USER MAY ADD HIS OWN
```

    DATA ENTRY, REMOTE BATCH, WORD PROCESSING
(AP) HOST/TERMINAL COMPATIBILITY, DEVICE INDEPENDENCE
    ON LINE TEST AND VERIFICATION, REMOTE MAINTENANCE, UP LINE/DOWN LINE,
    VIDEO SCREEN MANAGEMENT, MENU SELECTION, APPLICATIONS LIBRARY

tions, and network primitives, which are the set of basic commands characterizing the network architecture and its subsets.

A balanced network (not to be confused with a balanced protocol) pays due attention to resources and to objectives. It gives the proper identifications (Table 13.1) and ensures software support to both node-to-node communications for basic transmission functions and end-to-end solutions including the overall transmission integrity.

The host-to-host protocol takes the applications data from the user program and adds on a protocol header. As the message is sent into a computer network, the subscriber-to-network protocol adds on its own protocol information. Then the link control procedure adds on more information, and the network itself adds on subnetwork control fields. It is in the format of the messages flowing through a computer communications network that the concept of a protocol hierarchy is most evident.

Routing

Messages are transmitted in a given form and through an established path, called the route. Routing is the process of creating the route. This is done through software at the level of the node. A fixed route involves one and only one route

Table 13.1
Identifications

User Equipment	Communications Equipment
Packet type	Priority, if any
Session number	Origination address
Send sequence number	Destination address
Receive sequence number	Incarnation number
Author	
Sender	
(Mailbox)	
Annotations	

between two stations in a network. A variable, or dynamic, route presupposes the capability of switching. The routing process should adapt to changes in the network topology and traffic, and this principle influences its functions. The routing program must be efficient enough to run in real time, as the inputs change, it must have a higher priority than data handling, and it must be adaptable to changing conditions in the environment. A network can become badly congested if obsolete routing processes are used in the face of new traffic patterns.

Variable routing coinvolves tables in the memory of the node or switch for the optimal uses of resources, congestion, flow control, delay analysis, and so on. Among the typical routing elements we distinguish the following:

Index to the routing tables

Index to the group code tables (on disc)

Static and dynamic status and parameters for lines

List of destination routing mnemonics for each assigned group code

Corresponding logical identifier for each of the codes used, for further defining the routing

Additional routing information that will yield a logical identifier

List of increments to line and station tables ordered by the logical identifiers

Routing control commands can establish alternate routing, duplicate delivery, and routing report requests, specified by the operating environment.

Point-to-point and multipoint circuits are examples of fixed routing, whereas classical circuit switching might be taken as a type of variable routing, though it does *not* involve the services offered by packet switching.

The procedures to be observed in establishing a routing discipline are deterministic (fixed) and are isolated. Each node probes the communications system but does not share information with the other nodes; this approach can be heuristic. When each node, probing, shares the information with the other nodes, it is distributed. Finally, the control must be centralized. One master node (in Tymnet, for example) calculates for the whole network the variable routing.

Routing procedures must respond to two basic questions. One is what is to be done at the node level, which brings up the two issues of traffic requirements and the "reachability" matrix (Table 13.2). The second question is the criteria of efficiency, among which we distinguish not only cost considerations but also reliability, availability, accuracy, error detection and control, and adaptability.

Adaptive routing is preferable because it offers optimization with respect to delays, shared resources at node and link levels, better throughput, and lower overall cost for about the same service.

A basic reference in terms of routing procedures is pipelining.

Networks must transmit multiple messages between source and destination, calling for high reliability and good throughput. Throughput is studied in relation to distance, source and destination, line speed, and size of packet. For optimization the last of these is balanced with, and limited by, the first two.

Figure 13.2 diagrams the functions of a routing algorithm, in which the data loads, both present and expected, the cost targets set by management, and the network services, all enter into the equation. Evaluation of performance is indivisible from function. The algorithm should be adapted as quickly as possible to the correction of unfeasible routing; it should run uniformly over all the nodes it affects, and the goals of processing should not interfere with routing. If one node starts to send incorrect routing data, the networking as a whole will be disturbed.

Routing must be carefully examined in relation to cost. The elements of cost include the following.

Nodal bandwidth: When a node is designed to perform routing besides other functions (e.g., error correction, processing), then routing must have priority.

Nodal delay: Delay at the node should be evaluated as a function of routing calculation, matrix update, store-and-forward capabilities, and error detection.

Table 13.2
Forms of the Matrix at the Node Switch

Routing Input Data	Routing Output Data
Adjacency matrix Existence of lines between nodes	Reachability matrix Existence of paths between nodes
Traffic requirements Binding of traffic to destination nodes	Traffic assignment Total path perspectives

Figure 13.2

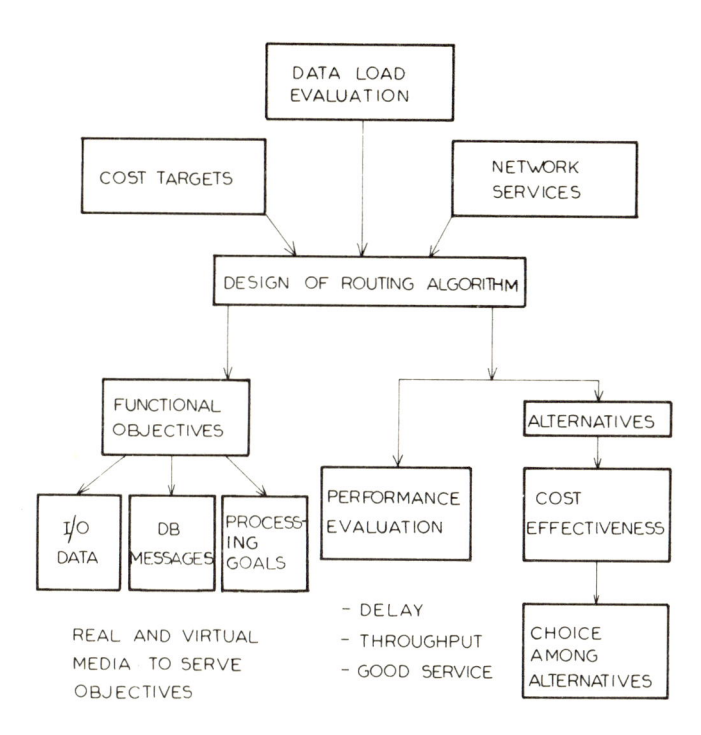

```
                    DATA LOAD
                    EVALUATION
                         |
    COST TARGETS ────────┼──────── NETWORK SERVICES
                         ↓
              DESIGN OF ROUTING ALGORITHM
              ↓              ↓              ↓
         FUNCTIONAL    PERFORMANCE    ALTERNATIVES
         OBJECTIVES    EVALUATION          ↓
         ↓   ↓   ↓                       COST
        I/O  DB  PROCESS-               EFFECTIVENESS
       DATA MESSAGES ING                     ↓
                  GOALS                   CHOICE
                         - DELAY         AMONG
    REAL AND VIRTUAL     - THROUGHPUT    ALTERNATIVES
    MEDIA TO SERVE       - GOOD SERVICE
    OBJECTIVES
```

Nodal storage: The examination of storage takes into account such elements as the reachability matrix, the algorithms, data transit, and input–output buffers.

Line bandwidth: The messages to be routed, the choice of path, the length of message, and the housekeeping information, all condition the line bandwidth and are necessary for the reliable operation of the network.

Line delay: Generally, line delay increases linearly with the frequency of message routing and quadratically with the length of message, but it decreases with the line bandwidth.

The choices to be made are fundamental and are reflected in the network architecture. Figure 13.3 dramatizes this point. The Decnet protocol DDCMP is composed of a header and a trailer, primarily addressed to the communications level; between them are the networking and data sections, the latter consisting of routing and the logical link. Routing thus is included in the architecture; the logical link is discussed in the following section. Notice that other layers, a fifth or an eighth, say, have not yet found themselves in network routines.

Figure 13.3

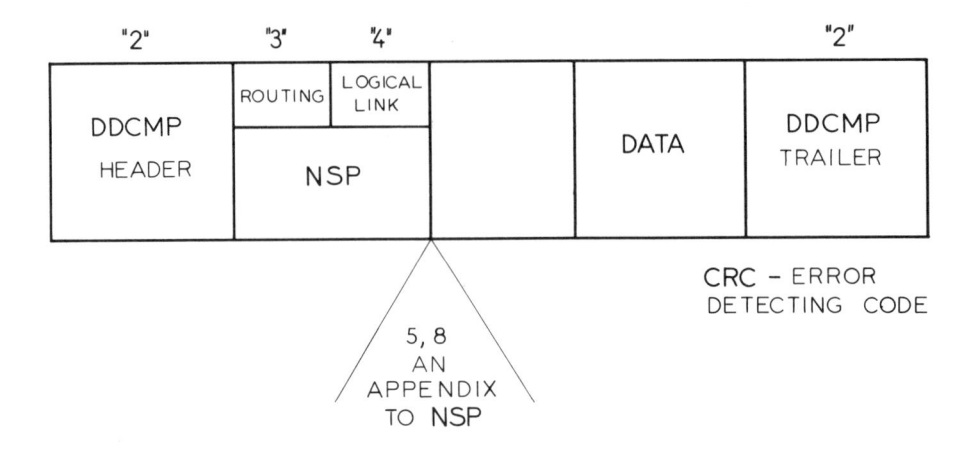

```
  "2"        "3"    "4"                            "2"
┌─────────┬───────┬────────┬──────────┬─────────┐
│         │ROUTING│LOGICAL │          │         │
│ DDCMP   │       │ LINK   │   DATA   │ DDCMP   │
│ HEADER  ├───────┴────────┤          │ TRAILER │
│         │     NSP        │          │         │
└─────────┴────────────────┴──────────┴─────────┘
               ╱      ╲              CRC - ERROR
              ╱  5, 8  ╲             DETECTING CODE
             ╱    AN    ╲
            ╱ APPENDIX   ╲
           ╱   TO NSP     ╲
```

Virtual Circuits and Datagrams

The layer next up from routing imposes a choice between virtual circuits (logical circuits, virtual calls) and Datagrams, the two chief processes possible in packet switching.

With Datagrams solutions are long messages divided into sections (typically of 256 or 512 characters each) individually routed through a packet switching network. Technically, a Datagram is a packet of information sent by one DTE to another as a standalone block traveling pseudorandom routes. The disadvantages of this arrangement are that packets may arrive at destination out of sequence (Figure 13.4) or they may get into an endless loop of nodes and never be delivered; the user, not the network, must cure such troubles. The chief advantage of the concept is that the network is kept simple and the user has more flexibility, since all packets are independent and not associated with a continuous stream of data, as they are in a virtual circuit. Datagrams are also advantageous when two separate networks in the packet-switching mode are interconnected.

Among the issues to be resolved are reasonable flow control at the network interfaces, packet size, identification of Datagrams, possible need for confirmation of delivery, and notice by the network of nondelivery.

For networks operated and maintained by the company that has intelligent terminals, Datagrams are a very workable good solution.

A virtual circuit is superior to Datagrams in that it obeys the X.25 standard and the network, not the user, is responsible for reassembly of messages in the right order and the decision about what to do in case of failure. On the other hand, the

Figure 13.4
The risk with Datagrams

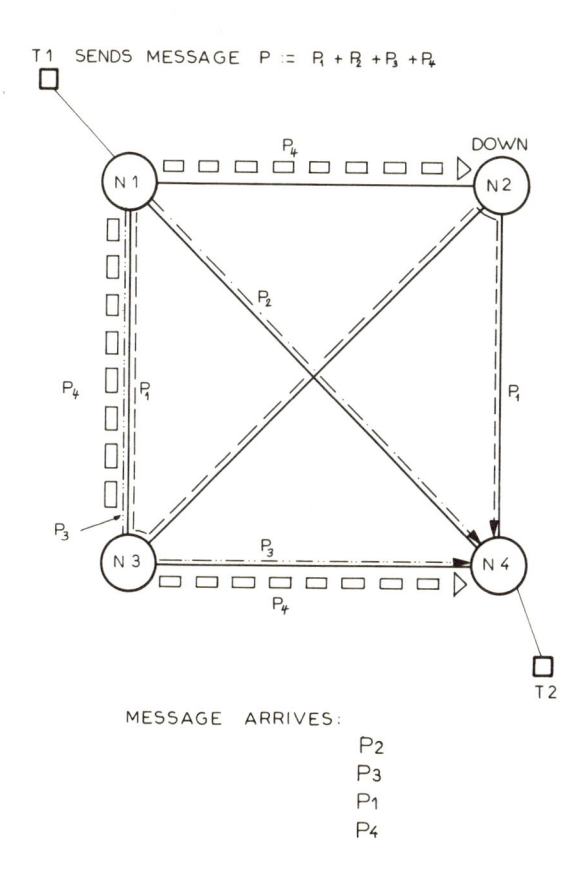

T1 SENDS MESSAGE $P := P_1 + P_2 + P_3 + P_4$

MESSAGE ARRIVES:
P_2
P_3
P_1
P_4

network operating system is very complex. Not only must each network ensure the basics, but it may also provide optional features. The optional facilities for all users of virtual circuits include priority or normal traffic, reverse charging, throughput selection, and closed user group.

A virtual circuit is a bidirectional association between a pair of DTEs; over it all data are transferred in packets.

A permanent virtual circuit is a permanent association between two DTEs; it is analogous to a point-to-point private line.

A switched virtual circuit is a temporary association between two DTEs and is initiated by a "call request" packet to the network.

The calling DTE will receive a response indicating whether the called DTE accepts the call. If for some reason the switched virtual circuit cannot be established, the network will transfer clearing call progress signals to the DTE indicating the reason.

A DTE may have many switched and permanent virtual circuits in operation at the same time over a single physical circuit. The number and mixture of permanent and switched virtual circuits is determined by requirements.

The virtual-circuit call method allocates a logical channel identifier, or logical channel number (LCN), to each call establishment. Packets with the same number then travel through a "virtual circuit" established for this connection, and the network guarantees the order of packet arrival. The virtual call has a better regulated message flow than Datagrams.

Technically, the virtual circuit, the bidirectional association, is characterized in recommendation X.25 as a full-duplex transmission path with integrity and accuracy of data, flow control mechanisms, supervisory and control signaling mechanisms, and sequenced data flow.

With virtual calls a specific path is set up from source to destination at the time a call is set up. If outage or noise occurs, an alternate path may be chosen. Once a path is selected and established, it is used for the transmission. When transmission is completed, it is terminated. Hence there is no risk of messages out of sequence or of endless loops, but more control than with Datagrams needs to be exercised at each node, which in turn means more software and more responsibility laid on the network.

Programs control exchanges between a DTE and another, remote DTE. An applications program prepares a logical message, which it prefixes with the symbolic name of the destination DTE. The data are then transferred to a communication access method queue, where the communication-related preparation of the message will be taken care of. While the channel controller is transferring the message over the channel to the communications control program, the latter handles the network-related functions: segmentation of message, if it does not fit into a single packet, code translation, and gathering of statistics.

Choosing Virtual Circuits or Datagram

The choice between virtual circuit and Datagram largely centers on how much is expected from the network versus how much is expected from the host computers and terminals.

To some extent the virtual circuit is a replacement for the circuit-switching or leased lines largely used at present for data communications purposes. The calling DTE goes through a call-request phase to establish a connection with the called DTE (terminal or computer); this is analogous to dialing into a circuit-switched network. A complete address must be given, just as a complete telephone number must be dialed. Once connection is established, the data phase is entered. When data transfer is complete, the terminals must clear connection before they can place other calls. Packets are delivered in the order in which they are sent. The network takes all the responsibility for the sequence as well as for error detection and recovery.

The Datagram is more like a telegram than a telephone call. Fully addressed, individual packets may be entered into the network at any time by a sending terminal. They may be delivered, however, in random order to the various recipients. The host computers are responsible for sequence and error control.

Carrier organizations worldwide are planning on virtual-circuit service because they believe it reduces disruption for their customers. They also feel that sequence and error control are their functions under the "value-added" coverage.

Supporters of the Datagram say it costs less, since less demand is placed on the network, and they also point out that host computers perform error checking in any case.

Since each approach has its advantages, it is wise to examine each carefully with a view to cost and performance. Congestion is a major factor, especially in internetworking and subnetworking. To study congestion control, for instance, we might experiment with the alternatives, virtual circuits and Datagrams, through simulation and thus establish for each the facilities, constraints, errors, and so on (Figure 13.5). The subject of congestion is covered in the discussion of flow control.

Connection and Transmission

Beyond routing, and within the realm of procedures, the communications mechanism needs a number of basic operational commands. These are structured around the concept of "conversations" between DTEs: connection, transmission, reception, interruption, disconnection.

Figure 13.5
To study congestion control, simulate effects of different methods. Simulation should consider end-to-end and all interleaved resources, including constraints, routing algorithms, and errors.

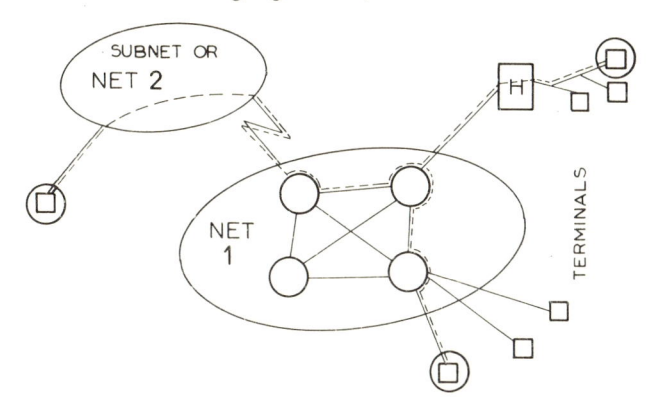

The first command is connection, the creation of a data path (virtual circuit or Datagram) between the requesting DTE and the addressed DTE. The receiving DTE is given the identity of the sender and offered some user's information, a password or identification code, for example. If the request is accepted, the data path will be created. Otherwise, the requested DTE may send back a message specifying why the connection is not possible.

Next is transmission, the actual sending of information over a data path. In packet switching the data paths are full duplex; data may be transmitted by both DTEs simultaneously.

In reception the information from a data path is synchronized with transmission via a flow control mechanism. Both DTEs on the logical link may be issuing transmitting and receiving commands simultaneously, but the flow may be heavier in one direction than in the other, depending on the communications requirements.

Interruption is a notification to the DTE on the other end of the data path of some unusual event or condition. It differs from normal transmission in that it does not require a message-receive message, it usually includes only a small amount of data, and those data must be passed on quickly. Typically, they are passed on via some such expeditious technique as an asynchronous software mechanism.

Disconnection is the destruction of a data path. The command is used on completion of the data exchange; the link is destroyed, and the resources are returned to the network. The command to disconnect may be used prior to actual completion of the connection if there is a lack of resources, or the requested object does not exist, or some other specified condition takes place.

Node-to-Node Protocols

As we have said, a protocol is a formal set of conventions, but in the literature the term is used also in another sense: the provision of the routines necessary to ensure communications between two pieces of equipment, a node-to-node protocol being an example; see Figure 13.6. It will be noted that a process-to-process or a host-to-host protocol is at a higher level than, for instance a node-to-node protocol.

Every time one protocol communicates by means of a protocol at a lower level, the lower accepts all the data and control information of the higher and then performs a number of operations upon it. Usually the lower protocol takes the data and control commands, treats them uniformly as data, and adds on its own envelope of control information.

In the following paragraphs we shall discuss the functions performed by the lower, or node-to-node, protocols and the higher protocols within Arpanet. Arpanet was developed by the Advanced Research Projects Agency of the United States Department of Defense.

Figure 13.6
Each protocol of a higher level is more critical than a protocol of a lower level. A typical hierarchy consists of a number of protocols such as node-to-node for typical transmission functions and end-to-end for dealing with the overall transmission integrity. The applications, or user, level is still higher.
N = network.

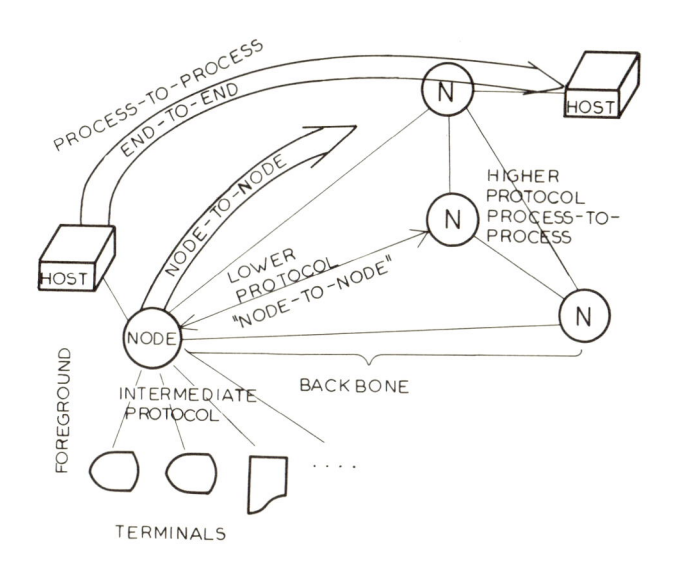

The IMP-to-IMP Protocol

The communications subnetwork of the Arpanet is composed of high-speed circuits and interface message processors (IMP). The IMPs are minicomputers that act as store-and-forward message-switching computers and as front-end processors for host computers.

The lowest protocol of the Arpanet is the IMP-to-IMP, which is for reliable communication among IMPs. It handles flow control and error detection and correction in a manner similar to the basic control procedures discussed earlier. Another of its functions is routing. In the network are at least two paths from every source to every destination. The routing routine in each IMP attempts to transmit a message along that path on which the total estimated transit time is least. The estimates appear in routing tables in the IMPs and are updated dynamically according to delays estimated internally and by neighboring IMPs. Such estimates are based upon length of queue and recent performance of the connecting communication circuit.

The IMP-to-Host Protocol

The protocol on the next level up permits the transmission of messages between IMPs and hosts. Combined with the IMP-to-IMP protocol, it creates a virtual path between host computers. A host computer is a computer connected to the communication subnetwork of the Arpanet that provides computing services to network users.

The IMP-to-host protocol permits a host to transmit messages to other hosts on the network and to receive information on the status of those messages. Furthermore, it constrains the host computer in its network transmission such that it makes efficient use of the available communications capacity without locking out other computers from a portion of that capacity.

Host-to-Host Protocols and Higher

Higher still is the host-to-host protocol, which allows hosts to initiate and maintain communication between distributed computers. A process (e.g., a user program) running on one computer and requiring communication with a process running on a remote computer may request its local supervisor to initiate and maintain the link under the host-to-host protocol.

The protocol utilizes the lower protocols in its implementation. It maintains the responsibility for initiating links between processes, on remote computers and for controlling the flow between those processes.

Let us add that there is no absolute standard today for the host-to-host protocol. Yet we need a way to control the activities end to end and host to host. One protocol, the X.C., defines certain norms, but it is not a standard; it is applied by some users as a special-purpose layer within the host.

The protocols discussed so far were designed as a set of communications primitives for relieving users of the details of operating systems. Still higher stand the user-level protocols.

14

The X.25 Recommendation

A standard protocol enables users with diverse terminals to access the network and to communicate with one another. The wider the use of a given protocol, the broader the movement of data over the network. The basic rule is that all parties clearly understand the sequence of actions appropriate to the data communications. The binary synchonous mode, XDLC, and so on, afford the user access to the network. The XDLC, as we have said, is designed for a network with packet-switching services. It so standardizes the format of the packets that the network has the information necessary for handling each one of them. It cannot, however, perform the tasks discussed in chapter 13, such as routing each packet, checking its path along the network, and delivering it to its destination.

Specifications must be laid out to enable recipients to obtain the degree of accuracy they want. This has been the object of Recommendation X.25 as approved by Study Group VII of the CCITT. The X.25 has gained widespread support from common carriers, manufacturers, and many expanding commercial and governmental enterprises. The standard was derived from diverse, practical experience gained from experimental networks in the United States, France, England, Canada, and Japan. It defines a packet-level protocol that allows a DTE to establish simultaneous communication with one or more DTEs on a network; it also enables the flow of these communications to be controlled.

Its functions include the routing and virtual-circuit procedures, and others, which we shall examine later. The objectives of X.25 may be phrased briefly as the following: universality in the sharing of resources, flexibility among different user systems, error detection and correction end to end in the transfer of data, and the least possible concern of the user with the mechanics of routing, monitoring, and so on. In sum, the layers to which it addresses itself are those we discussed in chapter 13.

172   *Data Communications for Distributed Information Systems*

The X.25 is the highest level in network operations and specifies the manner in which users establish, maintain, and clear calls through the network. It details the manner in which control information and user data are structured into packets. The packet header contains control and addressing information; this is most important, because a single physical circuit can thus support communication to numerous terminals and hosts at the same time. It is not necessary that the network and the DTEs (the terminals or hosts) work on the same protocol; see Figure 14.1. The network may work with X.25, but the terminals, or at least some of them, may be asynchronous or binary synchronous, in which case interfaces (gateways) are provided. The opposite may be the case, in which the DTEs are working on the X.25 but the subnetwork to which they are attached follows a different discipline.

What Is X.25?

In preceding chapters we have noted that the DTE (terminal, host) needs a hardware interface, the DCE, that this interface is standardized by the CCITT, and that it connects the DTE to the physical (communications) link. For the physical link there is a management discipline, provided in packet switching by the data link control, the XDLC, and several of its dialects, the SDLC, HDLC, ADCCP, and others. Let us remember that in their original version they were unbalanced

Figure 14.1
The internal subnetwork protocol may not be X.25, since the subnetwork tends to optimize transit time. Gateways (repacking) introduce possibilities of error.

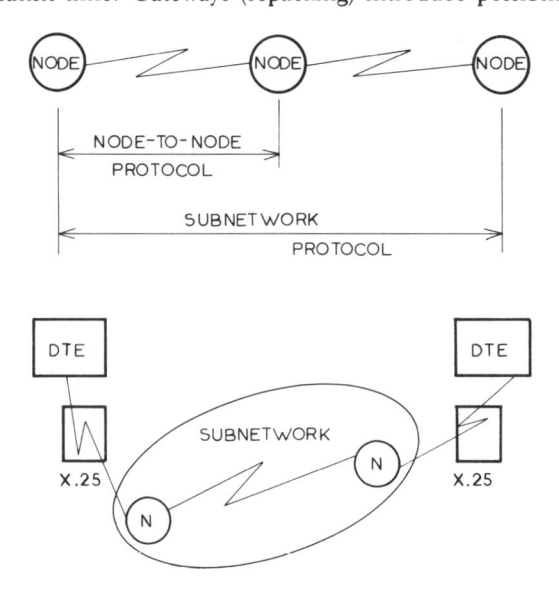

protocols and that LAP B was developed as a balanced version of data link control. Further, as we know, communications services alone, though necessary, are not enough; we need network services, routing being one of them. Thus physical link management and network services interface between the communications devices on one side and the user programs and data bases on the other; see Figure 14.2. (Once more we should note that X.25 does not meet the requirements of access to data and that higher disciplines are needed for that.)

We have already discussed the component parts of the bit-oriented frame-level protocol. The data packet format under X.25 is composed of the packet header, including packet type and logical channel number (identifier), and the user data. The logical channel number locally identifies the virtual circuit at the interface between the DTE and the network. Different channel numbers are used for a given virtual circuit to two or more DTEs. They are chosen independently. The choice of a logical (or virtual) circuit automatically means that the logical channels used at each end are occupied. This does not prevent other logical channels between the DTE and the network from being free. More precisely, the logical channels associated with permanent virtual circuits are permanently occupied; therefore the associated numbers cannot be used for any other purpose, although the bandwidth is still available for other calls. The logical channels associated with switched virtual circuits, though, are initially all free and could be used by the DTE to originate new calls or to receive incoming calls from the network. The logical channel number, then, identifies all data transfer, supervision, and flow control packets associated with that call, until the call is cleared. When all logical channels designated for use with switched virtual circuits are occupied, a new call cannot be established until a data communication is terminated and one of the channels again available.

Figure 14.2

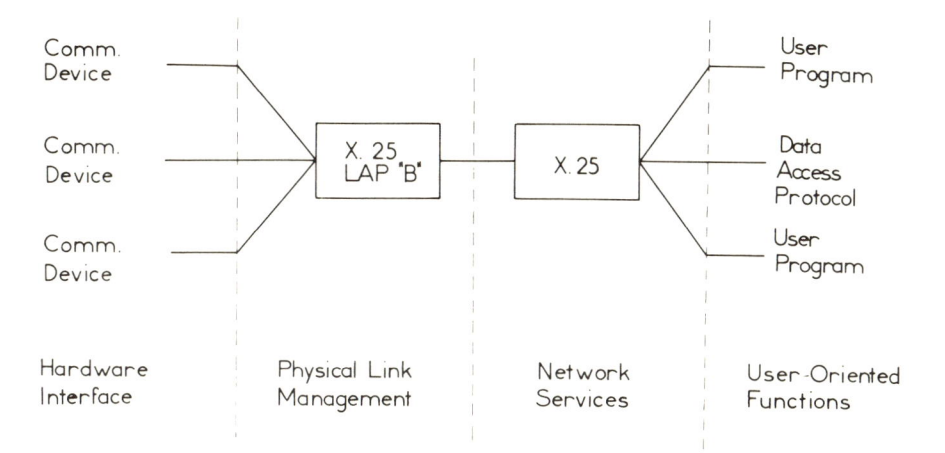

```
Comm.                                                   User
Device                                                  Program

Comm.                    X.25                           Data
Device                   LAP "B"          X.25          Access
                                                        Protocol

Comm.                                                   User
Device                                                  Program


Hardware        Physical Link         Network        User-Oriented
Interface       Management            Services       Functions
```

Call establishment starts with a "call request" by a DTE (Figure 14.3); this, too, is a packet. The logical channel number chosen by the DTE is 12 bits long. Another byte is dedicated to "type" the call request, say. Network address of the called DTE is composed of a string of binary coded decimal digits, the length of which is indicated and depends on whether the call is to another DTE or to a network node; if the former, the addresses are 8 decimal digits long. The facility field is present only when the DTE requires some indication in the call request packet. User data follow the facility field; they may contain any number of bits up to a given maximum length. (Datapac, for example, has a maximum of 16 bytes.)

To repeat: the first 2 bytes of information in the packet header or, more accurately, the first 4 bits and the next 12 bits, identify the destination of the packet; this is the logical channel number or logical channel identifier. The 4-bit field marked "ID" in Figure 14.3 can have only one of two values: either 0001 or 1001. The value 0001 signifies that the packet is being transmitted to an individual terminal or computer directly; the value 1001 is used for sending a transmission to a device via a cluster controller.

The two fundamental types of virtual circuit are the permanent and the switched. In the permanent one, linking terminal to computer, for instance, a

Figure 14.3
Call request packet format. The bits are transmitted starting with the low order, the bytes starting with number 1.

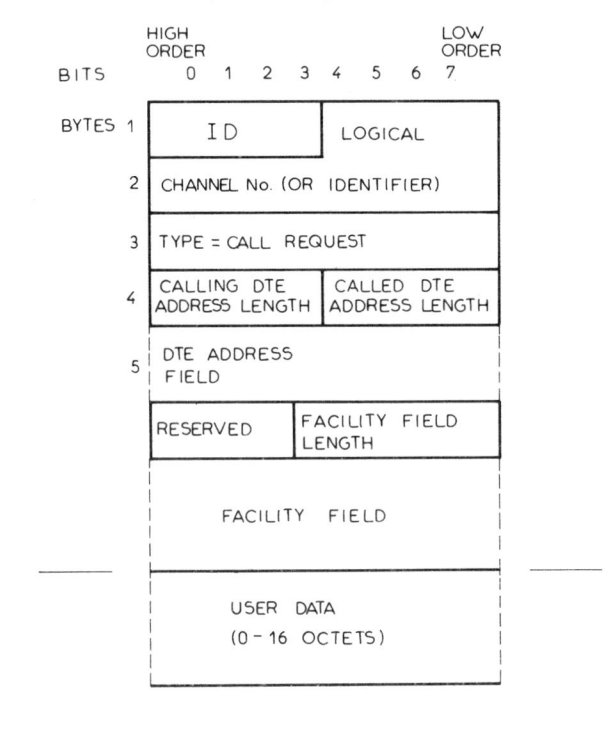

logical channel number is assigned by agreement at the time the service is initialized. In the switched, the circuit is under control of the DTE and of the network (dynamic solution); hence a mechanism is needed, and this is the call request packet, which lets the user place a call to a specific DTE. Each such attachment is assigned a number, as in the telephone network.

The call request packet assigns a currently available logical channel number, which is active for the duration of the call. It is short, compared to the generally much longer DTE attachment number; at the completion of the call, it is released for reuse.

With 12 bits available for the channel number, up to 4,096 virtual circuits may be supported simultaneously, meaning across a single physical connection to the network. (X.25 is, in a sense, the equivalent of a packet-oriented time-division multiplexer offering, in theory at least, up to 4,096 simultaneous logical connections.)

The control field within the packet header plays a role similar to that of the control field in the link header. It indicates whether the packet is a call setup request or a data transfer and whether an interruption of the device at the other end is required or the flow of data should be temporarily stopped. It also is used in error detection and control and in the handling of exceptional conditions.

The Communications Session

An X.25 data communications session is a typical transmitter–receiver dialogue: the transmitter first issues an inquiry, the receiver responds positively, the transmitter then transmits the text, the receiver continues to respond positively, and the process continues until a mutually understood end sequence occurs. If errors are found in the transmission, the packet is retransmitted.

Some networks offer further facilities to subscribers, such as a priority class of traffic, closed user group, and reverse charging. Reverse charging, for instance, may be specified in the call request packet; then the called DTE will be charged for the call *if* it accepts that call.

One outstanding advantage of the standard is built-in error-free data transmission: by means of error detection and retransmission techniques the network offers extremely low probabilities of undetected errors. The standard helps extend the network's internal protocol right up to the host computer interface by establishing, maintaining, and clearing calls and by managing the flow of data to and from the network, but it does not attempt to specify the characteristics of the virtual-circuit service.

Because a packet network can perform character set translation, totally dissimilar and hardware-incompatible terminals can communicate with each other. A basic cost advantage appears to derive from cluster configurations, when a moderate number of terminals are simultaneously connected through the network to various processes.

When a calling terminal or host wishes to establish a virtual circuit, the called DTE will receive an incoming call packet on a logical channel. This includes the logical channel number chosen by the network and used for the duration of the call, the network address of the calling DTE, and any facilities requested by the caller. A DTE actuates acceptance by transmitting a "call accepted" packet specifying the same logical channel number as in the incoming call packet. If it refuses the call, it transmits a clear request packet with the appropriate channel number. After the virtual circuit is established, data transfer takes place in both directions in accordance with data transfer procedures. When the transfer is completed, either DTE may issue a clear request packet. The logical channel reverts to the free condition on receipt of a "clear confirmation" packet from the node.

Notice the following: Data packets can be transferred on a virtual circuit only after that circuit has been established. Data packets transmitted before a call is accepted will be treated as an error condition by the network. Data packets transmitted after clearing procedures have been initiated by the remote DTE will be discarded by the network.

Data packet transfer is guaranteed (in terms of "send sequence") through a sequential numbering module 8. The first data packet to be transmitted is numbered 0. This numbering makes both the network node and the DTE able to detect the loss of data packets and to control flow across the modem. The send sequence is the P(S). Each data packet also carries a packet receive sequence number, P(R), which authorizes the transmission of additional data packets.

Figure 14.4 integrates what has been discussed so far by comparing the SDLC line access protocols with the X.25 discipline. It will be appreciated that the packet header (simplified in this diagram to its fundamentals) adds very little in terms of overhead, so the overall efficiency of packet-switching protocols is well argued.

Comparing Protocols

Digital control protocols are becoming standardized, and the packet protocol is favored by advanced users and for good reasons. The standard interface discipline it imposes more than offsets any inefficiencies or extra costs. The packet level, as discussed in the preceding section, is very efficient. The frame level (XDLC) adds some extra bytes but compares very favorably with the now aging binary synchronous protocol.

It is exactly because of these advantages that many users are attracted to XDLC, but bisync will be with us for some time to come. The real reason is investments: it is not conceivably possible to change all at once all the DTEs that are installed and operating now. Other reasons are functional: efficiency is usually a matter of volume (economies of scale play a major role), and since the more advanced protocols (packet switching for example) require sophisticated equipment, volume production and consumption are the best way to reduce unit costs. Economies of scale and economies of function are not uniform or self-evident. The Bank of

The X.25 Recommendation 177

Figure 14.4

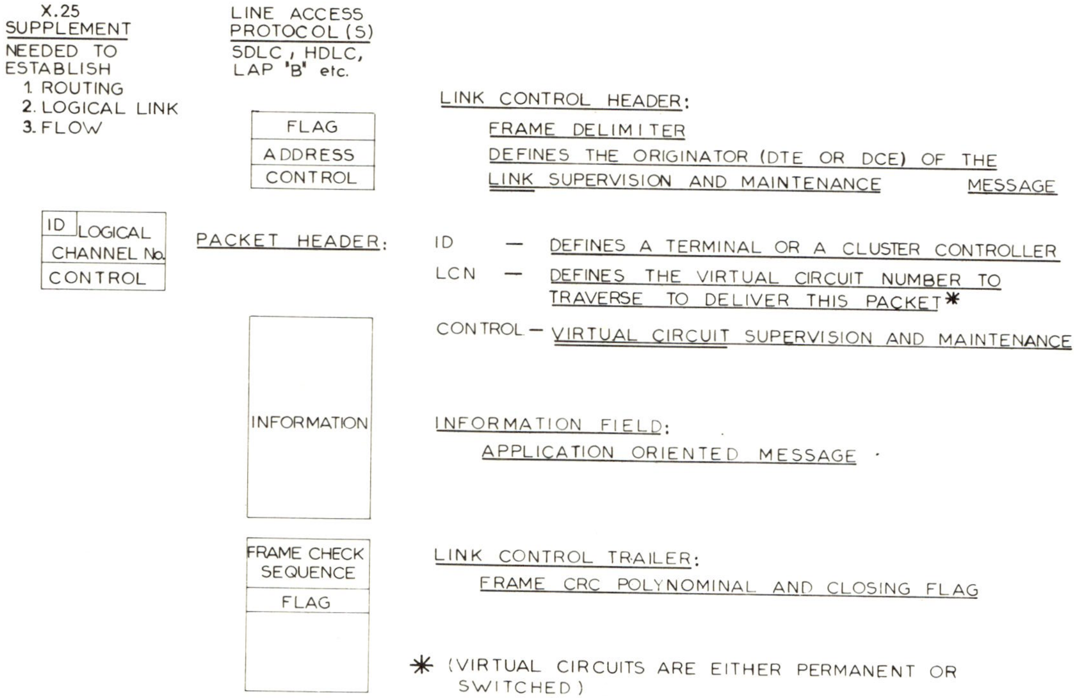

X.25 SUPPLEMENT NEEDED TO ESTABLISH
1. ROUTING
2. LOGICAL LINK
3. FLOW

LINE ACCESS PROTOCOL(S)
SDLC, HDLC, LAP 'B' etc.

| FLAG |
| ADDRESS |
| CONTROL |

PACKET HEADER:

| ID | LOGICAL CHANNEL No |
| CONTROL | |

| INFORMATION |

| FRAME CHECK SEQUENCE |
| FLAG |

LINK CONTROL HEADER:

  FRAME DELIMITER
    DEFINES THE ORIGINATOR (DTE OR DCE) OF THE
    LINK SUPERVISION AND MAINTENANCE MESSAGE

  ID — DEFINES A TERMINAL OR A CLUSTER CONTROLLER
  LCN — DEFINES THE VIRTUAL CIRCUIT NUMBER TO
        TRAVERSE TO DELIVER THIS PACKET*

  CONTROL — VIRTUAL CIRCUIT SUPERVISION AND MAINTENANCE

INFORMATION FIELD:
  APPLICATION ORIENTED MESSAGE.

LINK CONTROL TRAILER:
  FRAME CRC POLYNOMINAL AND CLOSING FLAG

* (VIRTUAL CIRCUITS ARE EITHER PERMANENT OR SWITCHED)

178   *Data Communications for Distributed Information Systems*

America uses three distinct disciplines for its distributed information system network:

Packet switching, among modules and among the four computers in the same module

Binary synchronous communications for the TRW banking terminals

Asynchronous communications for the money dispensers

Exactly because we foresee that packet and binary synchronous protocol structures (and also asynchronous ones) will intermix in networks, we foresee the need of gateways. The same is true of segmenting and grouping packets, between packet-switching networks operating at different packet sizes. In other words, networks of links and processes will need to interface various protocols. Most large organizations, for example, will have a line that has a binary synchronous terminal on it and will want to plug it into a larger network that is basically a packetized ring network. Asynchronous requirements, on the other hand, are not only survivals of older, starlike networks but also newer ones. Most cash dispensers are asynchronous, and that goes for point-of-sale terminals too. What is more, the numbers of both those terminals and automatic teller machines will substantially increase as time passes.

Since applications environments vary widely, for the necessary flexibility, protocols must have two basic modes of operation: the normal response mode, projected for centralized systems in which a primary station polls the secondary station, and the asynchronous response mode, for situations in which either station may transmit at any time.

Protocols are continuously undergoing revision, the balanced mode of operation being an example. We defined balanced or symmetric operations as those in which neither station is designated as primary or secondary. Let us recapitulate:

The XDLC is a type of protocol, not a specific one; it is designed to serve the communications layer.

X.25 is a superstructure, compatible with and higher than the XDLC: it is designed to serve the networking layer.

The link access protocol LAP A was unbalanced: it had primary and secondary stations.

The LAP B was balanced: it had only primary stations.

Because various protocols are used in a network, gateways must be implemented.

The X.25 standard describes several levels of interfacing. At the physical level the electrical connection between the modem and the DTE is defined. Hence X.25 takes advantage of the standard X.21 for full-duplex synchronous transmission. At the communications level the X.25 interface describes the link access protocol that is responsible for the management of the link between the DTE and the modem.

The X.25 Recommendation

At this layer X.25 uses a subset of XDLC for framing, transparency, error detection, flow control, and so on.

At the next level X.25 describes a packet level procedure for control of virtual calls through a public data network. It may even describe a packet assembler and disassembler function. The latter involves a procedure within the node. Its goal is the handling of virtual terminals.

Rules can and have been established for the use of mixed protocols; it is not necessary to have a uniform protocol throughout. We can use locally those protocols which are the most efficient, given the application.

Flow Control

We have seen how both routing and virtual circuits are assured by the X.25 protocol and how this is done, but we must now see that routing and the establishment of a virtual circuit, though necessary, are not enough; flow must be controlled.

A basic difficulty in logical link control is how to match the sender's transmission rate with the receiver's ability to accept traffic. A good solution is an explicit allocation of resources. The receiver clearly notifies the sender of its ability to accept traffic. Flow control aims to prevent the sender from overflowing the receiver's buffers by not transmitting data too fast for the receiver. Sequence and flow control procedures can, in fact, be combined, the latter using the sequence numbers for received ready (RR) and received not ready (RNR) administered by the virtual circuit.

Flow control leads to the subject of what are called windows. A window is a logical path to be opened between two processes before data is passed (as used in flow control management). Determining window size is important. The size should indicate the willingness of the receiving process to provide buffer space (Figure 14.5); in different terms, the window size might represent exactly the available buffer space that the user has offered for receiving (this is the conservative strategy), or it could reflect a buffer space expected on the basis of previous allocations (the optimistic strategy).

A window operation is presented in Figure 14.6. The window size K permits a maximum of 6 packets to be outstanding at a given time. The lower window edge, or last P(R) received, is 3. With the transmission and acknowledgment of packets, the lower and upper window edges rotate. A receive ready packet indicates the willingness to receive K data packets. A receive not ready packet indicates a temporary inability to accept additional data packets.

A reset procedure reinitializes the flow control on a virtual circuit to the state it was in when the virtual circuit was established. All data and interrupt packets in transit at the time of resetting are, then, discarded. The reset procedure may be initialized by a DTE by transmitting a reset request packet. When the node com-

180   *Data Communications for Distributed Information Systems*

Figure 14.5
An early computer data ring for optimal flow. Similar solutions may be used today in networks, for windows.

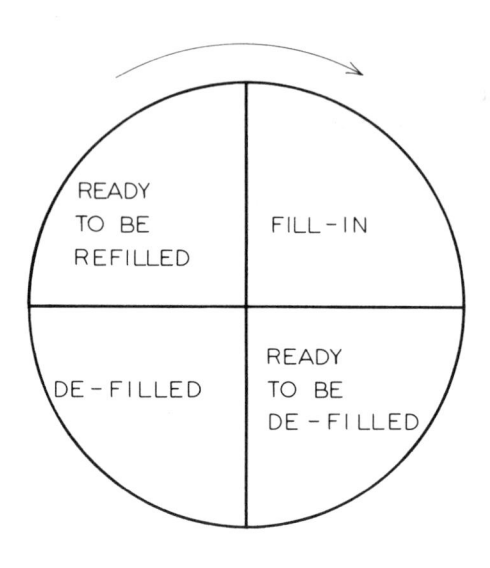

Figure 14.6
Window size $K = 6$

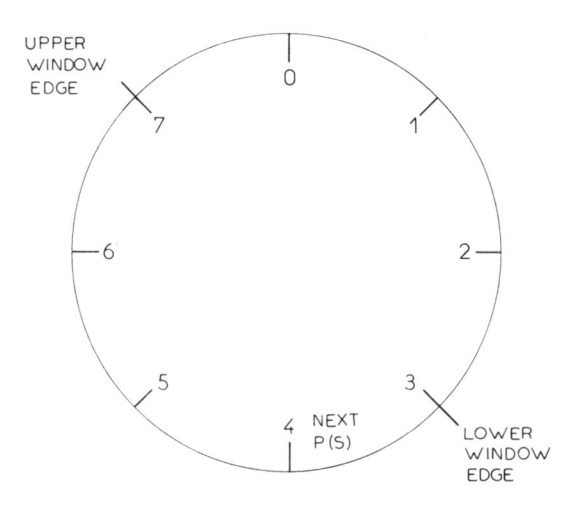

municates that the virtual circuit is being reset, it is done through a reset, or restart, indication packet.

The terminal or host uses a restart procedure as a mechanism for recovery from failures. A restart request packet is equivalent to a clear request on switched virtual circuits. A node issues a restart indication packet when the user has failed to follow the correct restart procedure or when the network has experienced a catastrophic failure.

Goals in Flow Control

A good flow control scheme must handle a long spectrum of problems that result from preventing buffer overflow in the receiver. As we have seen, the flow control strategy should consider the buffer space offered by a receiver (user). The goals and methods of flow control are as follows.

End-to-end: Flow control for a particular level of protocol should be exerted at the point closest to the final destination.

Congestion prevention: The flow control strategy should prevent queueing of messages in the protocol module so that module resources may handle messages that have a high probability of being delivered immediately.

Deadlock prevention: When congestion does occur, resources must be available to handle traffic-clearing messages.

Interplay with subnetwork: The interface between modules representing levels of protocol often causes flow control problems.

Such mechanisms may exist at each level of protocol as well as between levels of protocols. To work properly, they assume that "flow control information" is passed from the receiver to the sender. The information ordinarily reflects the receiver's ability to buffer data. It often also represents a count of some resources: a unit of buffering of a message queue element. But, as usual, reduced to its fundamentals, the mechanism reflects the interplay between available resources and the demands for their use.

Congestion Control

Congestion is a prominent concern in the design of message- and packet-switching networks. It occurs when the rate of arriving traffic exceeds the service rate provided by the network. Control procedures are of two types. End-to-end control places restrictions directly at the message source by monitoring the number of messages on the logical connection "source to destination." Local control places restrictions on the number of messages at each node of the logical connection between a source and a destination node. It has been shown that neither end-to-end control nor local control alone is sufficient to manage congestion but the two combined can potentially solve the congestion problem. Experiments have demonstrated what alternative solutions might offer. For instance, probabilistic routing is more successful than deterministic routing for congestion in locally controlled networks. The inclusion of random routing may enhance its usefulness by furnishing an analysis of alternative routing, but the most critical consideration is the steady collection of factual and documented traffic statistics.

Internetworking

The emerging network architectures, such as IBM's Systems Network Architecture, SNA, and Digital Equipment Corporation's Decnet, can ultimately coexist with public packet networks and private user's systems, given the required interfaces (gateways, internetworking nodes). An example is the recent implementation of an SNA interface by IBM World Trade for the Datapac network in Canada and the Transpac in France. IBM's network interface adapter (NIA) generates a polling routine that makes a 3270 cathode ray tube think it is being interfaced with the network. The adapter takes information from the terminal and translates it into the protocol for data link control, for transmission over the packet network. A protocol thus must be defined for signaling and data exchange.

It is advisable, however, to use operational features compatible with X.25. The following would be desirable for internetworking connections as well as for the host interface.

Extended numbering at the link level would permit more unacknowledged packets to be outstanding on the circuit; this is particularly important for long-delay channels such as satellite links.

Extended numbering at the packet level, or variable packet size per call, also would address the long-delay problem.

Accounting information on call setup and clearing packets would allow a schedule of international tariffs to be established.

It is proper to add that, where network interconnection is concerned, many problems remain. The international standardization effort is still lagging. A new common base of reference, X7X, addresses itself only to the signal level; it is a superstructure of X.25. Any new recommendation, however, that is to become an end-to-end standard must tackle the user-level protocols.

Datagrams as a choice over virtual circuits must also be settled. From certain viewpoints it is simpler to interconnect nets through them than through virtual calls; they have the lesser requirements for support services, logical complexity, and buffering. If virtual calls are adopted, the gateway has to keep status reports for, say, 4,096 of such calls, and this can be a heavy duty. Datagrams do not pose such requirements, though each one may need a fair amount of header and trailer

The X.25 Recommendation   183

data to support itself. This leads some to believe that virtual calls have the greater conceptual simplicity.

Acknowledgment, too, needs to be redefined for internetworking (Figure 14.7). As it now stands, an ACK will carry to DTE A a message that is valid only within the borders of Network I, to which it belongs. Documentation is another difficulty. Poorly documented networks may send an ACK, but we don't really know to what extent that ACK is valid.

Other problems arise from technical questions. For instance:

How to exchange more data than a given network can carry (under, say, X.25).
How to charge for internetworking calls.
How to effect conversion from one packet length to another (X7X specifies 128 octets as a maximum, but some networks, e.g., Datapac, allow 256).
How to "split up" the long messages (it should be done within the X7X framework).
How to assign the window sizes between internetworking points.

Figure 14.7
Here ACK means to DTE A that it is all right only to the border of Network I to which it belongs.

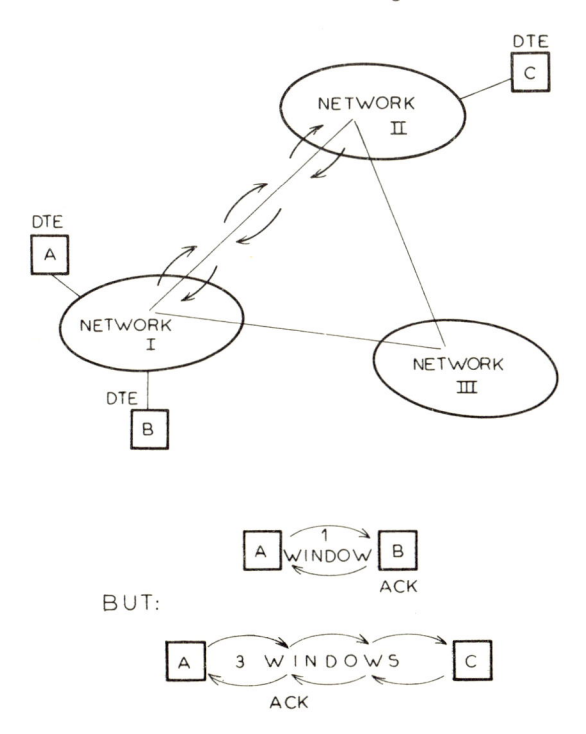

We might also point out that the experimental networks are more interested in the development of X7X than the commercial value-added carriers, and this somewhat dampens user interest.

Several of the solutions being considered today are based more on the circumstances of business transactions than on economics, service to the user, technology, and good sense.

15

Session and Presentation Control

References have been made in preceding chapters to the advantages of layering. Each layer achieves its functionality both by itself and by making use of the services of the layer just below it. Further, the modularity offered through layering helps ensure that a layer's services are independent from the protocols or implementations actual at that level. A level's particular protocols and their implementation are transparent to the user of that level, which makes it possible to replace them, when appropriate, with other protocols.

Reference also has been made to the fact that, at least so far, there has been no standardization for layers beyond networking, and that standardization is needed to make every process addressable to every other, so that they may exchange information independently of their location, the logical or physical characteristics, and the specific goals at the time of the needed exchange. These are the background reasons. The possible solutions outlined in the preceding chapter aim to ease the dialogue at the user's site, but it is also good to look at the work the standards institutes and associations are putting forward.

An effort in the right direction has been undertaken by ANSI (with the participation of IBM, AT&T, Honeywell, Digital Equipment Corporation, Burroughs, Univac, CDC, and Xerox, among the manufacturers, and the United States government and Boeing among the users). ANSI divides the functions beyond networking into three major blocks, which are session control, presentation control, and process control, the last embracing the actual handling of applications programs, data base management, and file access.

Figure 15.1 goes a step beyond the ANSI definition: session and presentation control are kept intact, but process has been broken down into three layers, in anticipation of future needs.

Notice that networking is, as always in this book, divided into two layers. The definition of data transport has been enlarged, too.

Figure 15.1
Interfaces

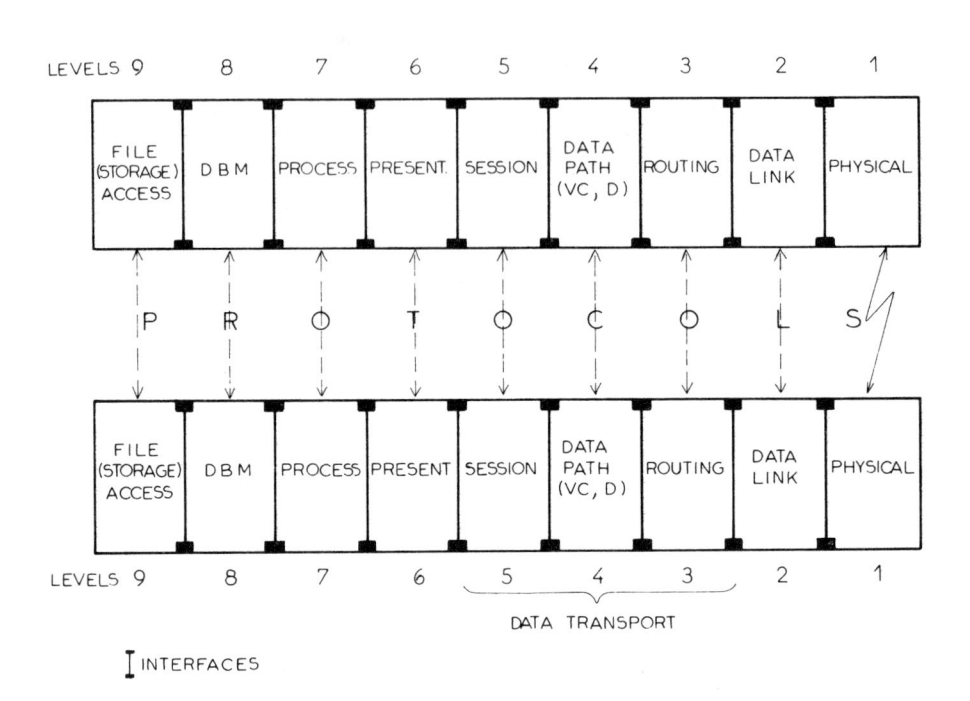

[Figure: Two rows of protocol stack boxes connected by PROTOCOLS arrows. Top and bottom rows each show Levels 9 through 1: FILE (STORAGE) ACCESS | D B M | PROCESS | PRESENT. | SESSION | DATA PATH (VC, D) | ROUTING | DATA LINK | PHYSICAL. Levels 5 through 3 of the bottom row are bracketed as DATA TRANSPORT. A legend shows ⊥ INTERFACES.]

Some of the definitions advanced by ANSI and applicable at all levels of reference are the following:

DTE: an addressable endpoint at a location, i.e. a place where things happen

Connection: a logical association capable of transferring data between DTEs or processes

Data unit: a quantity of data and control information transferred as a unit over a connection

Data assurance unit: a quantity of data whose successful transfer over a connection is acknowledged

Data flow unit: a quantity of data whose transfer over a connection has been authorized

Data mapping unit: an entity used to map a data unit of the next level up onto a data unit of the current level

The Purpose of Session Control

Session control takes care of the logical aspects of transmission from one process to another, whether local or remote. Let us say that process A wishes to communicate with process B. This may be done through a terminal addressing the central memory of a mainframe or take place within the host. Whichever the case may be, it will, most likely, involve routines in the applications program library, routines in the utilities library, and data base elements. The operator of a DTE (and the program running in the central memory) will need assistance at the session level or else should be clearly knowledgeable about these three things. The session establishment and control commands are oriented to applications programming, but the data entered or removed and their form of presentation follow the specifications of file design and data base management.

Functionally, rules and supports are necessary to control and interpret the operation of devices at the work station, to execute commands on behalf of the process or processes, to receive commands from the corresponding process or processes associated with the session, and to pass them on to the process of the work station in question.

Typically, in a communications environment each work station has a mailbox name. Process A says to the session control, "I give you the mailbox number, but you must do the rest." Session control must establish whether this is to be a one-way or two-way operation and the degree of priority. The set of rules by which a session is established, maintained, and terminated covers the logical aspects of the transmission: process to process, local, or remote. Control information must assure log on and log off and a number of programmatic interfaces. The latter regard the rules by which a person–information dialogue is interpreted, so as to make available to the user the data asked for. To send, receive, establish, maintain, and terminate are activities largely falling within the scheme of Figure 15.2. Session control complements the networking operations (data path, routing) and provides the section of transport control nearest the user.

This brings us to the subject of functionality and of interfaces. Transport control aims, overall, at a reliable transfer of data between endpoints, across a communications network. The virtual circuit of Datagram provides the interconnection services with a packet-switched network. Session routines see to it that control is exercised over a person–information dialogue session.

It follows logically that the information given to session control must be enough for a decision whether this is a local or a remote request, to call the right programs into play. If it is not a local request, then session control must establish a conversation with the fourth level, data path (refer again to Figure 15.1), actuating the proper interface, and since next to the data path lies the routing, the third level, it must also look into that, for information about routing patterns and for specifications. Then it must face the other way and look at the sixth level, presentation. At this interface, session control causes the reliable transfer of data between the presentation control modules supporting processes in a network of work stations or

Figure 15.2

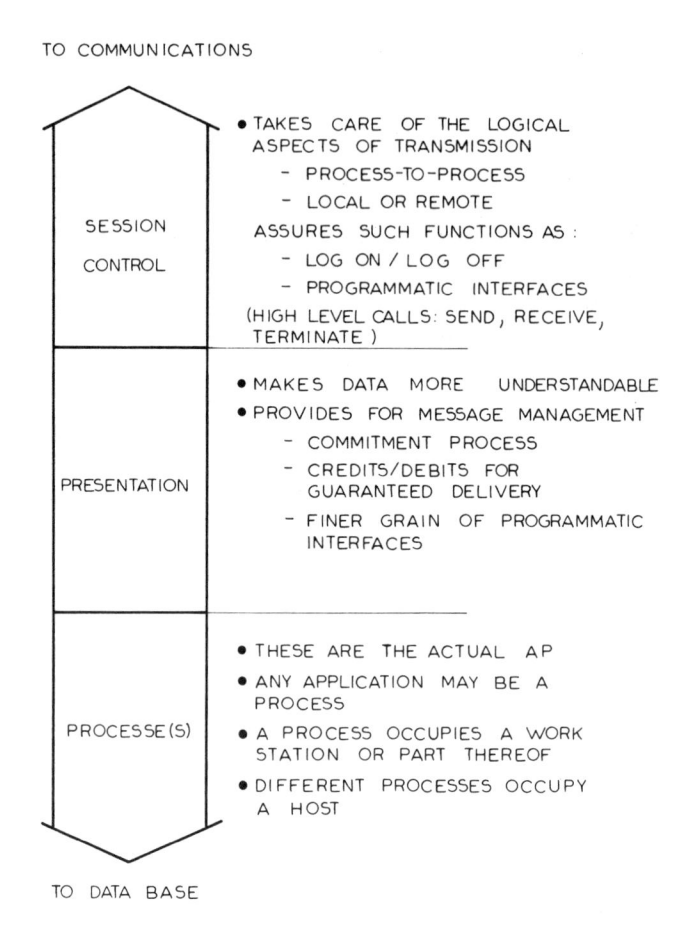

TO COMMUNICATIONS

SESSION CONTROL
- TAKES CARE OF THE LOGICAL ASPECTS OF TRANSMISSION
  - PROCESS-TO-PROCESS
  - LOCAL OR REMOTE
- ASSURES SUCH FUNCTIONS AS:
  - LOG ON / LOG OFF
  - PROGRAMMATIC INTERFACES
  (HIGH LEVEL CALLS: SEND, RECEIVE, TERMINATE)

PRESENTATION
- MAKES DATA MORE UNDERSTANDABLE
- PROVIDES FOR MESSAGE MANAGEMENT
  - COMMITMENT PROCESS
  - CREDITS/DEBITS FOR GUARANTEED DELIVERY
  - FINER GRAIN OF PROGRAMMATIC INTERFACES

PROCESSE(S)
- THESE ARE THE ACTUAL AP
- ANY APPLICATION MAY BE A PROCESS
- A PROCESS OCCUPIES A WORK STATION OR PART THEREOF
- DIFFERENT PROCESSES OCCUPY A HOST

TO DATA BASE

inside the host's main storage. This includes integrity and security control facilities.

Functionally, session control gives system-level support from log on to log off. Such commands as to edit, put in, test, and so forth should be covered.

In an interactive environment session control gives the video user, say, the same facilities given by intelligent devices. Some examples are simple ones, maybe an unlocked keyboard, and others complex, such as a full-width output review of an entire session. Session control should be designed to coexist with full-screen programs.

Among the basic functions we distinguish three: user support, tailoring to individual needs, and software for session "streams," as follows.

User support dynamically redefines part or all of a user's display environment; it should be possible to accomplish this function at any time during the session.

The ability to tailor the operation of the terminal to the user's individual needs demands considerable flexibility, since the user's needs may change from day to day and even during one session.

Software receives input from, and places its output in, session streams.

A stream may be thought of as a sheet of paper that one may both write on and read from; it is called a virtual sheet of paper (VSP), and, like paper, may be stacked. The same is true of data within the stream; each line of data that enters a stream is placed next to the preceding one, top to bottom, like lines of copy on paper. Just as lines of copy fill a page, data fill up streams of fixed capacity. When this happens, we say that a stream "wraps around." Not only lines in a stream but also streams in a DTE may reach a limit. Theoretically there is no limit to the number of streams a user may have, but practically a limit is set by the size of the memory.

ANSI and Session Control

We have said that the functions of session control are not yet standardized and that they are fairly complex. The software support and the interfacing with adjoining layers define whether a session is possible or not possible and allowed or not allowed. If all prerequisites are met, session control can inform the process that an exchange of data is in order. Then it will proceed to initiate the session, activate its side of transport control, and (when at the receiving end) put in action the quarantine. Procedures for quarantine are those which ensure that no access to a message or file is possible before the successful completion of the intended communication.

ANSI has proposed certain other terms, which it defines as follows.

A *session-quarantine unit* is a quantity of text that cannot be released to the receiving process until the sending process signals its completion.

A *session-commitment unit* is a quantity of data transferred during a session. It ensures the accomplishment of an element of work that is indivisible, from the point of view of consistency; for instance, it may concern itself with the consistency of data base updating across a distributed system.

A *session-interaction unit* is a subdivision of a session commitment delimited by the passing of control of a session from one work-station process to its corresponding process. Whoever is in control of the session may request termination or some other type of interaction.

A *session-recovery unit* is a quantity of data transferred during a session-commitment unit. Typically, it synchronizes the data transferred with respect to the checkpoints of the cooperating work-station processes.

A *session data unit* is a unit of data transferred between a pair of processes using a session. It is of a size that is defined independently of the size of the transport network data unit just above.

A *session data mapping unit* is an entity mapping the data unit of the next level above onto a session data unit.

This leads our discussion to the subject of presentation control.

Presentation Control

Different computer and communication equipment manufacturers have different notions of what presentation control is. Sometimes they interchange "session" and "presentation." Furthermore, in spite of the efforts extended by ANSI (in the X3 SPARC Study Group) there is no general agreement yet on the standardization of this level. The area of presentation control is, therefore, still in need of a proper definition, but by and large its activity is to adapt the information-handling characteristics of a given process to the requirements of session control and of the corresponding processes.

A process, as defined hereby, supports application and system activities, definitely including exchanges of information by which cooperation is achieved end to end with other processes. We must point out, however, that presentation control as defined by ANSI is one layer, but it really should be defined as two: a "basics" layer that includes what is projected by the current standardization effort (as discussed in this section) and an "add-on" layer that is distinctly oriented to industry and other segments of society. In that way each major segment—banking, merchandizing, manufacturing, law enforcement, and so on—may develop functional, user-oriented solutions, thereby enhancing communication between persons and data, or information.

For a better understanding of the currently projected functions of presentation control, we outline below the mission of the interface with the lower-level session control procedures, already defined.

Follow-up on establishing, maintaining, and terminating sessions, including requesting creation of a process when specified

Delimiting of data enclosures

Preparing the necessary delimiters for addressing work stations via mailboxes, a function of session control

Notifying processes upon receipt of data and data enclosure delimiters

Making data more understandable through segmenting, blocking, etc.

Providing for message management beyond the level of buffering data and controlling flow (proper to session control)

Actuating the commitment process

Providing credits and debits for guaranteed delivery

Supporting data operations beyond checkpoint, recovery, and commitment (proper to session control)

Providing the finer grains of programmatic interfaces

The protocol followed in presentation control is a set of rules by which support is given to a session for establishing, maintaining, and terminating a data transfer. The interface with session control contains the format by which control information is passed on and the rules by which it is interpreted for the transfer of data.

Specifically, presentation control adapts the existing specialized information-handling characteristics of a process to the session control interface. This calls for transforming commands, and data, to accommodate differences in sending and receiving formats, data types, data codes, and data representations; these may exist not only between different DTEs but also between different processes in the same host.

To accomplish these functions in an able manner, presentation control needs to make data more understandable, assure a reasonable homogeneity of language between processes and DTEs, adapt requests, if virtual terminals are used, to the specific machinery existing in that location, and translate local names, if programs use them, into a common reference. It must further make sure of the necessary compacting and decompacting, the enrichment of information, and the encrypting and decrypting as required.

This is, in brief, a commitment process to which could be added other functions as necessary, within a specific operating environment. For each one of them debits and credits must be given for guaranteed delivery—one of what we have called the finer grains of the programmatic interfaces.

Notice that session control and presentation control are necessary whether or not the networking and communications layers are used. Figure 15.3 exemplifies the case of the local terminal. Logical procedures for a data link probably will not be necessary, in which case the physical media should connect directly with session control.

Figure 15.3
The case of local terminal. (FA, file access; DBM, data base management; PRO, process; PRE, presentation control; SE, session control; DPA, data path; ROU, routing; DL, data link; PH, physical medium)

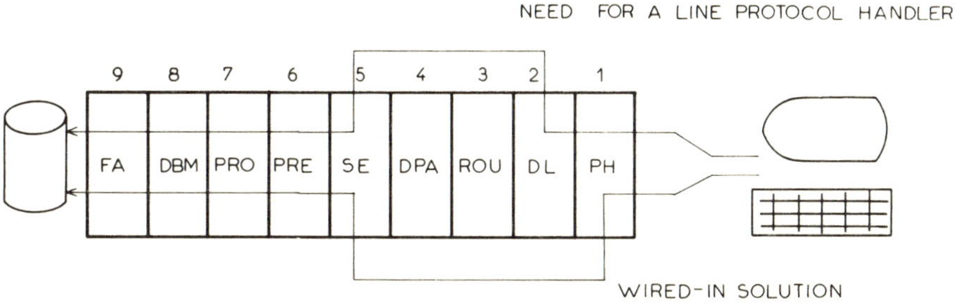

A Process-Level Protocol

A protocol for the process level, the seventh in Figure 15.1, supports applications and system activities, including the exchange of information between processes residing in the DTE or in the same host. The processes are actual applications programs and any such program may be a process. Processes occupy a work station or part thereof, and a protocol must guarantee that different applications programs cooperate in the achievement of the objectives and requirements. From presentation control to data link, all lower levels are designed to facilitate this; indeed, that is the purpose of data processing and data communications systems.

As ANSI aptly delineates, the objects of interest at the process level will be specific to each broad applications field. For a bank's current-accounts protocol, they will be customers, balances, accounts, deposits, withdrawals. For a manufacturer's order-entry protocol, they will be customers, sales orders, products, inventories, in-process orders, bills, receivables. For a distributed data base access protocol, they will be files, records, sets, items, access requests, processes, data descriptions. For a programming language, they will be procedures, statements, labels, items references. Regardless, the end point is file access, the ninth layer in Figure 15.1.

The multiplicity of tasks and interests sees to it that a process-level protocol is defined in terms of the data formats and their interpretation, the presentation control services, and the session control services. Each and all of these levels must take into consideration the control procedures for integrity and security—their object, extent, design, and impact.

Notice that the eighth level, the data base management system, determines whether it can have direct access to the data asked for by a process or whether it requires help from a surrogate data base process at some other session node (Figure 15.4). Activities relating to data base management and file access (ninth layer) will bring into play routines that may be typed according to processing: transaction processing, program development, file transfer protocol, integrity control protocol, and terminal interaction protocol. These call for fairly different data-handling methods.

Such protocols thus specify the rules by which the information passing between processes of two DTEs, or between processes within a host is put into format and interpreted.

Many different interprocess protocols exist, but they fall into two major classes: basic information systems and applications systems. As of now, neither particularly conforms to any standards, though both badly need to.

Establishment of a session, high-level language interfaces (possibly converting the language statements into packets, observing chosen protocols), data base inquiries, data audits, and software transparency (whether remote or local) are among the functions in great need of standardization. They largely pertain to the fifth to ninth layers, where much of the attention in network studies is now focusing.

Session and Presentation Control   193

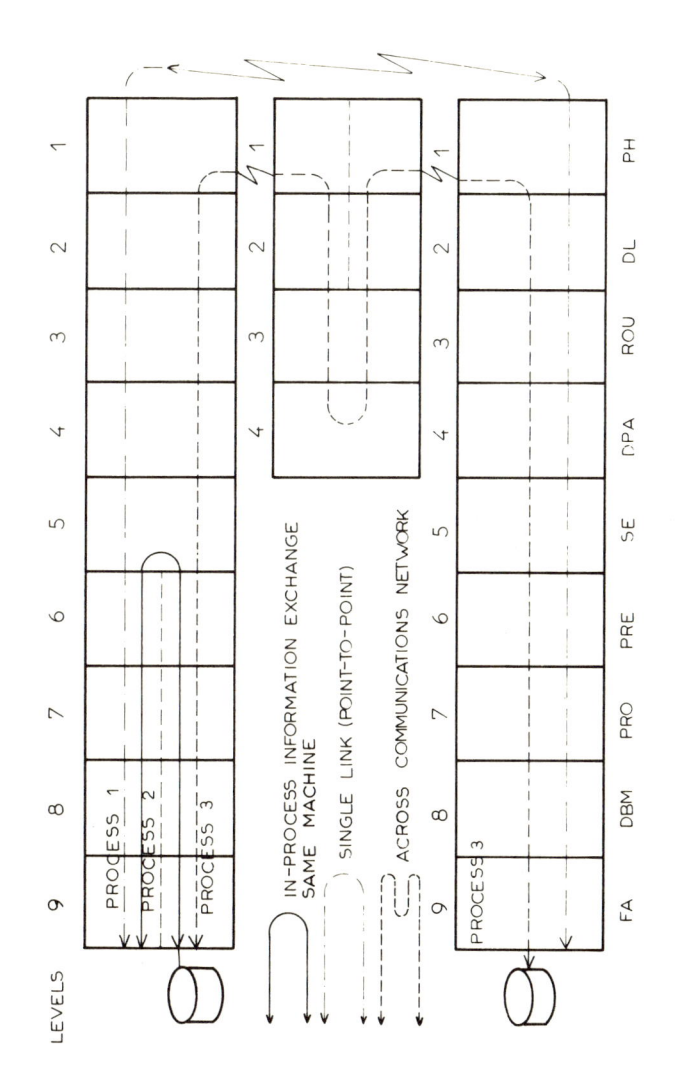

Figure 15.4

16

Communications Software

Computer and data communications systems are combinations of subsystems made to work together by software, which allows users to control the components of the system. Control must necessarily be appropriate to a particular environment. The requirements follow the environmental and operational perspectives. For instance, a priority structure calls for a provision relative to resource allocation.

Usually a data communications system encompasses many tasks. Task-to-task switching *must* be accomplished, calling forth a rational approach to server programs.

Routines handle the characteristics of each individual service component. Figure 16.1 identifies five classes of prerequisites: overall performance, communications control, terminal control, network control, and network operations. The last two are the object of the network architecture; the first two, of the system architecture. Terminal control concerns both types.

The software-implemented communication functions include the following:

> Storage and forwarding of data
>
> Routing
>
> Switch monitoring
>
> Flow control
>
> Congestion control
>
> Error detection and correction
>
> Response handling
>
> Security control
>
> Interrupt

Figure 16.1
Software functions for data communications

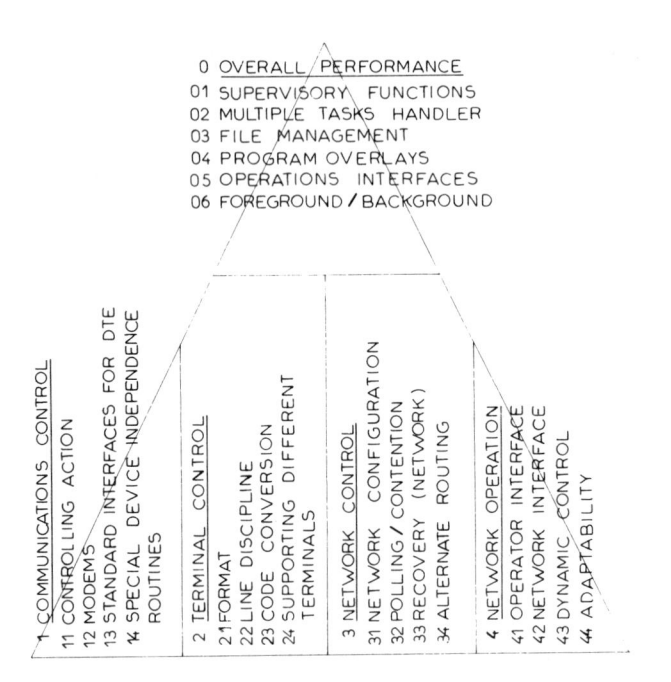

```
                    0 OVERALL/PERFORMANCE
                    01 SUPERVISORY FUNCTIONS
                    02 MULTIPLE TASKS HANDLER
                    03 FILE MANAGEMENT
                    04 PROGRAM OVERLAYS
                    05 OPERATIONS INTERFACES
                    06 FOREGROUND / BACKGROUND
```

1 COMMUNICATIONS CONTROL
11 CONTROLLING ACTION
12 MODEMS
13 STANDARD INTERFACES FOR DTE
14 SPECIAL DEVICE INDEPENDENCE ROUTINES

2 TERMINAL CONTROL
21 FORMAT
22 LINE DISCIPLINE
23 CODE CONVERSION
24 SUPPORTING DIFFERENT TERMINALS

3 NETWORK CONTROL
31 NETWORK CONFIGURATION
32 POLLING / CONTENTION
33 RECOVERY (NETWORK)
34 ALTERNATE ROUTING

4 NETWORK OPERATION
41 OPERATOR INTERFACE
42 NETWORK INTERFACE
43 DYNAMIC CONTROL
44 ADAPTABILITY

Terminal handling
Information display
Line concentrating
Statistical calculations
Customer billing

The network functions must be first defined and then documented (Figure 16.2). The structure of the network, its topology, the projected usage, the operating environment, all influence to a considerable extent the goal and mechanics of software implementation.

Like any other logical support, communications software must be thoroughly tested. Not having proper program and system tests and the tracing of hardware, software, and data errors can be disastrous. A good rule is this: test the software often for "bugs" and establish a maintenance and stand-by policy. We shall examine the details in this chapter.

Figure 16.2
Network functions

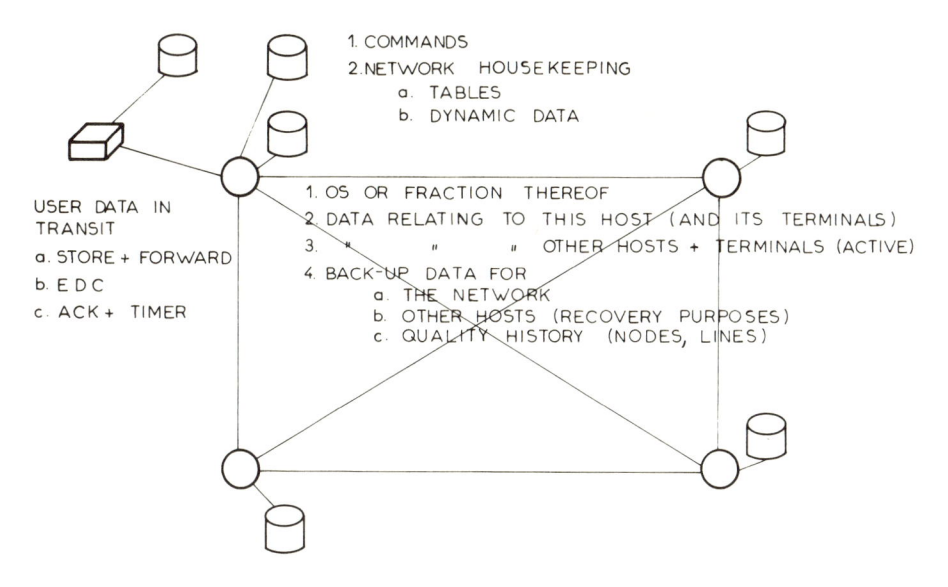

1. COMMANDS
2. NETWORK HOUSEKEEPING
   a. TABLES
   b. DYNAMIC DATA

USER DATA IN TRANSIT
a. STORE + FORWARD
b. E D C
c. ACK + TIMER

1. OS OR FRACTION THEREOF
2. DATA RELATING TO THIS HOST (AND ITS TERMINALS)
3. "   "   "   OTHER HOSTS + TERMINALS (ACTIVE)
4. BACK-UP DATA FOR
   a. THE NETWORK
   b. OTHER HOSTS (RECOVERY PURPOSES)
   c. QUALITY HISTORY (NODES, LINES)

Developing the Software

The software for a data communications system aims at an efficient management of the hardware resources. In an interactive environment this means a service responsive simultaneously to many users. The prerequisites of the service are security for each user's resources, systematic job rotation, program-loading and storage, and interfaces with a variety of peripherals.

The user's tasks must be protected against alteration and destruction. The size of the memory must be decided upon (sometimes during the initialization dialogue); it varies according to the user's need. Every effort should be directed toward security.

A network's resources may be shared among multiple users by means of an interrupt-driven, time-slice facility. Interrupt packets may be transmitted by the network before all the other packets awaiting transmission and delivered to a DTE even when it is not accepting data packets. Interrupt packets contain neither send nor receive sequence numbers. They handle interrupt conditions, which are signaled between DTEs without being subject to the flow control imposed on data packets. The acceptance of an interrupt, however, must be confirmed before a second interrupt is allowed to cross the DTE. Algorithmic solutions will control the status of a process awaiting input or output.

When interrupts occur, an interrupt handler mechanism, activated by a clock, gains control, and then a procedure is followed that is peculiar to a given communications system—that is specially designed for it, in fact. The handling of interrupts is an example of how the software of a data communications system serves to structure that system. Software controls the interrelationships among hardware components, for example, by ensuring the potential communication path between two terminal devices or between a terminal and a host.

The software itself may be regarded as a system and its structure discussed in terms of the programming language used to construct it. The hardware may be regarded as having a static structure; programmed activity would have a dynamic structure. The static structure discloses the kind of faults that might exist in a system and the provisions that have been made for dealing with them. The dynamic structure, which is equally important, deals with the effects of these faults and how, or whether, the system will tolerate them and continue to function. The activity of a data communications system may be visualized in terms of many different structures, depending on one's point of view.

One basic, well-established concept of the dynamic structure of a system's activity is the process. Of vital concern is sequence or flow control in process structuring, namely, the creation, existence, and deletion of a process.

In choosing to regard a system (or its activity) as a collection of components, and to concentrate on their interrelationships while ignoring their inner details, we deliberately consider a particular abstraction of the total system. We usually identify a set of levels of abstraction, each of which might relate to the whole system or just a part. The importance of levels of abstraction is that they enable us to cope with the combinational complexity that would otherwise be involved in a data communications system constructed from a very large number of very basic components. When we define interrelationships among subsystems, we impose a structure on a system and describe how components are constructed, related to one another, and functioning.

Figure 16.3 illustrates the complexity of topology. Other things being equal, the number of connections increases exponentially as a function of the number of components, and although the physical links in a network will not be $n(n-1)/2$ for n nodes (chiefly for reasons of economics), they will surely be greater than n to take advantage of the possibility of alternate paths. The effect on the routing algorithm is evident.

Software Functions

Special software is needed for the user of a computer and data communications system, and it may be divided broadly into two parts, communications and data bases. The functions relative to communications are the following:

1. Convert high-level statements (of the user programs) into packets to be handled by the transmission subsystem.
2. Divide messages into packets when they are too long for the transmission subsystems and reassemble them after transmission.

Communications Software 199

Figure 16.3

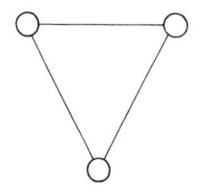

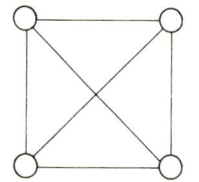

$$\frac{n(n-1)}{2} \quad \text{NUMBER OF CONNECTIONS}$$

n = NUMBER OF COMPONENTS

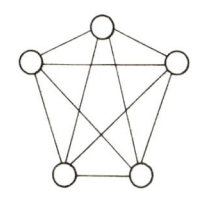

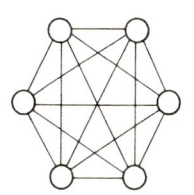

3. Make sure that the network protocols are observed.
4. Use numbers for maintaining correct sequences.
5. Perform local flow control.
6. Queue the messages and handle priority.
7. Correlate requests and responses to the requests.
8. Determine where a requested function is performed, or where requested data reside.
9. Establish communications with the node that owns or controls the requested functions or data.
10. Obtain that node's agreement to establish a session.
11. Exchange information about protocols to be used in the communication.
12. Check that the communicating nodes have the resources, such as buffering, necessary for the communication.

The primary components of the communications software necessary at the level of the local host or intelligent DTE are driver and handler routines for computer communications, line control and task-scheduling routines, and a message-handling and routing package. Other necessary software are programs for logging message traffic, routines for operator communications, a switchover and switchback capability of the communications lines in case of processor failure, applications support and interface routines, link-handling routines, and a switchover-switchback capability for disc storage in case of processor failure.

Some of the software will be oriented to the data base, as we shall see; still other software will concern transaction-processing support routines and a significant amount of system support and utility programs. Such software would supplement the subsystems for communications support and for particular applications. The following are necessary for network control and monitoring: program and data file transfer, data file display, and peripheral status display. Further software functions are gathering of system statistics, display of system statistics, system resource enabling and disabling operations, remote resource enabling and disabling, system maintenance support, system access control, system initialization. All of these are the *components of data communications systems*. To recapitulate:

The *operating system* controls the overall functions of the processor.

The *applications system* consists of the programs that act on the messages received and transmitted.

The *communications control system* assembles the message received and passes it to the applications system; it also prepares messages for transmission and passes them to the line handler.

The *line handler* provides the primary control of messages to and from the communication line.

The *supporting services* are for maintenance, reliability, and supervision, such as loopback testing and downline loading.

We shall speak of these fairly sophisticated functions shortly, but let us first look at two issues that condition the degree of complexity one may be willing to adopt.

The first issue is the state of the art (Figure 16.4). The ability to utilize more and more complex systems grows with experience, both our own and that of others. Another factor is our goal, which may be expressed according to whether or not to use human intervention at the local site and how large a network to use. Ideally, one would not wish human intervention, because it costs money and produces errors, but the software then becomes that much more complex. That is why most software developments in data communications started with the prerequisite of a pushbutton approach. Moreover, they are slowly moving away from it through other methods (downline loading, upline dumping, and loopback programs), as we shall see.

The second issue, relating to what we can do in the way of automatic pushbutton functions, is the capacity of the memory of the machine (Figure 16.5). Memory is not as expensive as it was in the early 1970s, but it is not yet as inexpensive as it will be in the early 1980s. A minicomputer typically has a capacity of 16, 32, or 64 kilobytes. Three things share the memory: operating systems, applications programs, and terminals. An on-line terminal generally needs 1 kilobyte or more of central memory which helps determine how many terminals a minicomputer can manage. Usually, at the minicomputer level, an operating system consumes between 35 and 50 percent of central memory—an efficient one at that. Another 25 to 30 percent is taken by the applications programming (often squeezed in with overlays). The balance is taken by the terminals. The limits of communications software are set.

Communications Software 201

Figure 16.4
Levels of complexity: one machine, two machines (automatic modem), *n* machines, and *m* persons, where $m > n$.

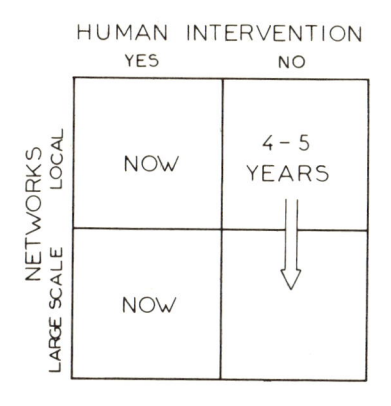

	HUMAN INTERVENTION	
	YES	NO
NETWORKS — LOCAL	NOW	4-5 YEARS
LARGE SCALE	NOW	

Figure 16.5
Capacity of memory machine. (KB, kilobytes; MB, megabytes; T, terminal)

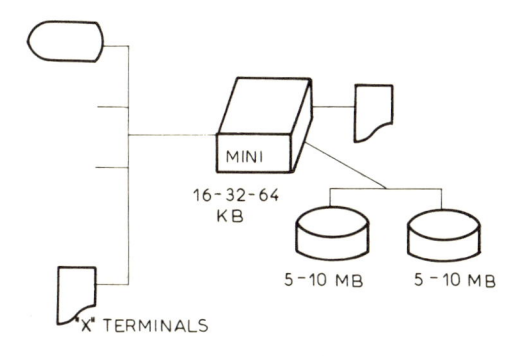

MINI
16-32-64 KB
5-10 MB   5-10 MB
"x" TERMINALS

OS	8	12	24 KB
AP	4	8	24 KB
TERMINALS (1 KB/T)	4	10	16 KB
	16	32	64 KB

Downline Loading, Upline Dumping, and Loopback

Downline loading, or memory deposit, is an integral part of a distributed operating system. It is the process by which a host or a DTE sends to other DTEs. It makes no difference whether it handles applications programs, data, other operating systems sections, or a maintenance discipline. At the user level, we speak of three types of configuration: one with no disc, one with no people, and one with no disc and no people (Figure 16.6).

Downline loading has no disc. It is the typical job of a concentrator and requires a minimal memory at the periphery. (The term comes from the practice of hierarchical systems.) Downline loading helps the communications linkage to test for failures and actuate other devices from remote locations.

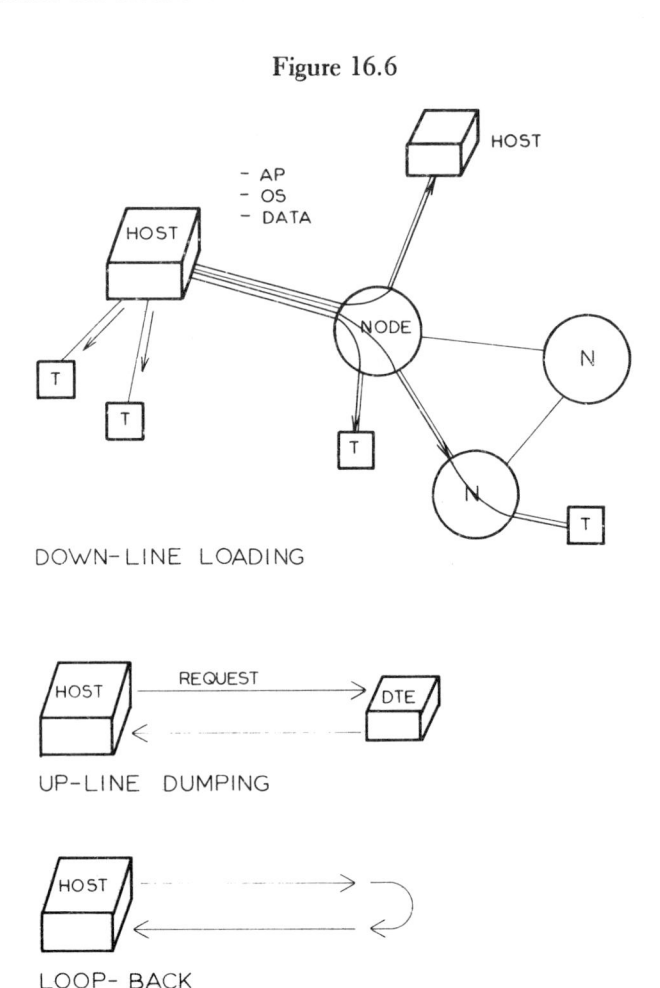

Figure 16.6

Upline dumping, or memory examination, involves no people. It is a means by which the host checks the operations and errors of other DTEs. A host may request from a DTE a particular file, or send information, ask to have it treated by a terminal, and then examine whether or not it has been altered.

Loop testing, or loopback, involves neither people nor discs. It tests the data link. It allows one to send a pattern down the loop, turn it around, and examine the results.

Software should make it possible to push a button at one terminal and reload a program at another terminal or host computer (where what is stored is available). At the on-line maintenance level such facilities allow network element-testing, data communications tests, and connection-tracing. To test network elements one must decide whether to work from the *host outward* (toward the front end, concentrators, terminals) or from the *terminal inward* (toward the concentrators, front ends, hosts). The decision has evidently an effect on the design and development of the software.

Data Base Support

A key software feature is the file management system that supports large data bases and runs them. This may involve automatic record-packing, efficient record-level directories, and the security and integrity of the file.

System software should make it easy to add new applications to the system. It must support maintenance of the data base and handle it separately from the applications, easing the job of the applications programs and making access to the data base applications independent. Figure 16.7 diagrams the general flow of events. Ten steps are indicated, starting with the request posed by the user program and ending with the provision of called-for data elements. (A full description is beyond the scope of this book.)

The following are twenty functions of the software for a data base. Inevitably, most of them are also the functions of communications systems.

1. Insert and interpret end-of-record and end-of-file indicators.
2. Transfer whole files, portions of files, records, or fields, as instructed.
3. Perform end-to-end acknowledgments and checking of sequence numbers.
4. Operate batch controls.
5. Perform checkpoint restart.
6. Recover from a reset or restart condition in the transmission subsystem (if possible, without breaking the session).
7. Proceed with code conversion, as necessary, if several codes are used in the system.
8. Insert and delete files.
9. Search a file or dispersed files to find information according to keys.
10. Determine where needed data are located.

Figure 16.7

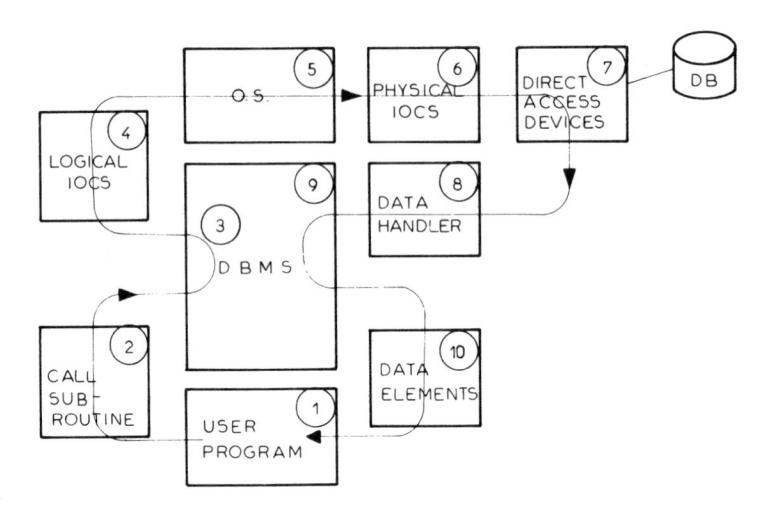

[Diagram showing components: LOGICAL IOCS (4), CALL SUBROUTINE (2), O.S. (5), DBMS (3), PHYSICAL IOCS (6), DIRECT ACCESS DEVICES (7), DB, DATA HANDLER (8), (9), USER PROGRAM (1), DATA ELEMENTS (10)]

11. Put the data in a format for output (to fill a screen, print tables, and so on).
12. Add appendages to data, such as page headers, dates, page numbers, and repeated information.
13. Provide for information enrichment on the basis of applications (e.g., substitute coded identification numbers for repetitively used screens, formats, messages, or segments of text).
14. Operate menu selection of other dialogues in which only the results of the dialogue are transmitted.
15. Conduct data base interrogation dialogue that assists an operator of a terminal in formulating queries.
16. Permit users to refer to virtual terminals and also to use other virtual machines.
17. Permit programmers to use *logical* input–output capabilities and to map them to the characteristics of specific machines.
18. Provide users with access to more than one transmission subsystem.
19. Perform routines for reducing the number of bits transmitted (compaction, zero, blank suppression).
20. Make the operation of the transmission subsystem transparent to the user.

System Design Requirements

Let us put the foregoing into some perspective. Communications software must exercise extensive supervision over the controlling and monitoring of the message-handling functions of the system. Controlling and monitoring include such items as command, response, alarms, reporting, repair of message, and retrieval of data. In any and every computer and communications network the programs manage all supervisory functions (reports, retrievals, table change). In general, one or more DTEs may be designated for the system's supervisory position.

The communications software must provide for:

Routing control

Skip poll, resume poll

Hold and release

Test

Message repair

Inquiry and response

Commands may be classified as of five major types: line control, message queues, routing, privileged control, and alarm monitoring, which are described below.

Line control controls the flow of traffic for a line. It may give the command to skip polling or resume polling for a terminal, a line, or all lines, or it may control output by commanding a hold or reset for a terminal, a line, or all lines, or it may monitor the commands for the purpose of acquiring statistics.

Message queues control the queues of messages handled by the network.

Routing monitors the routing facilities. The routing-control commands can establish alternate routing, duplicate delivery, and routing report requests.

Privileged control is for such tasks as direct retrieval, fault isolation, and configuration control. Configuration control involves host-interface configuration, processor or disc file configuration, and system thresholds and reporting intervals.

Alarm monitoring handles messages that alert the system to some abnormality or status change. The following are the conditions usually subject to alarm monitoring:

Line failure and line restoration

Front-end failure and restoration

Terminal failure (polling or addressing) and restoration

Excessive number of messages in queue

Buffer availability

Secondary storage failure

Switchover and recovery execution or failure

Abnormalities in host processor

Alarms generated by the system may apply to a center or to the network. The first type of alarm concerns the computer-center hardware and software, such as disc files, magnetic tape units, system control, monitoring functions, overlay failures, and so on. The second type concerns the lines, terminals, line termination units, and so forth.

Alarm messages usually include the time of occurrence and some text identifying the terminal or line affected and describing the abnormal condition.

The reports give information about traffic and equipment relating to lines, terminals, and processors. They may be displayed so as to alert personnel of the conditions. They are of three kinds:

> Generated and delivered to the reports position when requested by the supervisor.
>
> Generated periodically, at predetermined time intervals, and delivered automatically to the reports position.
>
> Generated periodically, at predetermined time intervals, and delivered automatically to terminals.

The Implementation Schedule

Finally, by way of conclusion, Table 16.1 presents an implementation schedule for data communications. Two words of caution are necessary.

First, this schedule, largely derived from data communications experience, does not reflect anything nearly as complex as the computer and data communications systems described in this book. Rather, the table is drawn from a condition of transition, from an on-line environment operating for a number of years but under stress because of rapidly multiplying requirements (number of terminals and applications) to a structure much expanded and more sophisticated. An example is the change from a mainframe (and primitive front end) to a specialized communications hardware and software able to handle, say, over a thousand terminals and a network control center. Typically, such a conversion would leave intact the original centralized nature of the network.

Second, the schedule in Table 16.1 presupposes a project team with able specialists under a competent leader. Skill and knowledge are the basic ingredients of a good data communications system. It is not enough, though; just as vital is to put in charge a person who knows how to get work done, respect timetables, and draw out of everyone the best each can contribute. Projects do not conform to timetables of their own. They must be managed with an iron hand and with persistence, against odds, and through the labyrinths of company politics.

Communications Software 207

Table 16.1
Implementation Schedule for Data Communications

Function	Men	Weeks* Unit	Sum
1. Functional description (preliminary proposal)	4	4	4
2. Complete specifications	4	8 to 12	16
3. System design (startup)		1	17

4. Hardware list
    Order hardware
    Programmer training
    Installation site
		4 to 7	24

5. Interface specifications (if data communications must interface to other systems)		1	25

6. Software development
    Modules
    Design reviews
		16 to 20
		(in parallel)
			45

7. Acceptance test procedure		1	46

8. Acceptance test
    Hardware
    Software
    Communications
    Personnel
		10 to 12	58

9. Installation check-out
    On-site tests
    Functional acceptance
    Test transactions
    Total transactions
		2 to 3	61

10. Editorial documentation (review)		2	63
11. Complete acceptance test		3 to 4	67
12. Pilot branch sites		8 (1½ years)	75

*Time scales are not linear. If 2 to 3 men work on this project, it may take roughly 8 calendar months.

17
A Network Operating System

In a computer and data communications network, the architecture provides the logical design, the engineering the physical design, and the software the dynamics of the situation.

How is the network going to work? The logical design includes three groups of commands. The first is the basic commands, which create communications paths and use them to pass data. The second is file-sharing, which permits a DTE to transfer or request data from a file or input–output in another DTE. The third is program control, which allows a DTE to start and stop the execution of programs on another DTE of the network.

The preparation of a processor for on-line operation involves some primary tasks, such as initialization (loading with no record of prior activity), checkpoint (the process of recording dynamic status), and recovery (reinitializing, using the last recorded status).

Recovery is the fundamental activity allowing the system to resume operations. Initialization consists of loading the resident software in the central memory and then extending control to the applications initialization process. This includes the functions of (1) establishing the disc configuration and setting up the disc addresses, (2) initializing the data–channel interfaces and the disc-file control parameters, (3) reading the overlays (for instance, from tape to disc) and building the overlay index, (4) loading the tables resident in high-speed memory, (5) modifying the tables for initial conditions, and (6) handling the queue tables and building the checkpoint directory.

During operation the status of the system will be checkpointed periodically for use by the recovery functions in restoring the system after outage of a processor. Included in this operation is the handling of queue pointers for all store-and-forward status traffic, status indicators for circuits and terminals, circuit, line, and terminal tables as an alternate routing requirement and, generally, system-configuration data.

The preparatory work pinpoints the need of a description of the data to be checkpointed. The same is true in defining checkpoint frequencies and identifying the calls to be issued for checkpoint functions.

Finally, as in checkpointing, the basic recovery procedures must be part of the network's operating system, such as reading checkpoint data and setting up operating parameters.

The application recovery routines are dumping other functions, ceasing polling of procedures, transmitting notice of canceled messages, retransmitting all messages in process at time of failure, sending go-ahead messages to nonpolled DTEs, and restoring status, message queue, and log locations.

An organization such as that described is, to a considerable degree, influenced by the structure and the functions of computer-oriented operating systems. Today network operating systems are added into maxicomputer operating systems (particularly transaction-oriented routines and front-end applications), and not vice versa. This is an unfortunate result of past practice and of present technology.

Architectural extensions are built on the primitives of the operating system. The reasons are historical. New developments might make networking functions the primitives for the operating system, and then the operating system will be less dependent on location; the scheduler will reside in one computer, the "swapper" in another, while the device drivers will be scattered. But even today the aim is to have no human intervention and no pushbuttons, the host doing all the work down line, as we have stated.

Designing a Basic Operating System

The design of an operating system to serve a given architecture must above all consider and reflect the goals of the network. A network for data communications may be used in three different ways: for remote communications, the primary aim being to move information from one place to another, for the sharing of resources (resources in one system shared by other systems), and for distributed information, involving autonomous computers designated for problem handling by a division of labor or immediate access or specialization.

Remote communication, the first above, involves a large number of terminals geographically distributed but connected in an arbitrary topology. The network would have relatively few large host computers. Other things being equal, this is the least complex operating system of the three network types.

Because the major computer-run resource today is the data base, resource-sharing networks will be using data base systems to make their contents locally available, but fundamentally such networks will be centralized storage systems, transferring files or information elements to remote line printers or plotters.

A Network Operating System   211

Distributed information systems will incorporate the foregoing characteristics but use advanced technology to reduce cost by distributing the storage of the user locations and sharing low-usage devices among many systems, providing for both local and remote access to files in a widely distributed data base system.

The software of a communications network will not only see that the right things happen at the right time but also effect "reconciliation." Since the different elements are not homogeneous, the codes and speeds, the terminal classifications, the data bases, their sizes, and their use must be made to work together very precisely by means of logical functions.

The location and availability of terminal and host, the support of data input (rates, codes), the loading projections, and the protocol requirements are factors in the design of software. Others relate to growth: percentage utilization, future throughput projections, and physical limitations of sites or hosts

Figure 17.1 presents a comprehensive view of the requirements, outlining the component parts and their interrelationships.

At the level of the host, the low or high speeds of the circuits, the hardware or software front-ending, and the line discipline should determine the operating system's software. The requirements of terminals will revolve around low or high speed, hardware or software implementation, and interactive or batch operation.

Figure 17.1

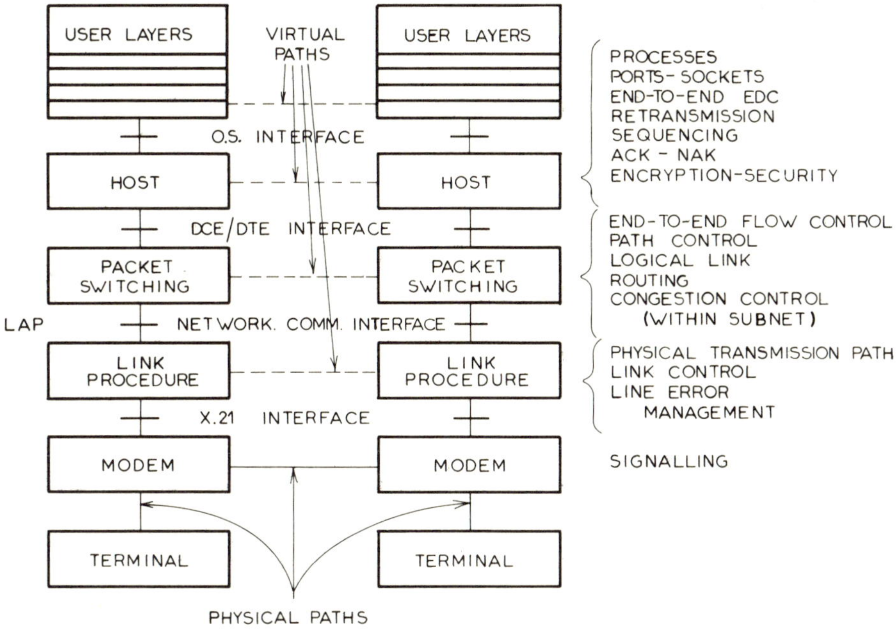

These have an impact on what is necessary in terms of buffering, switching and routing, line discipline, turnaround, and delay.

Switching and routing must be studied, not only in regard to the function involved, but also in regard to destination control overhead, monitoring needs, and methods of error control. This leads to diagnostic services, namely the signals required, the procedures used, and the control overhead.

The throughput requirements call for an examination of turnaround, of delay in forwarding, of multiplexing, and of buffering. The network startup has its prerequisites, many of which are related to software; such is the case of testing and of the procedures needed for access.

Operations must steadily be upgraded, expanded, and maintained. Distributed systems versus centralized ones, diagnostic services, and reconfiguration are other examples of needed support. It is, therefore, no wonder that the development of a comprehensive software able to cover these services entails a large investment. Table 17.1 outlines the investments made by one leading computer manufacturer in developing his network architecture.

The Software "Constant"

The sources of heterogeneity within a computer network and among communicating networks are the hardware components, the operating systems, and the applications software. In the typical case heterogeneity of components results both from the use of hardware devices and software routines and from the variety of functions the network is expected to perform.

Table 17.1
Investment in Network Architecture by a Manufacturer

	Completion (%)	Design (man-years)	Observations
Data link	95	10	X.25 capability in process of development
Routing	80 }	30	Design follows layered solutions
Virtual circuit	90 }		
File access	70 to 80	15	Intermediate step to data base management system
Data base management system	0		
Information enrichment	0		

Signal carriers (wires and microwave links) work with different transmission techniques, and the irresponsible switching by telephone companies among differing media throws the user's network out of synchronization. At the local site processors and terminals of different architecture and word sizes work differently, and within the same processor some devices, such as line printers, may be variously controlled. Interfaces at devices and signal carriers with different operating modes call for extraordinary ingenuity from designers of software. We should not forget that operating systems themselves may be multiprogrammed, real time, batch, or time sharing. The users' applications also are various. Programs employ networks in various ways, and file systems and data bases have different access modes and formats.

All this underlines the need to have, somewhere, a sort of constant, a base of reference. The constant would be to software what the "bus" is to hardware (Figure 17.2). With this concept, within a network the software might be treated as if it were a hardware component, without undergoing revamping (portability).

A careful study of what should be included in the operating system and how it should be distributed is the only way to give the software modules the advantages of interfacing. Functions should be defined a priori, among them network control, routing of message traffic, system protection, logging and journaling, queueing, tag build, and output services. Each would be divided into subfunctions. For example, system protection would include control of memory and disc overwriting, monitoring of failures, and management of traffic flow, and network control would include configuration management, communication line monitoring, message queueing, assignments of centralized privileges, isolation testing, and table changes.

The exact divisions and subdivisions are a matter of choice; no two systems are alike, but a functional orientation would permit a subdivision of the elements such that they might be organized in the concentric manner shown in Figure 17.3. Here use is made of the fact that complex problems may be divided into specialized parts, the latter organized in a modular fashion; then together the modules constitute the components of the network operating system. This organization is a valid framework within which portions of a complex problem may be defined and solved. The solutions may be tested independently and later integrated into the total system.

Let us always remember that the problem with software is testing: we must spend at least half of our time and effort in testing the product. The task is simplified if we deal in small lots. Let us not forget, either, that a new, "announced" architecture fundamentally represents a software adjunct to existing processors and operating systems, extending the systems by offering new network capabilities. The modular aspect is, therefore, once again underlined.

Properly designed, software makes networks and users share resources, communicate between distributed components, and move data to and from terminals, at the same time and fairly efficiently Properly designed, the operating system is

Figure 17.2
The information-passing mechanism inside the computer.

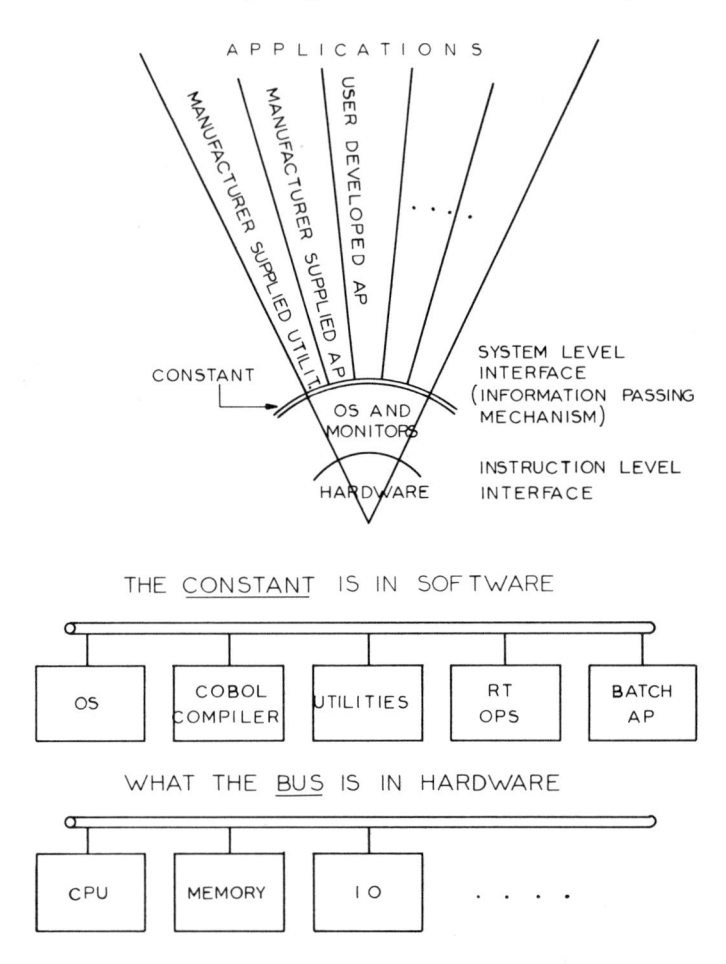

[Diagram: A fan-shaped diagram showing APPLICATIONS at top spreading out, with labels MANUFACTURER SUPPLIED UTILIT, MANUFACTURER SUPPLIED AP, USER DEVELOPED AP, converging down through OS AND MONITORS to HARDWARE. CONSTANT label points to the OS and Monitors layer. Labels on right: SYSTEM LEVEL INTERFACE (INFORMATION PASSING MECHANISM), INSTRUCTION LEVEL INTERFACE.]

THE CONSTANT IS IN SOFTWARE

[Bus diagram with boxes: OS, COBOL COMPILER, UTILITIES, RT OPS, BATCH AP]

WHAT THE BUS IS IN HARDWARE

[Bus diagram with boxes: CPU, MEMORY, IO, ...]

optimized with respect to the three network types we have outlined. All-inclusive designs will not work; they are cumbersome, ineffective, and resource-consuming.

Some Historical Background

Regarding the fundamentals, the basic purpose of any operating system is to get a group of people to share a complex computer installation in so efficient a manner as to maximize the throughput of their jobs.

In the early days of computing the entire installation was, practically speaking, allocated to one user at a time; most of the operations were manual, and operating

A Network Operating System   215

Figure 17.3

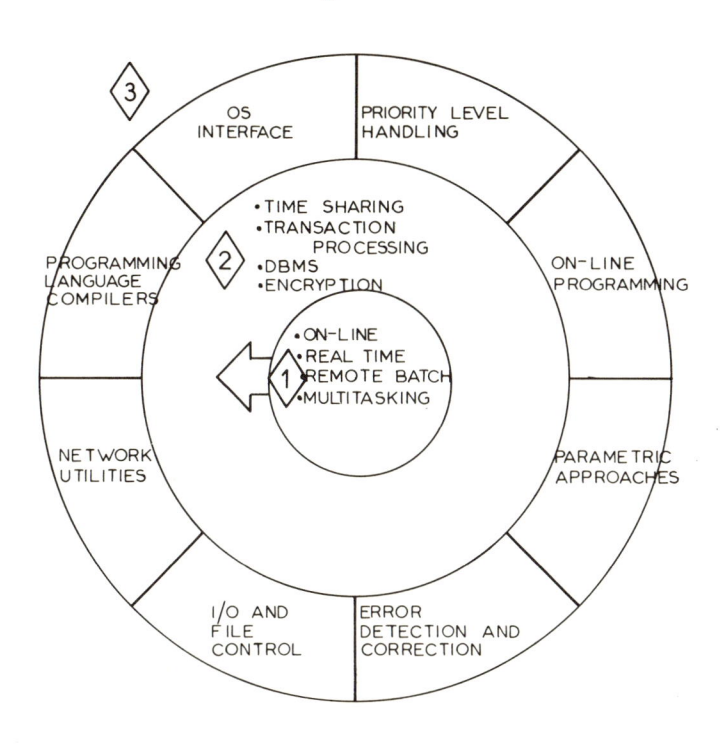

⟨1⟩ THE CORE OPERATIONS ARE FUNDAMENTAL.
FUTURE DEVELOPMENTS ARE GOING OUTWARDS

Inner core (1): ON-LINE, REAL TIME, REMOTE BATCH, MULTITASKING

Middle ring (2): TIME SHARING, TRANSACTION PROCESSING, DBMS, ENCRYPTION

Outer ring (3): OS INTERFACE, PRIORITY LEVEL HANDLING, ON-LINE PROGRAMMING, PARAMETRIC APPROACHES, ERROR DETECTION AND CORRECTION, I/O AND FILE CONTROL, NETWORK UTILITIES, PROGRAMMING LANGUAGE COMPILERS

system software was almost nonexistent. Standard software was therefore introduced to facilitate the complicated task of operating the different units of a modern computer.

For example, input–output control systems (IOCS) were devised, the backbone of which is (usually) a parametric processor program that drives the input–output system or, more precisely, the input–output control routines. It manages the device drivers, to which are connected the peripheral's controllers, each controller running one or more devices. Supervisors (monitors) interrupt processing, job scheduling, and resource allocation. This software constitutes the basis of any modern operating system, and the user communicates with it by means of an appropriate command language.

At this point we might note the historical development of operating systems, because we can detect a cycle repeating itself:

1953, Computers and maxicomputers

1957, Input–output control systems

1964, Disc and other operating systems

1971, Minicomputers

1978, Microcomputers and microminicomputers

That is, we started with computers, then added something, and now are back to computers again. Of course, the minicomputer of the 1970s is much more powerful than the maxicomputer of the 1950s.

Now let us see what was slowly added a quarter of a century ago to put some muscle onto the bare bones of computer systems.

First there was a single processor operating system. Then this started to become a fairly complex software system incorporating many different components. Components performing supervisory functions were frequently used. Prompt execution was essential. It was therefore expedient that some of them reside in the memory at all times. Less critical components were stored on discs so as not to overload the memory and were reloaded into the memory only when needed. Reloading was, and still is, done by erasing other programs no longer needed for current operations; this is known as "swapping." With this background we can return to Figure 17.3 and look at the process inside the first circle, the core of the procedure, which includes on-line, real time, remote batch, and multitasking.

A rational organization in successive layers is shown in Figure 17.4. Seven layers are identified, beginning with the most basic, the selector. The selector scans the stack of waiting tasks to find a process to start; then it transfers control to the starter. If there is a priority condition, a given task is pushed to the background and later moved to the foreground. The starter also will reestablish the process in its previous state.

Device availability routines, as the term implies, signal the availability of a device, or a data base element, to the next process awaiting access to that resource. Some associated routines are needed, such as an input–output interrupt handler, which converts interrupts from the various devices into device availability routines. Device drivers contain the supervisor and input–output programs. The supervisor is composed of subroutines, such as terminal control, including enabling or disabling, echoing, changing terminal priorities, and switching, as the need arises. The so-called DB locks in an operation associated with the data base. A file or information element in the data base might be locked by a previous user, in which case routines must see to it that a new request is added to the queue of jobs awaiting access to the data base. Conversely, as a user exits a data base, the file or information element must be unlocked.

Depending on system configuration, the input–output drivers may include storage media, line printers, and terminals. The handling of buffers is important, one solution being circular buffers filled from one end and emptied from the other; this permits the input–output handler a greater flexibility.

Figure 17.4

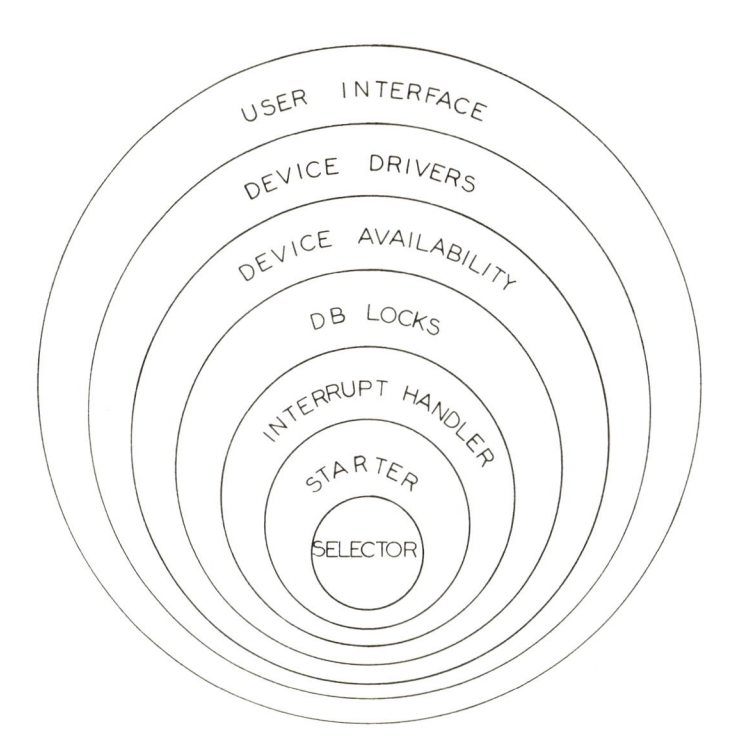

(concentric circles, from outermost to innermost: USER INTERFACE, DEVICE DRIVERS, DEVICE AVAILABILITY, DB LOCKS, INTERRUPT HANDLER, STARTER, SELECTOR)

Within the user interface the generation of reports is another vital consideration, since a great number of reports is necessary (soft copy rather than hard copy) to provide information on traffic and equipment status, relating to line, terminal, and processor activities. Reports that alert personnel to abnormal conditions or exceptions may be generated and delivered to the reports position when requested by the supervisor, or they may be generated periodically at predetermined intervals of time. A still better option is to generate reports periodically at predetermined time intervals and deliver them automatically to terminals; even information identifying no abnormal conditions is vital information.

The main parts of a typical communications-oriented operating system are the subject of the following sections.

Executive Functions

Executive functions are responsible for maintaining real-time supervision of the system environment. This assignment basically involves input–output control, including input–output scheduling, data transfers and device manipulation, job and task scheduling and the necessary resource allocation and event-monitoring, system communication along with input–output queue maintenance and console support.

Other functions under executive control are hardware error detection, recovery from errors, program error control, support for timing services, and the needed accounting procedures.

System Management

System management is primarily concerned with the nonreal-time parts of the operating system. These support both system and applications programs by means of such services as system generation, program maintenance, including that of libraries and catalogues, compiler interfaces, support utilities.

Within system management linkage must pass information between subroutines and furnish a common entry point. For instance, when a user task requests a service provided by the supervisor, a command must be issued containing an identification code designating the function to be performed. The handler should save the state of the task at the time of the call, examine the code, and select the proper system routine to be called. Returning the system routine to the handler restores the user to the precall state, adding the returned values. These are the basic parts of a multiuser time-sharing system.

Data Maintenance

Data maintenance allows the user to access and process data in general. It involves file management facilities, including directories, and user control of the access. Under data management are also the input–output support for different access modes (sequential, index sequential, random, and so on) and for file record, the facilities for file display and copy, and peripheral-device support, including format conversion and data editing.

Terminal-Handling

Terminal subsystems typically offer a particular service to the user and support a restricted class of terminals. The diversity of terminal subsystems is illustrated if we consider at least three different solutions for an equal number of requirements. The first is time-sharing programs which usually are general-purpose, primarily supporting low-speed typewriter terminals in a line-at-a-time mode. The second is job entry programs, which can be conversational approaches that support high-speed locally buffered cathode ray tube terminals in a full-face interaction mode.

A Network Operating System 219

The third is remote job entry subsystems, which support binary synchronous communication to remote batch terminals.

A ring of special software thus interfaces between the basic operating system and the functional programs, which are goal oriented (Figure 17.5). The latter are the link between the operating system's special software and the applications programming. A special software functional interface may, for instance, submit job streams to either of two batch-processing subsystems and return the printer or display streams to the user terminal.

Evidently, the design of future operating systems would be influenced by the requirements of networking, but today the design of entirely new operating systems for widely used central processing units is rather uncommon.

The system design problem faced by computer centers is to provide network service on a machine running an immense and amorphous collection of system software. This makes it necessary to add a network interface to an existing operating system by superimposing rather than by integrating, which would be more rational (Figure 17.6). Consequently, software development can be a major undertaking, particularly for operating systems on large-scale central processing units. That is why it is useful to examine the requirements of interfacing to existing systems.

Figure 17.5

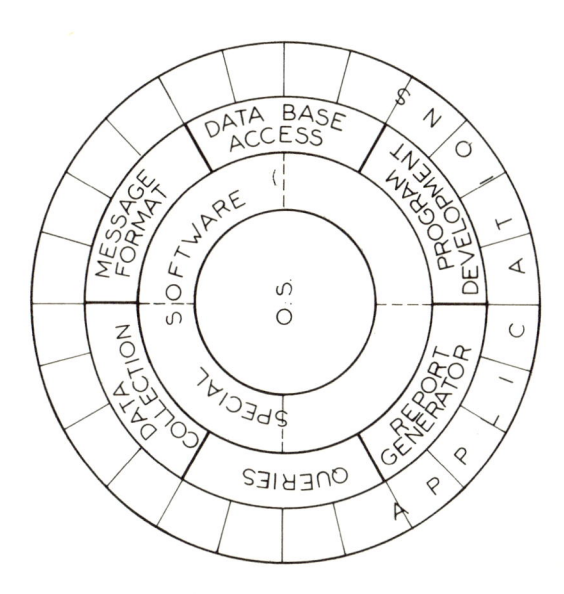

Figure 17.6

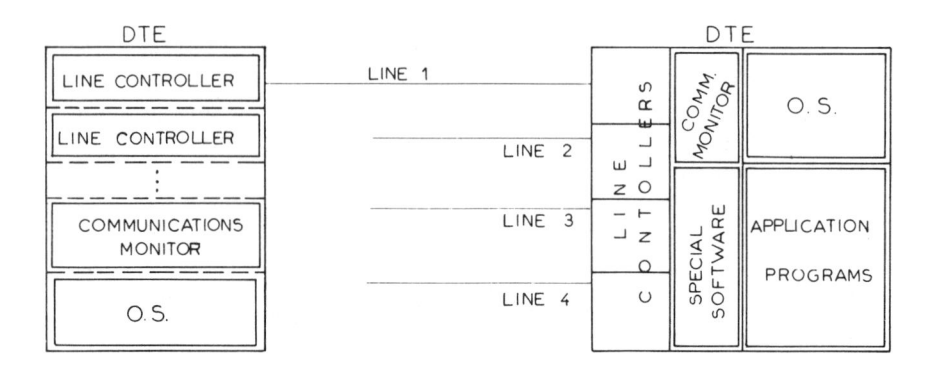

The Server System

Classic operating system functions, device routines (for instance, input–output operations), and channel interfaces (to pheripherals) constitute the traditional architecture of an on-line-oriented operating system (Figure 17.7). Now, they must be modified to achieve a high degree of true parallelism.

The object of server systems is service to the user. Terminal subsystems are of particular interest; they serve users communicating with terminals as input–output devices.

Present-day input–output devices controlled by a particular subsystem are logically and exclusively allocated to it by the operating system. The nondynamic nature of this so-called device binding, however, is a reflection of the batch-processing orientation of the past, and this approach is now changing. The problem now is to provide for interprocess communication through a standard, robust, and flexible mechanism that affords the explicit definition of interfaces and protocols.

New approaches must be applied to the management of terminals, input–output units, central memory, and the "processes" in the central memory.

The server, or terminal support software, must match symbolic port names, provide multichannel and bidirectional data transfer, disconnect signaling when a process dies, and queue and handle requests. To do so, it must run local resources, reach into remote resources, and provide what is necessary in terms of data communications facilities (Figure 17.8). Running local resources means to supervise control, file access, input–output with the network and, eventually, ensure encryption. Many facilities are needed. In the last chapter we spoke of two operating requirements, which are practically unknown with batch operations,

A Network Operating System   221

Figure 17.7

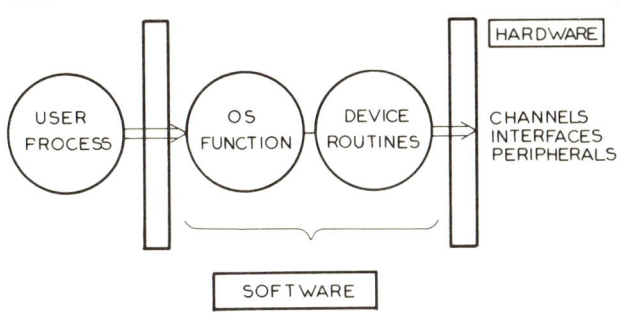

THE TRADITIONAL ARCHITECTURE IS:

[Diagram: USER PROCESS → OS FUNCTION → DEVICE ROUTINES → CHANNELS INTERFACES PERIPHERALS (HARDWARE); OS FUNCTION and DEVICE ROUTINES grouped as SOFTWARE]

NOW NETWORK REQUIREMENTS CALL FOR A "SERVER" SOLUTION TO THE "OS" FUNCTION

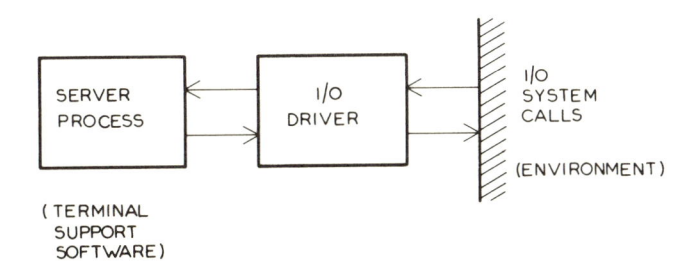

[Diagram: SERVER PROCESS ← I/O DRIVER ← I/O SYSTEM CALLS (ENVIRONMENT); (TERMINAL SUPPORT SOFTWARE)]

even with the classic star or hierarchical real time: downline loading, needed for unattended operations, and upline dumping (and loopback), necessary for network-testing and maintenance. Further faculties may be required. Debugging cross-net software is difficult; conventional "static" debugging techniques are totally inadequate. The ability to plant break-points and probe interactively is absolutely essential.

Users of Arpanet have pointed out the difficulty of trouble-shooting the cause of failure in a production system. Many subsystems and at least two host central processing units are involved in the simplest Arpanet operations.

To be able to ask the user–server system to report its status, we must implement not only novel but also intelligent solutions. Figure 17.9 shows three steps in the evolution of a local software solution to meet this end.

From the unintelligent and basically hardware terminal we progressed to an intelligent solution with a network interface, but it has not been enough. Hence the new server systems with the facilities of data base and message-handling, with a number of network interfaces, specialized by function, and with encryption.

Figure 17.8
(QL = query language)

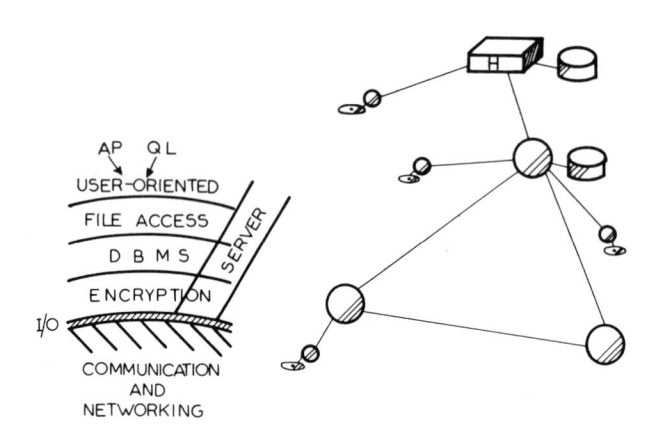

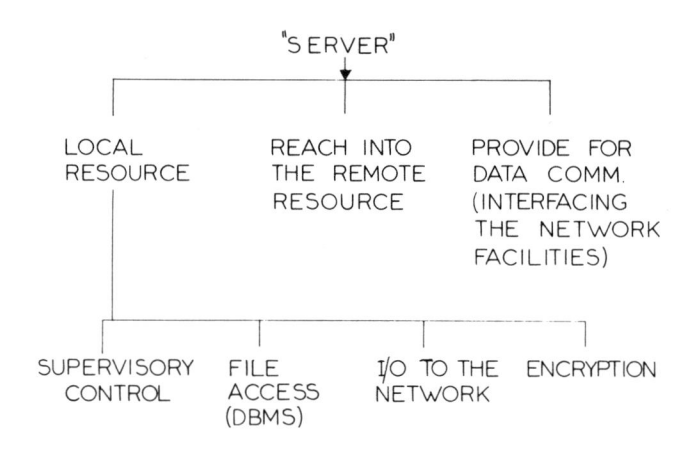

AP QL
USER-ORIENTED
FILE ACCESS
DBMS
ENCRYPTION
SERVER
I/O
COMMUNICATION AND NETWORKING

"SERVER"

- LOCAL RESOURCE
- REACH INTO THE REMOTE RESOURCE
- PROVIDE FOR DATA COMM. (INTERFACING THE NETWORK FACILITIES)

SUPERVISORY CONTROL | FILE ACCESS (DBMS) | I/O TO THE NETWORK | ENCRYPTION

A Network Operating System 223

Figure 17.9

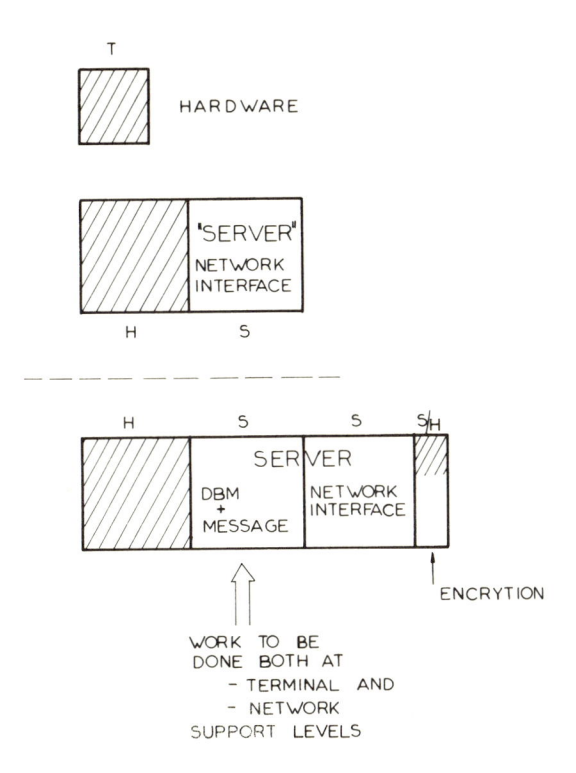

Distributed Operating Systems

It is not uncommon to see resident operating system routines occupy more than a quarter of the main memory, in this way reducing the amount available to users. In small systems the percentage can be even greater as, for instance, 8 kilobytes out of 16. Moreover, because of the numerous supervisory functions they have to perform, a substantial portion of the total execution time is spent by those routines doing administrative work, while the user tasks wait for the connection point to become available. Lastly, no matter how carefully programmed such systems are, they inevitably will be error-prone because of their size alone.

A number of changes and innovations in hardware as well as operating system structure and design have therefore been suggested, with the objective of improving overall performance by solving some of the problems outlined above. With respect to software we have, most notably, the development of synchronization primitives at low levels (semaphores) as well as at higher ones (mailboxes and monitors). Whether centralized or distributed, the operating system must ensure that the flow of information through the system is flexible and efficient.

Within the local site the distributed operating system contrasts with a traditional one, in which all input–output transfer involves the central memory. It makes feasible the exchange of data directly between any two peripheral units.

Furthermore, distributed operating system functions, or at least a good many of them, can be converted to firmware. Among the reasons for converting to software-plus-hardware solutions are:

Legal (patents, investment protection)

Marketing competition

New developments in products

Faster operations (e.g., compiler capability)

Standardization (normalization of certain operations)

Making feasible the breakup of the operating system and its distribution throughout the network

Reducing error probability

Providing efficient interfaces for device independence

The system must also make it easier to connect peripheral units from different manufacturers to a given computer (equipment independence).

Once a microcomputer can be programmed to handle a particular device, the actual interfacing problems are greatly reduced, as long as information transfers between system components are governed by a standard communications protocol.

INDEX

Abstraction, levels of, 198
Acknowledgment, 114, 143, 183
   as function of message delivery, 107
   utilization of supervisory frame in, 138–42, 151, 152
Access modes, 218
Access time, 47, 92
Acoustic coupling, 33
Acoustic mode, 38
Adaptive delta modulation (ADM), 21
Advanced Communications Control Procedure (ADCCP), 131, 136, 149, 172
Advanced Communications Service (ACS), 121
Airline reservation systems, 13, 87, 94
Alarms, 205–06
Algorithms, 137, 145
Alohanet, 22–23
American National Standards Institute (ANSI), 131, 185, 189–90, 192
American Telephone and Telegraph (AT&T), 3–4, 36, 94, 185
Analog repeaters, 91
Analog transmission, 32, 36, 38
   cost, 122
Applications program library, 78, 187
Applications programming (AP), 67, 219
Applications programs, 166, 185, 192, 200, 202

Applications standards, 156
Architecture, 195, 213, 220, 221
   of central processing unit, 61
   see also Network architecture
Arpanet, 5, 100, 157
   difficulties of, 221
   protocols within, 168–170
   as a standard, 110
Asynchronous time-division multiplexing (ATDM), 25
Automatic answering, 36, 38
Automatic calling unit (ACU), 36
Automatic teller machines, 178

Bandwidth, 27, 91, 173
   allocation of, 19, 25, 61
   definition, 28
   as problem in circuit-switching, 123
   voice, 17, 28
Banking industry, 12, 42, 87, 176–78
   data processing in, 3, 76–77, 94, 192
Baud, 27
Baudot code, 106
Binary data, serial, 38
Binary data wave, 34
Binary frequency modulation, 33
Binary synchronous communications (BSC, bisync.), 106, 112–15, 132, 178, 219

226   *Data Communications for Distributed Information Systems*

criticisms of, 114
Binary synchronous protocols, 112, 151, 176
Bit data transfer rate, 28
Bit error, 145
  causes, 103
  checking for, 152
Bit error rate (BER), 15–16, 122
Bit-oriented protocols, 152, 173
  dialects, 149
  using in a loop, 142–45
Bit sequence, 27
Bit stuffing, 137, 152–53
Blackouts, 76
Blocking, 26, 190
Broadband, 28
Broadcast, 28
Buffer(s), 27, 50, 53, 179, 216
Buffering, 58, 130, 181–82, 190, 212
Buffer overflow, 181
Buffer space, 179, *180*, 181
Bus drivers (busbars), 45
Byte standard (IBM), 152
Byte synchronization, 152

Call-clearing time, 102
Call request packet, 174, 175
Call setup, 151, 153, 175, 182
Call-setup time, 102, 122
Carrier, 28, 167
  common carriers, 17, 151, 171
Carterphone decision, 36
Cash dispensers, 178
CCITT (International Telegraph and Telephone Consultative Committee), 36, 57, 149–50, 171–72
Channel(s), 32, 98
  capacity, 16, 28
  characteristics, 35, 152
  relative importance of, to message, 97
Channel controller, 67, 166
Channel control programs, 67
Channel separation, 17
Character handling, 50, 67–70
Checkpoint/checkpointing, 142, 189, 209, 210

Checksums, 22, 23, 53
Cheque processing, 3–4, 87–88, 97
Circuit(s), 1, 26, 91, 153, 169
  assigning, 122
  definition, 25
  detecting disruptions in, 102–03
  inefficient use of, in circuit-switching, 122–23
  leased, 28
  logical, 164
  multipoint, 161
  point-to-point, 161
  shared, 121
  standards for, 150–51
  terrestrial, 144
  two-wire and four-wire, 34
Circuit chips, 52
Circuit data rate, 26–27
Circuit switching, 97, 103, 121, 151, 161, 166
  advantages/disadvantages, 122–23
  compared to network switching and packet switching, *124–25*
Clocking, 27, 35, 51
Coaxial cable, 15, 20, 23, 32, 57, 89, 108
Code(s), 27, 52, 61, 98, 122, 191, 211
  ASCII, 26, 114
  definition, 45
  as design factor, 70
  EBCDIC, 114
  effect on transmission format, 101
  identification, 168, 218
  operating, 90
Code conversion, 20–21, 48
Code sets, 26, 132
Code symbols in Morse code, 25–26
Code words, 26
Collisions between messages, 23
Commands, 128, 161, 168, 187–88, 209
  types, 159–60, 205
Commerce, United States Department of, 4
Communication costs as necessary business expense, 5–7, 11–12
Communication requirements, estimating, 7–10
Compressed pulse code modulation (CPCM), 20

Index   227

Computer systems, transaction-based, 87–96
  capabilities and limitations, 87–89
  changes in structure, 93–95
  choice of facilities, 89–90
  system requirements, 95–96
  types of communications links, 91–93
Concentration, 23, 25, 57–58
Concentrators, 12, 25, 58–61, 64–65, 157, 202–03
Conditioning, 15, 28, 34–35, 38, 123
Congestion, 167, 181
Congestion control, 153, 167, 181–82
Connection, 127, 167–68
  definition, 107–08, 123, 186
  multipoint, 126
  point-to-point, 126
  switched end-to-end, 127
Connectivity, full, 22
Contact, 105
  components of, 58
Content and sequencing procedures: see Bit-oriented protocols
Contention for transmission, 23, 61, 65
Control, 15, 27, 29, 151, 195, 220
  components of, 32
  definition, 45
Control bus in DTEs, 45
Control fields, 132, 160, 175
Controlling and monitoring, software supervision of, 204–05
Control messages, 153
Control program, 46, 166
Conventions, 57, 100–02, 105, 153. See also Protocols
Conversation characteristics, 24
Conversion, 27, 38
Credit verification by computer, 87
Cycles, 28, 33
Cyclic redundancy check (CRC), 70, 141

Data, asynchronous, 22
Data activity, statistical aspects of, 25
Data assurance unit, 186
Data base management, 62, 185, 187, 192

Data base management systems (DBMS), 62, 101
Data bus in DTEs, 45
Data clearance techniques/methods, 43
Data communication network, 15, 83, 89–90, 108
Data communications, 15–16, 122, 154
  compared to data processing, 73–86
  historical background and future of, 5, 29, 76–80, 90
  potential market, 94-95
Data communications systems, 70–72, 192
  components of, 200
  implementation schedule, 206–07
  tasks in, 195
Data compaction, 27
Data compression units, 84
Data flow, 53, 151, 166, 175
Data flow unit, 186
Datagram, 73, 103, 149, 187
  advantages/disadvantages, 164
  compared to virtual circuit, 166–67, 182–83
Data integrity, 70, 104
Data link control, 110, 141, 149, 151–53
Data link control procedures/protocols, 102–03, 145, 153, 172, 182
Data mapping unit, 186
Datapac network (Canada), 174, 182–83
Data path, 149, 159, 168, 187
Data processing, 5, 73–74, 154, 192
  historical background and future of, 76–80
Data stream, 14, 26
Data transfer, 153, 157, 176
Data transport, 185–86
Data unit, 186
Datex, 28
Deadlock prevention, 181
Decnet protocol (DDCMP), 163, 182
Dedicated data switch, 122
Defense, United States Department of, 5, 23, 168
Delay, 103–04, 212
Delta modulation (DM), 20
Diagnostics, 38, 58, 60, 65, 96, 129–30, 212

228   *Data Communications for Distributed Information Systems*

Dialogue procedures, 156
Dial-up circuit, 28
Differential phase-shift key (DPSK), 33
Differential pulse code modulation (DPCM), 20
Digital repeaters, 91
Digital transmission, 32–33, 36, 38, 122, 129
Disc(s), 47, 202, 203, 216
  storage, 94, 199
Disconnection, 108, 126, 167
Distributed computer networks, 75
Distributed data assurance, 110
Distributed data bases, 154
Distributed operating systems, 222–24
Distribution of load, 30, 70
Documentation, 183
Downline loading, 75, 95, 145, 200, 202, 221
DTE (data terminal equipment): *see* Terminal(s)

Echoing, 108, 216
Editing, 64, 67
Electronic Industries Association (EIA), 150
Electronic mail, 13, 14, 75, 81, 84
  Mailgram, 83
Electronic message systems (EMS), 81–83. *See also* Facsimile; Telegraph service; Telex
Endless loop, 164
Equalization, 34–35
Error(s), 6, 22, 122, 200
  components of, in message system, 102–03
  line errors, 35, 112
  tracing, 196
  undetected, 175
Error checking, 42–43, 50, 132, 167
Error control, 104, 108, 141, 153
  as feature of intelligent line, 58
  methods of, 212
  as responsibility of host computer, 167
Error correction, 35, 42–43
Error detection, 65, 112, 179, 218
Error detection and control, 105, 162

Error detection and correction (EDC), 31, 73, 90, 103, 110
  as component of transfer, 58, 105, 171
  as function of line controller, 50
  as function of network, 96, 169
  use of control field in, 175
Error detection and recovery, 167
Error rates, 28, 76, 88, 91
  influence of switching on, 32
Error recovery, 31, 114, 138, 151–52
Error signal, 20, 50
Establishment, 123
Ethernet, 23
Executive functions, 217–18
Extended numbering, 182

Facility field, 174
Facsimile, 1, 2, 22, 81
  as adjunct of copying, 84
  cost, 4
  requirements, 30
  statistics on, 83
  terminals, 13
Failure, recovery from, 181
Federal Communications Commission, 36
Feedback network, 20–21
File access, 78, 185, 220
  role in layering, 157, 192
File management system, 203
Flags, 132–38, 152–53
Flat-rate service, 11
Flow control, 73, 93, 171, 176, 179–81, 197–98
  goals, 181
  mechanisms, 166, 168
  at network interfaces, 164
  protocols and, 106, 169, 170
Foreign exchange (FX) service, 11, 42, 89
Frame, information:
  management frame, 138, *140*
  parameters, 132, *139*, 149
  supervisory frame, 132, *139*, 141
Frame sequence, 132, 141
Framing, 151–52, 179
Frequency, 15, 89, 91. *See also* Bandwidth
Frequency division, 21, 58

Frequency-division multiplexing (FDM), 17–20
  cost, 18
  rules and standards for, 57
Frequency spectrum, 15, 32
Front end, the, 76, 203
Front-ending, 61–70
  definition, 61
  functions, 64
Front-end processors, 65, 169

Gateways, 58, 61
  need for, 112, 172, 178, 182. *See also* Interfaces
"Go back N" technique, 141, 142, 144

Header, the, 141, 143, 163, 173–76
  components, 138, 172, 174–75, 182–83
  as function of message delivery, 107
Hertz, a, 28
Heterogeneity of components, 212
Hierarchical systems, 202
High-level data link control (HDLC), 131, 134, *135*, *136*, *139*, 149, 172–73
Host computer, 170

IBM (International Business Machines) 112. 131, 185
  predictions on communications costs, 5
  recommendations for electronic office, 75
  statistics on terminal sales, 93–94
IBM World Trade, 182
Identification, 101, 105, 109, 160, *161*
Identification numbers, 152
Identifying symbols, 128
Incarnation numbers, 145
Information field,
  structure of, 156
  upper limits, 141
Information flow, 75, 134
Initialization, 151–52, 209
Input-output control systems (IOCS), 215

Inquiry-response systems, 121, 123
Integrity, 188, 192, 203
Interface(s), 48–52, 65, 187, 192, 213, 220
  definition, 45
  developed for internetworking (*see also* Gateways), 182
  physical interface as first layer, 149
Interface message processor (IMP), 22–23, 169–70. *See also* minicomputer
Interfacing, 48–52, 57
International Standards Organization (ISO), 131
Internetworking, 182–84
Interoffice memos, statistics on, 90
Interruption, 108, 167, 168
Interrupts, handling of by software, 197–98

Journaling, 64

Keys, 102
Keywords, 98

Language use, statistics of, 25–26
Layering, 157
  advantages of, 185
Layers (levels), 150, 163, 178, 191, 216
  need for, 98, 149. *See also* Protocols
Leased facilities, 91, 121, 151. *See also* Private lines
Light-emitting diode (LED), 38
Line(s), 36, 70, 109
  full-duplex and half-duplex, 112, 132
  intelligent and unintelligent, 58, 151
  multidrop, 52, 93, 111
  point-to-point, 52, 93, 111
  public, 52, 92
Line adapter, 60, 61
Linear pulse code modulation, (LPCM), 20
Line control, 50, 67, 88, 205
Line controller(s), 50–52, 53
Line control procedures: *see* Data link control

Line discipline, 132, 211, 212
  synchronous and asynchronous, 111–12
  See also Protocol
Line management, 60–62
Line procedure: *see* Protocol
Line speed, 16, 60, 70, 123
Line turnarounds, 112, 143
Link(s), 23, 43, 88, 92, 105
  half-duplex/full-duplex, 15, 153
  logical, 107–08, 163, 168, 179
  physical, 145, 153, 172, 198
  purpose/functions, 32, 145
  types/arrangements, 15, 20, 91–93
  See also Channels
Link control, 106, 128, 179
Link control procedure, 110, 160
Link management, 141, 151
Logical channel number (LCN), 166, 173–76
Logical functions, 32, 211
Loop, 142–45
Loopback, 58, 75, 95, 200, 203, 221

Mailboxes, 78, 101, 187, 190, 223
Mail statistics, 81, 90
Mainframe, 76, 187, 206
  use of in front-ending, 61–62
Maintenance, on-line, 31, 73, 130
Manufacturing uses of data communications and data processing, 36, 94
Massachusetts Institute of Technology, 23
Master control numbering, 85
Master station responsibilities, 127
Maxicomputers, 94, 152, 210, 216
Memory, 31, 47, 70
  as component of computer system, 41, 52, 58
  management of, 105
  size/capacity, 189, 197, 200
Message(s),
  accountability for delivery of, 106–07
  definition, 97, 100
  in endless loops, 166
  length of, 81
  out of sequence, 166
  transmission formats, 88, 101, 153, 156, 160
Message fields, 101
Message flow, 50, 166
Message handling, 123
Message management, 50, 190
Message manipulation programs, 100
Message-rate service, 10
Message-switching, 16, 75, 85, 103, 121
  compared to circuit switching and packet switching, *124–25*
  development of, 32
Message systems,
  computer-based, 98–100
  performance criteria, 102–04
Message theory, 97–104
Message unit, 10, 11
Message unit charges, 10–12
Metropolitan-area service, 11
Microcomputer(s), 42, 53, 130, 224
  definition, 52
  as interface, 61
Microelectronics, effect on telecommunications costs, 5
Microfilm, 75
Microform (COM), 75
Microline controller, 70–71
Microprocessor(s), 53, 70, 130
  capabilities, 52
  as component of DTE, 41, 45
  as component of intelligent line, 58
  costs, 61
  definition, 52
  used for equalization, 35
Microverification, 53
Microwave links, 213
Microwaves, 15, 32
Minicomputer(s), 56, 130, 152, 200, 216
  costs, 53
  definition, 52
  IMPs as, 169
  as part of PBX system, 6
  projections for future use, 94
  storage capabilities, 47
  terminal as, 76
  typical, 90

Index 231

Miniprocessors, 61
Modem(s), 32–36, 78, 91, 152
  as element of transmission speed, 48
  half-duplex and full-duplex capabilities, 34
  levels of operation, 28
  standards for, 36–37, 149, 150
  synchronous and asynchronous, 35, 38
  technical issues with, 34–35
  testing, 35
  types, 35–36, 38
Modem series:
  103 Series (Bell System), 35
  201 Series (Bell System), 35
  208A Series (Bell System), 35–36
  209A Series (AT&T), 36
  212A Series (Bell System), 36
Modulation, 28, 33
Molecular-electron emissions, 15
Money transfers, 3, 103
Monitoring, 31–32, 38, 171, 200, 212, 218
Morse code, 25, 26
Multiplexers, 17, 25–27, 58–60, 175
Multiplexing, 23, 212
  definition, 57
  frequency-division, 17–20, 57
  propagation delays with, 26–27
  requirements of, 23
  time-division, 14, 18–20, 25–27, 31, 57

Network(s), 111, 123, 160
  circuit-switching, 150, 166
  components/design, 1, 89, 181
  costs, 6
  functions/goals, 196, 210
  levels of service, 74–75, 93
  packet-switching, 92, 164, 178, 181, 187
  private, 90, 155
  public, 175, 179, 182
  starlike, 76, 93, 178
  switched, 28–29, 38, 121, 129
  voice-grade, 29, 90, 122–23
Network architecture, 110, 163, 182, 195, 209–12
  based on network protocols, 153

  components, 159
  layered, 105, 149, 153
  relationship of XDLC to, 134
Network control, 73, 200, 213
Networking, 149, 153, 154, 185
  functions, 159–70, *160*
  layers of, 185, *186*
  relationship to traffic, 78
Network interface adapter (NIA), 182
Network management, 153
Network operating system, 209–24
  designing, 210–12
Network performance, 104
Network transit delay, 102
Noise, 28, 91, 166
  as cause of errors, 35, 103, 122

Ontyme, 84–86
Operating systems, historical development, 214–16
Optical fibers as transmission medium, 5, 32, 57, 128

Packet(s), 102, 151, 166, 173
  detecting missing or lost, 103, 152, 176
  "short," 26
  size, 162, 164, 178, 182
  standardization of format, 132, 171, 173
  structure, 132, 153
  as third level of protocol, 149, 176, 179
  types, 26, 176, 179–81
Packet assembler, 157, 179
Packet switching, 97, 121, 161, 171–72, 178
  advantages of, 103, 130
  compared to circuit switching and message switching, *124–25*
  cost, 130
  data paths in, 168
  development of, 32
  protocols for, 112, 176
PBX systems, 6–12
Peripheral interface adapter as component of DTE, 41

Personal identification number (PIN), 42, 89
Picturephones, 28
Piggybacking, 145, 151
Pipelining, 151, 162
Point-of-sale equipment (POS), 75, 178
Polling, 114, 128, 138, 182, 205
 as function of intelligent line, 58, 62
 half-duplex/full-duplex, 109
 protocols, 108
 as responsibility of master station, 127
Postal Service, United States, 75, 98
 revenues, 81–83
Presentation, 187, *188*
Presentation control, 185, *186*, 190–92
Priority, 187, 216
Private branch exchange, 3, 42, 89
Private lines, 38, 52, 122, 182
 costs, 5, 12
Privileged control, 205
Process, 190, 198
Process control, 185, *186*
Processor(s), 52, 58, 70, 157, 219
 preparation for on-line operation, 209
 statistics on, 75
Protocol(s), 70, 75, 105–19, 123–30, 170, 176, 178, 185, 224
 applications, 156–57
 bit-oriented, 90, 131–47
 communications level, 151–52
 comparing, 176–79
 definition, 57–58, 105
 digital control, 176
 functions of, 105
 host-to-host, 160, 168, 170
 IMP-to-host, 169–70
 IMP-to-IMP, 169
 influence on equipment, 65
 layering of, 105, 149, 153–56, 160
 modes of operation, 112–15, 151, 160, 172–73, 178
 necessity of, 121, 123
 nesting of, 149–57
 network, 100, 157, 172
 network access, 109
 node-to-node, 168
 packet-level, 171, 176
 in presentation control, 191
 process-level, 192
 process-to-process, 168
 reliability of, 106–08
 structure, 128, 149, *154*
 subscriber-to-network, 160
 transparent, 105–06, 108
 user-level, 156–57, 170, 182
 virtual, 105–06, 157
Protocol chips, 130

Quarantine, 189–90
Queues, queueing, 48, 65, 102, 104, 166, 181, 205, 210, 213
 as feature of front-ending, 61
 as function of software, 220

Radio, 15, 32, 89, 108
Rays, 15
Rear-end operations, 67, 76
Reception, 167–68
 definition, 107–08
Recommendation X.25, 164, 166, 171–84
 functions, 171
 goals, 149, 171
 X7X, 182–84
 See also Protocols
Recovery after outage of processor, 209–10
Reinitialization, 152
Remote files, access to, 157
Reset procedure, 179–81
Resource allocation, 31, 179, 195, 218
Resource sharing, 197, 210, 213
Response modes, 141
Response time, 65, 75, 108–09, 152
Restart procedures, 153
Retail industry use of telecommunications, 13, 42, 87, 94
Retransmission, 103, 107, 142, 152, 175
 after failure, 210
 automatic, 96, 122
Reverse charging, 175
Routines, 199–200, 210
Routing, 73, 90, 108, 122, 160–64, 179, 212–13

Index   233

adaptive, 162
alternate, 25, 61, 182
deterministic, 182
fixed, 161
as function of IMP, 169
as function of networking, 159, 173
as function of X.25, 171
probabalistic, 182
random, 182
relation of costs to, 162–63
as third level, 187
variable, 161–62
Routing algorithm, 31, 198
functions of, 162, *163*
Routing procedures, 161–62

Sampling, 19
Satellite(s), 5, 13, 23, 32, 57, 89, 128
delays in transmission, 23, 143, 153, 182
earth stations, 22, 94, 129
Satnet, 22
Scrambling, 34–35
SDLC: *see* Synchronous data link control
Security, 78, 97, 145, 192, 203
enhanced by front-ending, 65
Segmentation of message, 166, 190
Selecting/selector, 127, 216
Selective reject technique, 142, 144
Semiconductors, 30, 41, 52
Sequencing, 93, 107, 152, 166–67
Server systems, 220–23
Session control, 185, 187–92
function/purpose, 187–89
Signal(s), 27–28, 35, 36, 45, 89
conversion of, 41, 91
distortion, 35
elements, 26–27
functions, 27
level, 33, 182
in synchronous and asynchronous transmission, 34
Signal types:
analog, 28, 91
binary, 28, 33
digital, 28, 91, 129 (*see also* Facsimile Telegraph service, Telex)
discrete; 91

Software, 6–7, 100, 160, 168, 188–89, 195–207, 209, 211
costs, 52, 212
as data base support, 203–04
debugging, 221
development, 197–98, 211–12, 219
for front-ending, 64–65
functions, 130, 195–96, 198–201, 203–04, 219
need for, 98, 166
quality, 65
role in data concentration, 58–60
standard, 215
as support for minicomputers, 53
Specialization, 67
Speed, 84, 122, 134, 162, 211
of central processor or miniprocessor, 50
channel, 23, 97
influence of switching on, 32
transmission, 36, 60, 104, 112
Standardization, 90, 171–84, 185, 190
Standards, 131, 192
for data communications, 151, 155
for data processing, 155
for DTEs, 155
for modems, 150–51
for networks, 145
See also Protocols
Storage, 15, 31–32, 47, 64–65, 121
characteristics, 48
devices, 47, 52, 53, 55
interrelationship with transmission and switching, 32
as parameter of switched network, 29
Stuffing, 23
Sub-voice-grade lines, 32, 91
SWIFT system, 103
Switch(es), 32, 78, 157
types, 30, 121
Switching, 16–17, 29–32, 61, 161, 212, 213, 216
as design parameter, 15, 29
developments in technology, 16
disciplines, 30–31
importance of, 129
quality of service, 31–32
techniques, 121
Switching centers, 3, 30–31

234   Data Communications for Distributed Information Systems

Switching equipment: see PBX
Synchronization, 15, 19, 50, 105, 110, 152–53
  loss of, 26, 213
Synchronous data link control (SDLC), 131, 135–39, *139*, 149, 172
  line access protocols, 176, *177*
  loop application with, 143–45
System management, 218
Systems Network Architecture (SNA), 182

Tarriffs, international, 90, 182
Telecommunications, 1–14
  benefits of, 12–13
  costs, 1–5, *2*, *13*
  future systems, 13–14
Teleconferencing, 84
Telegraph service, 28, 30, 81, 97–98, 108
Telenet system, 108
Telephone(s), 16, 28, 81, 98, 104, 108
  costs, 3–6
  statistics, 3–5, *13*
  as terminal equipment, 1, 41
Telephone calls, statistics on, 81
Telephone lines, 13, 28, 50
  capacity, 14
  limitations, 48
Telephone Monitoring Systems, User's Checklist for, 8–9
Teleprocessing, 46, 94
Teletype, 1, 41, 111–12
Telex, 13–15, 98
  statistics on, 81
Terminal(s), terminal equipment (DTE), 1, 12, 25, 32, 41–56, *153*, *191*, *200*
  asynchronous/bisynchronous, 172
  batch-oriented, 115, *118–19*
  capabilities, 53, 90
  characteristics, 76, *122*
  costs, 5, 42
  definition, 186
  interactive, 115, *116–18*
  projected needs for, 5, 94
  requirements of, 172, *211*
  transmission speed, 48–52
  #2740 and #2848 (IBM), 115
  #2780 (IBM), 53, 115
  See also Telephone; Teletype
Terminal, intelligent, 15, 42–43, 103, 123, *164*, *199*, *221*
  definition, 31
  effect on messages, 150
  memory capabilities, 53
  storage capabilities, 47
Terminal, unintelligent (passive), 42, 43, 76, 123, 157, 221
Terminal control, 157, *195*
Terminal-handling, 218–20
Terminal interface message processor (TIP), 157
Terminal management, 62, 220
Terminals for asynchronous and synchronous protocols, 115, *116–19*
Termination, 123
Testing, 32, 35, 61, 65, 75, 110, 202, 212, *221*
  automatic, 89
  software, *196*, *213*
Throughput, 61, 65, 70, 104, 162, 165
  definition, 102
Time-assignment speech interpolation (TASI), 23–25
Time division, 21, 58
Time-division multiple-access (TDMA) bus, 22
Time-division multiplexing (TDM), 14, 18–20, 25–27, 57
  problems of, 31
Time sharing, 61, 103, 121
Time slots, 21–23
Tolerances, 34–35
Traffic, 22, 78, 79, 181, *213*, *217*
  analysis, 32
  collecting and monitoring statistics, 26, 182
  deferred, 32
  flow, 16, 32, *205*
  logging, *199*
  patterns, 161
  priority, 165, 175
Traffic management, 60, 123
Trailer(s), 141, 143, 163, 182–83
Transaction Network Service (TNS), 87–89
Transaction telephone, 42

Transfer, 58, 105
Transmission, 17, 19, 25, 26, 29, 167, 168, 187
 asynchronous/synchronous, 34, 52, 110–12, 137, 149
 bidirectional, 34, 90
 capacities, 32
 definition, 34, 107–08
 delays, 27
 direction/path, 52, 166
 integrity of, 160, 166
 operations executed during, 48–49
 rates, 35, 179
 speed, 32, 38, 48–52
 technical aspects, 15
Transmitter-receiver dialogue, typical, 175
Transpac (France), 182
Transparency, 26, 114, 134, 179, 192
 of data, 26
 file, 145
 of links, 134, 137
 network, 25
Trunk lines, 23, 130
Tymnet, 162

UDLC, 131
Univac, 53, 185
Upline dumping, 75, 95, 200, 221
 definition, 203
User-level systems, 156
User operations, 154, *156*

Value-added networks (VAN), 90, 92
Virtual call(s), 164, 166, 182–83
 control of, 179
Virtual channel, 105
Virtual circuit(s), 73, 102–03, 149, 164, 166–68, 175, 187
 costs, 103
 establishing, 176, 179
 types, 165–66, 173–75

Virtual-circuit procedures, 171
Virtual path, 169
Virtual terminals, 156–57, 179
Vocabulary, problems of, 27–28
Voice and data transmission combined, 12–16
Voice-grade lines (telephones), 6–7, 28, 33, 38, 97–98
 capacities, 32, 35
 characteristics, 34
 requirements, 15–16
 speeds, 91
 use in computer systems, 87
Voice protocols, 130
Voice traffic, 15–16, 130, 122–23
Voice transmission, requirements for, 19, 23

Western Union, 83
WATS (wide-area telephone service), 11, 36, 92
Waveguide transmission, 13
Waves, 32, 33
Wideband, 15, 32, 84, 91
 definition, 28
Windows, 179, *180*
 sizes, 183
Wire as transmission medium, 32, 52, 108, 213

X.25: see Recommendation X.25
XDLC protocol, 131–47, 151–53, 171
 characteristics, 134
 commands, 145, *146–47*
 comparison of dialects in, 134, *136*
 fields, 136–41
 as frame-level protocol, 149, 176, 178–79
 objectives, 145
 things it will not do, 134–36
Xerox Corporation, 23, 185